RECOVERY FROM NARCISSISTIC ABUSE, GASLIGHTING, CODEPENDENCY AND MANIPULATION (2 BOOKS IN 1)

UNDERSTAND A NARCISSISTS DARK PSYCHOLOGY + ESCAPE TOXIC FAMILY MEMBERS & RELATIONSHIPS

NATALIE M. BROOKS

CONTENTS

NARCISSISTIC MOTHERS AND ADULT DAUGHTERS

LIFE BEYOND THE NARCISSIST - THEIR DARK PSYCHOLOGY, GASLIGHTING AND MANIPULATION EXPLAINED

NARCISSISTIC MOTHERS AND ADULT DAUGHTERS

RECOVERY FROM A NARCISSISTS ABUSE, GASLIGHTING, MANIPULATION & CODEPENDENCY + ESCAPE TOXIC FAMILY MEMBERS (SELF-LOVE WORKBOOK FOR WOMEN)

INTRODUCTION

Welcome, brave soul, to a book that understands the dance between a narcissistic mother and her adult daughter—a dance that is as complex as it is painfully intimate.

> "Every adult daughter of a narcissistic mother has lived a life where her own reflection was never her own. It was always a mirror of someone else's expectations."

Does this strike a chord in your heart? Have you ever felt lost in the maze of your mother's needs and wants, unable to find the thread of your own desires and hopes? If these questions echo with the sound of your own story, you are not alone.

My name is Natalie M. Brooks, and I've walked the road you're on. I have learned through experience, and now my mission is you. Yes, you—because together, we can navigate this journey from pain to empowerment. I believe in the transformation that comes from interacting with words, stories, and exercises that don't just offer insight but lead to real-life change.

This book isn't a passive read; it's a call to action. Its pages are rich with expert insights, each one a stepping stone towards breaking the cycle of narcissistic abuse. But more than that, this book offers you interactive elements—reflection prompts, journal entries, and actionable steps—so that you can apply what you learn in real-time.

Divided into four parts, we will begin by understanding the 'What and Why' of a narcissistic mother's behaviors. Then, we will delve into the 'How'—how it affects you and how to cope. The third part explores the 'Strategies' for setting boundaries and healing. Finally, we culminate with 'Beyond Survival,' a guide to thriving and creating a life of your own design.

You may have scars, doubts, and unresolved pain. Your struggle is seen and acknowledged here. This book is crafted not just with information but with empathy, and it aims to give you a lantern to illuminate the path forward.

While professional help from therapists or counselors is invaluable for navigating these waters, this book is a powerful friend at your side. It complements the support you seek or may already be receiving, equipping you with additional resources for your toolkit.

As we take this first step together, I extend my hand to you. It's time to reclaim your reflection, discover your voice, and rewrite the narrative of your life. The road will not always be easy, but every step is a step towards freedom.

Turn the page. Your journey towards understanding, healing, and growth begins now. Together, we will emerge not just survivors, but victors. Welcome to your new beginning.

1

THE ANATOMY OF NARCISSISM: UNVEILING THE MASK

When we start to peel back the layers of what it means to have a narcissistic personality, we're diving into a world that's much more than just thinking highly of oneself. It's about a deep belief that one is better than others, an ongoing need for other people to see us as great, and not being able to truly understand or share the feelings of others.

The idea of narcissism isn't new. It comes from an old story from Greece about a guy named Narcissus. He saw his face in the water and couldn't stop looking at it because he loved how he looked so much. He couldn't pull himself away, and it shows us a picture of what it means to be totally wrapped up in oneself.

Sigmund Freud, a famous thinker on how our minds work, dug deep into this idea of narcissism. He connected it to how we see ourselves, either feeling top-notch or not worth much at all.

These days, there's a whole list of signs that experts use to figure out if someone has what's called Narcissistic Personality Disorder. This list is in a big book that doctors use to understand different mental health conditions.

Now, imagine a huge iceberg floating in the sea. We only see a tiny bit of it sticking out of the water, right? But underneath, there's so much more. That's kind of like a person with narcissism. On the outside, we might see someone who seems super confident and like they have it all together. But what most people don't see is what's hiding deep down—maybe feelings of not being good enough or really big fears.

Even though folks with narcissism may look like they love themselves a whole lot, they might actually be dealing with a tough time feeling valuable or truly loved. And the stuff they do that can hurt or control others, like playing mind games or pushing people around, those are often ways they try to keep feeling okay about themselves.

So, when we think about narcissism, it's important to remember the big picture. It's not just about someone thinking they're the best. It's about what's going on under the surface, the things we don't see that drive the behavior we do see. This understanding is key, not just for knowing what makes a person with narcissism tick but for understanding how they affect those around them and themselves. It's about seeing the whole iceberg, not just the tip.

NARCISSISM IN COLOR: OVERT, COVERT, AND MALIGNANT NARCISSISM

Narcissism comes in different ways, like a few colors in a big box of crayons. Each color has a special look and shows up in its own way. Let's peek into three common types: overt, covert, and malignant narcissism.

First, let's imagine a person we know as an overt narcissist. They're like a person who stands in front of everyone, talking loudly about how cool they are. They love the spotlight and think they're better than everyone else. An example that might come to mind is a mother who always tells people about the great things she's done. She talks about the awards she won years ago like they happened yesterday. Let's say she's at her daughter's birthday party. Instead of letting her daughter shine, she tells everyone about the time she was the star of her school play. She talks and talks, and doesn't see how it makes her daughter feel small and ignored. This mother doesn't mean to hurt her daughter's feelings; she just can't see past her own need to be noticed.

Next is the covert narcissist. They're trickier to spot. Think of them like the person at a get-together who doesn't brag out loud but still finds a way to make everything about them. They might act sad or hurt to get what they want. Let's look at a mother again, this time one who is a covert narcissist. She might say, "After all I've done for you, you can't do this one little thing for me?" She makes her daughter feel guilty for having her own life or wanting to spend time with friends. This mother plays the role of someone who has been wronged to make her daughter do things for her.

Finally, we have malignant narcissists. They can cause a lot of harm because they mix their self-love with mean behavior and don't care about the rules. A malignant narcissistic mother might tell her daughter cruel words or, worse, hurt her to show who's the boss. She does this to keep a tight grip on power and to always come out on top in their home. When her daughter tries to stand up for herself, this mother might lash out or punish her in ways that are too harsh.

Each type of narcissist has its own way of acting around others. Overt narcissists are easy to spot because they're always talking themselves up. Covert narcissists keep it on the down-low but still twist things to make themselves the main point. Malignant narcissists are harmful, using fear and hurt to stay in charge. Recognizing these types can help us understand why some people act the way they do, especially if they are close to us, like a family member. Knowing is the first step to handling these situations better and taking care of ourselves and our loved ones.

THE MAKING OF A NARCISSIST: GENETIC, ENVIRONMENTAL, AND PSYCHOLOGICAL FACTORS

Understanding narcissism can be like trying to solve a puzzle with many pieces. It's not something people choose like a new outfit or what to eat for breakfast. Narcissism is like a big pot of soup made up of different ingredients. The ingredients are the things in a person's life, like their genes, the way they were raised, and their very own personality.

Let's start with genes. Just like how you might inherit your dad's nose or your mom's eyes, you can also get ways of thinking and acting from your parents. Scientists have done a lot of looking and learning to find out that narcissism is partly written in our genes. Imagine genes as a book of life with lots of different stories. Some of these stories can tell if a person may act in ways that are seen as narcissistic. For instance, if a mom carries these stories, she might pass them on to her children, like a family recipe.

But genes are just the start. Imagine you are coloring with blue and yellow crayons. On their own, they are just blue and yellow. But when you mix them together, you get green. This is like how our world shapes us. The 'mixing' part comes from the places and people we grow up with. This includes our parents and the kind of home we have. If a little boy or girl is always told they are the best no matter what, or if they are treated very poorly, they might start to think they are more important than others or that they must always be perfect. This can be one way a person grows to show narcissistic traits. They use it as a shield to protect their feelings.

Lastly, there's the part that's all about who we are inside - our personalities. Some kids are born leaders; they're not afraid to stand up first or talk loud. If a kid like that doesn't get kindness and support at home, they might use their strong will in ways that seem selfish to others. This is because our surroundings can push our personality to show itself in different ways, just like how wind and sun can make a tree lean and grow in a certain way over time.

So, narcissism isn't a simple matter of a single cause. It's the outcome of genes, environment, and personality dancing together through someone's life. A lot like a three-layer cake, each layer plays a part, and you can't have the full cake without all of them. People with narcissistic traits didn't just wake up one day and decide to be that way. It's important to remember that it's a complex mix that made them who they are. Understanding this is like finding the corners of a puzzle—it's the first step to seeing the bigger picture.

THE NARCISSIST'S IMPACT: A RIPPLE EFFECT

In the shadow of a narcissistic mother, a child often carries silent wounds and struggles that seem invisible to the outside world. This is a truth not easily spoken but felt deeply by those who live it. Imagine a daughter: she may grow up under the gaze of a mother who seems like all love and light to friends and strangers. Yet, at home, the story is different. The mother's mirror is one-sided, reflecting only her own needs and desires.

For this daughter, her life can feel like a constant, uphill quest to win her mother's love—a prize that feels forever just out of reach. She might study longer, practice harder, and smile brighter, all with a hope that somehow, it'll be enough to catch her mother's eye and, more importantly, her heart. This belief that perfection is the ticket to affection is heavy, coating every choice and every dream. The weight of this expectation whispers to her: "Only the best is worth my love."

This unending drive for the flawless performance does not come without cost. The price is paid in self-esteem that seems to ever dwindle, flowing away like water through fingers, no matter how tight the grip. A slight mistake, a small error, and her world tilts—a reminder from her mother that love is earned, not given freely. It's a powerful lesson packaged in disapproval, one that can shape a lifetime of searching.

These children, including the daughter in our story, might long for their mother's tenderness, her attention, and her gentle, unconditional support. Yet, they often face an emotional desert—a place where the nurturing rain of affection seldom falls. This daughter might sit in her room, grappling with a sense of neglect that gnaws at her, feeling like a plant trying to thrive without water in barren soil.

The impact of a narcissistic mother's neglect is not limited to a solitary relationship either. It spreads like a slow poison, reaching the roots of other family ties. The mother's need for control and manipulation can twist the family dynamic into knots. Sisters and brothers, fathers and other relatives, can become pawns in a wider game that the mother plays, often without fully realizing it. And the daughter? She might find herself alone, cocooned from genuine connection by her mother's maneuvers—a lonely figure in a crowded home.

This daughter's experience is not a singular tale; it reflects the story of many who have had to navigate the treacherous waters of growing up with a narcissistic parent. Every day is an act of resistance against the pull of this toxic tide, trying to keep afloat in a sea where waves of manipulation crash relentlessly.

To shoulder this reality, to understand it and speak of it, is the beginning of a journey. It's a path that wanders through pain and confusion but also heads toward healing and self-discovery. The daughter's tale, like that of so many others, is one of resilience—

however, much it might be tested by the turmoil of a love that must be fought for, instead of freely given.

2

UNMASKING THE NARCISSIST: THE MOTHER-DAUGHTER TUG OF WAR

Navigating the relationship between a narcissistic mother and her daughter is like moving through an invisible emotional war zone. This war zone is often hidden from the eyes of others. To people not in the family, the mother may seem very loving and kind. But the truth of her behavior often shows up only when they are alone with her.

In this war zone, daughters feel stuck. They try very hard to make their mother happy while also dealing with their feelings. It's like they are caught in a confusing world where things often don't make sense. This confusion can make daughters second-guess what they think and feel. They might always be on edge, silently asking themselves questions like, "Am I remembering this right? Did that really happen the way I think it did?"

Walking on eggshells—that's how life feels for these daughters. And that isn't an easy or comfortable walk. They live each day not knowing what might upset their mother or cause her to say harsh words. This kind of worry isn't just something they feel in their minds; it can actually make their bodies feel bad over time. They might have trouble with stress that doesn't go away, feel tired all the time, or even get sick more often.

This worry doesn't just stay within the walls of home, either. It travels with them into the world, shaping how they interact with friends, co-workers, or partners. Those same patterns of anxiety that they learned in their dealings with their mother might show up again and again, affecting their chance to have good, caring relationships with others.

A narcissistic mother typically finds ways to make her daughter's emotions work for her. She might always be asking for more love, more time, more of everything from her daughter. If the daughter tries to share how she feels or what she needs, the mother might ignore her or make her feel like her feelings are not important. Other times, she might use guilt to keep her daughter close and in control, making her feel wrong for wanting her own life or happiness.

As the daughter grows, so does the feeling that she must always put her mother first. She learns to leave her own needs and wants on the side, not seeing them as important. This can lead her to feel lost or confused about who she is and what she really wants in life.

Understanding these patterns is a big step for daughters. They can start to see that their struggles are part of a bigger picture, one where they have been trying to make sense of their mother's difficult behavior. This knowledge can be powerful. It can help them seek change and growth and take back control over their own emotional health.

THE NARCISSIST'S PUPPET SHOW: ROLES AND MANIPULATIONS

In a world where a mother looks only to herself, her daughters might feel like characters in a play, each one given a part that shines a light on the mother's own dreams or fears. The "perfect child" is like a living trophy, showing everyone how great the mother wants to seem. This daughter has to be the smartest, prettiest, and best at everything, not for herself, but to make her mother look good.

On the other side, there's the "scapegoat," the daughter who gets blamed for anything that goes wrong. If the mother is upset or things aren't perfect, it's the scapegoat's fault. This daughter carries a heavy weight, always feeling like she's not good enough, because her mother's anger and sadness are often dropped onto her shoulders.

These daughters might feel stuck, like they can't ever just be themselves. They try hard to fill the role their mother has given them, but the truth is, these parts were never meant to fit. They were made by the mother, for the mother, and they don't leave much room for who the daughters really are.

The ways a mother like this gets her daughters to stay in these roles can be hard to spot. Tactics are like invisible strings that pull the daughters this way and that. One tactic is making the daughter feel guilty. For example, the mother might say, "After all I've done for you, this is how you treat me?" This makes the daughter feel like she owes her mother for simply being her child.

Another trick is called gaslighting. This is when something clearly happened, but the mother twists it, saying it didn't happen that way or didn't happen at all. It's like the daughter starts doubting her own mind, which can make her feel crazy.

Sometimes, the mother acts like she's the one who's hurt, making it seem like the daughter is the problem. She may even turn the siblings against each other, making them compete for her love or approval. These games can make a family feel more like a battleground than a home.

For daughters trapped in this world, learning about these games can start to change things. Knowing about the guilt, gaslighting, and other tricks can help them see they're being played. It's like seeing the strings on a puppet for the first time; once they see them, they can start to cut them.

Breaking these strings won't be quick or easy, but it is a step toward fixing their hearts and taking back their power. It starts with seeing their own value and knowing that these games aren't fair or right. They might need to take a step back from their mother or even get help from someone who understands these tricky family problems.

In the end, it's key to remember that how the mother acts says more about her own troubles than anything about the daughter's real worth or what she can do. The journey to stand on their own might be long and filled with bumps, but it's a path to a life where they can be truly themselves, not just a piece in their mother's game.

THE GOLDEN CAGE: THE EMOTIONAL TOLL OF BEING A NARCISSIST'S DAUGHTER

Growing up with a mother focused mostly on herself can be really hard on the heart. When a mom always thinks she's the most important person, it can make a daughter feel like she's not good enough. Many daughters end up feeling shaky about themselves. They may worry a lot, feel very sad, or have trouble making good friends. Some daughters might feel like something is wrong with them, not seeing that the way their mom acts is not okay.

Daughters of such moms often believe they are not worth much and might feel guilty for no reason. They start thinking maybe they are the reason things go wrong. This isn't true, but it can be tough to see that. Daughters might get mixed up about what love should look like. They might think when someone tries to control them or tells them what to do all the time, it means that person cares. But that's not right, because real care and love let you be yourself.

Moms who always need to be the star can make their daughters hide what they really feel and need. It's like daughters learn to lose touch with the real person inside them. They grow up thinking they need to make their mom happy to be loved. So they might say 'yes' to everyone, trying to make them pleased, and forget to look after themselves.

Starting to really listen to their own feelings and putting themselves first sometimes is a big step for daughters like this. Healing from this kind of hurt isn't straight like an arrow. Daughters working on feeling better might find some days harder than others. That's okay. Healing takes time, and it's normal to feel stronger some days and less so on others.

When a daughter starts this tough road to feeling better, it's super important to do it gently. They should try to make friends who get it, join groups where people share the same struggles, or talk to someone who knows a lot about feelings, like a therapist. Friends, people who have been in the same boat, or a counselor can offer a shoulder to lean on.

Looking after themselves with kindness should be a big part of getting better, too. Daughters on this road should do things that make them feel calm and happy. Taking care of their own hearts and bodies is a way to say "I am important." This is how they start fixing the pain from the past and building a life that's healthy and full of light. It's all about taking small, steady steps toward loving themselves just as they are.

3
LIGHTING UP GASLIGHTING: DISSECTING A NARCISSIST'S GO-TO TRICK

When you think about a dance, you might picture people moving to music with steps that match a rhythm. Now, imagine a different kind of dance, one that's not about fun, but about tricking someone. This is what we call the "Deceptive Dance" of gaslighting. It's not a real dance, but a way to talk about how somebody can secretly control or confuse another person. Let's dig deeper and learn about this tricky behavior, especially when a mother doesn't act in the kind and loving way we expect.

The word gaslighting might sound strange, but it has a story. Imagine a movie from long ago, called "Gaslight," where a husband plays mind games with his wife to make her think she can't trust her own thoughts. From this movie, we got a name for when one person makes another doubt what they know to be true.

So, how does this show up with mothers and daughters? Think about a time when you remembered something clear as day, but someone told you it never happened, or twisted the story. This can shake you up and make you think, "Am I remembering wrong?" If a mother, who is supposed to be loving and truthful, does this often, it can really confuse her daughter. When the mother denies things that happened, lies, or bends the truth, it's not just a simple fib. It's gaslighting.

It is tough when the mother who should have your back is the one spinning your reality. Maybe one day, she says something mean, and the next day, she insists she said no such thing. You start to question, "Did I make that up?" No, you didn't. That's gaslighting in action, and it's a favorite trick for moms who can't see past themselves. They use it like a secret weapon to keep their daughters under their thumb, doubting their own memories and feelings.

Understanding gaslighting is like shining a light on a shadow. Suddenly, what was hidden becomes clearer. You realize it's not you with the problem; it's the gaslighting that's muddying the truth. This clarity is powerful. It can't undo the past, but it can change how you deal with the present and future. It's the first step in learning how to protect yourself from these psychological games.

Don't forget, the Deceptive Dance of gaslighting is a choice by the one doing it, not a mistake. Narcissistic moms choose to make their dance tricky. When you learn their steps, you can decide not to dance along.

Grasping all this might be hard, especially when it's about your mom. But it's the starting ground to taking back your trust in your own thoughts and feelings. In the next part, we'll talk about how to spot these gaslighting moves and the signs to watch for, so you know when this Deceptive Dance is happening. This knowledge is your shield and your path to standing strong in your own truth.

ECHOES IN THE FOG: RECOGNIZING SIGNS OF GASLIGHTING

In this chapter, we will explore the signs of a specific kind of trouble that can happen between a mother and her daughter. This problem has a big name: gaslighting. Understanding gaslighting is important because it can make a daughter feel very mixed up inside. It's like a game where the rules keep changing, and it's hard to know what's real. Recognizing the signs can be the first step in making things better.

One sign of gaslighting that daughters may notice is the feeling of being confused a lot when they are with their mothers. Imagine you are pretty sure you remember something one way, but your mother keeps telling you it happened a different way. It can make you question yourself. You might even start to wonder, "Am I going crazy?" But no, you're not going crazy; you're just in a tough spot where what you believe is being questioned.

Here's an example: let's say you remember putting your keys on the kitchen counter, but your mother insists you never do that. She tells you you're forgetful and careless. If things like this happen often, you might start to doubt your own memory.

Second-guessing oneself is another common sign. If you find you're always asking yourself, "Did I really say that?" or "Was I wrong about what happened?" even though you used to be sure of your memory, then you might be experiencing gaslighting. This can make you feel like you can't trust your own thoughts.

Another thing that might happen is you might start saying "I'm sorry" all the time. It can get to a point where you say it even when you've done nothing wrong. You might apologize just to keep the peace or because you think it's what your mother wants to hear. You might even feel like you can't do anything right.

The last sign we'll talk about in this part of the chapter is fear or anxiety about sharing your ideas or feelings. Let's say you're worried about how your mother will react if you tell her something. You might be scared she'll get mad or make fun of you, so you keep quiet instead. If saying what you think or feel always seems to bring trouble, that can be a red flag that something is not right.

These signs of gaslighting, like feeling confused, doubting yourself, saying 'I'm sorry' too much, and being scared to share your thoughts, can weigh heavily on a daughter's heart. If you see these signs in your relationship with your mother, it's not your fault, and you're not alone. Remembering that what you feel and think is important is a step towards a healthier relationship, whether with your mother or anyone else who might be gaslighting you. The next sections of this book will guide you on what to do if you find yourself facing these challenges.

THE SMOKY MIRROR: THE IMPACT OF GASLIGHTING

When we talk about gaslighting, we're discussing a very tricky and hurtful way of twisting someone's reality around. Imagine someone, in this case, a mother, consistently telling her daughter her thoughts and feelings aren't true or real. As one can imagine, this can really mess with a daughter's mind over time.

Let's delve into how this kind of mind game can shake a daughter's mental health and make her think less of herself. It's not just something you brush off like dust on your jacket; it can stick with you, deep in your thoughts.

Anxiety is like having a worry bug whispering in your ear all the time, making you fret over things big and small. Depression is like a heavy blanket that makes it hard to get out of bed, enjoy things you used to, or see hope on the horizon. It's tough stuff, and when a daughter is constantly gaslighted, she's more likely to carry these burdens. She's told her feelings are wrong so often that she starts to distrust the very emotions that make us human. With the lines between what's real and what's not blurred, the fear and sadness can take over.

Imagine you're standing in front of a mirror, but the mirror is lying to you about the person you are. This is what constant self-doubt does – it eats away at a daughter's sense of self, the feeling that she is good enough just as she is. When a mother, someone a daughter looks to for honest advice and love, tells her she's remembering things wrong or making stuff up, it chips away at her confidence, bit by bit, until there's barely anything left.

It's strange but true that someone can still depend on a person who's treating them badly. If a mother keeps telling her daughter that only she knows what's best, the daughter may start to believe that she can't make good choices on her own. It's a trap that keeps the daughter tied to a relationship that hurts instead of helps, even though she knows deep down it feels wrong.

Now, imagine living in a world where your map is always getting scribbled on – where your compass doesn't work. It'd be terribly hard to navigate, wouldn't it? Long-term gaslighting can twist a daughter's belief in what's real to the point where trusting her own ideas and what she sees or hears feels impossible. It's like having glasses that don't let her see clearly, leaving her to stumble and doubt herself.

All of this can sound scary, and it is. But it's really important to know that none of it is the daughter's fault. If you find yourself relating to this, understand that you can find your way back to trusting your-self. Speaking to a friend, a counselor, or anyone you trust can be a first step in cleaning that mirror, fixing that compass, and lifting off that heavy blanket. The journey back to seeing and accepting your true, wonderful self can be challenging, but it's definitely worth it.

BURNING THROUGH THE FOG: COUNTERING GASLIGHTING

When someone tries to make you question your own thoughts and feelings, it's like they're playing a sneaky mind game. This is known as gaslighting, and it can happen to anyone, even from someone as close as a mother. It's tough, but there are ways to fight back against it and take back control of what's real for you.

Let's start with the first thing you can do: believe in your own experiences. Your life is like a story, and you're the one living it. Sometimes, when people cast doubt on what you remember or how you feel, it's like they're trying to rewrite your story. Stand firm in your truth. It can be super helpful to write down what happens to you—sort of like keeping a personal history book. This isn't just any notebook, though; it's your journal. Whenever something feels off, write down what happened, how it made you feel, and why it bothered you. Over time, seeing this written record can help you see patterns and trust your own memories and emotions more.

Now, even the strongest of us can wobble a bit when we're up against someone who keeps trying to confuse us. That's why it's important to have people we trust to talk things over with. Friends, support groups, or a counselor can be like mirrors reflecting the real you back when the gaslighter tries to blur your self-image. These good listeners can offer the kind of validation that says, "Hey, you're not making this up. I see what's happening and I've got your back." This outside perspective can be like a lighthouse guiding you through a fog of doubt.

When it comes to dealing with a mom who's gaslighting, setting boundaries is key. Imagine painting a clear line around yourself. Not everyone is allowed to cross it, and that includes mom. Let her know what is not okay to say or do. That might mean hanging up the phone when she starts telling you how you "should" remember things or kindly but firmly changing the subject when she doubts out loud how you said you felt about something. It's not about being mean; it's about protecting your space and your mind.

Lastly, there are these neat tricks called grounding techniques that can keep your feet planted firmly in your own reality. When you feel like you're starting to slip into that place where you're doubting what's true, try this: Look around and name five things you can see, four things you can touch, three things you can hear, two things you can smell, and one thing you can taste. It's a bit like doing a systems check to remind yourself that you're here, now, and connected to the world around you.

In the face of gaslighting, taking these steps isn't just helpful; it's about claiming back your story and the main character—the real you. By trusting your memories, leaning on others for support, drawing lines of protection, and staying rooted in the present, you're turning the pages back to where they belong, in your hands.

SHINING THE LIGHT: RESOURCES FOR HELP

In the journey to healing and finding one's footing after being caught in the shadows of a narcissistic mother, resources are like rays of light piercing through a long night. They offer guidance, support, and understanding that are essential for daughters who have been victims of gaslighting—a confusing dance where their reality is constantly questioned and warped by their mother's manipulative tactics.

One invaluable resource is the National Domestic Violence Hotline. It isn't just a lifeline for those in physically abusive relationships; it also provides support for those trapped in the silent turmoil of mental and emotional abuse that gaslighting entails. One phone call can connect daughters with a caring person who understands the complexity of this form of abuse. The hotline isn't only about crisis intervention; it's equally a resource for information and a starting point for understanding that the daughter's experience is valid and not an illusion.

"The Gaslighting Recovery Workbook" by Amy Marlow-MaCoy is like a map for navigating the confusing landscape of emotions and memories that gaslighting can leave behind. It's a book filled with practical exercises which are simple to engage with—even for those who have no prior knowledge of psychological terms and concepts. These exercises are tasks one can do alone, jotting down thoughts on paper, examining personal experiences, and slowly untangling the intricate web of a gaslighted reality. It's a step towards reclaiming one's thoughts and feelings, which is vital in the healing process.

Another powerful tool in the digital age is the online support community, such as the subreddit r/raisedbynarcissists. Here, the internet becomes a gathering space for souls who have walked similar paths. It's both eye-opening and comforting to read the stories of others who have lived through the same type of experiences. People share advice, support, and empathy, showing that even the most isolating experiences can be shared and understood by a wider community. This sharing can reduce feelings of loneliness and the false belief that one somehow "deserves" the gaslighting they have endured.

Perhaps one of the most impactful resources is finding a mental health professional with a specialization in narcissistic abuse. Unlike friends or family members who may offer well-meaning yet uninformed advice, these professionals bring a deep understanding of the nuances of narcissism and gaslighting. Therapy with such a professional isn't a one-size-fits-all approach; it's a customized path to healing shaped by understanding each individual's story. Through this guidance and support, daughters of narcissistic mothers can learn strategies to protect themselves from future gaslighting and rebuild their self-esteem.

The journey is long, and the healing process is not linear. However, the presence of these resources provides a constant reminder that no one has to walk this path alone. Each step taken with the aid of these supports is a step towards a healthier, brighter future—one where a daughter's reality is her own, her voice is strong, and her life is no longer overshadowed by doubt and manipulation.

4

THE GOLDEN CHILD AND THE SCAPEGOAT: THE NARCISSIST'S CHESSBOARD

At the heart of a family steered by a narcissistic mother is a complicated web of roles she hands out to her children. This is the landscape where her children learn who they are in her eyes, and it can greatly shape how they see themselves as they grow up.

The golden child in the family is the one who can do no wrong in their mother's eyes. This child receives heaps of praise, more attention than siblings, and maybe even special treats or privileges that the others don't get. Why does the narcissistic mother do this? She sees the golden child as a shiny mirror reflecting back all the good things she thinks about herself. It's as if she is saying, "Look at my child, so smart, so good, so much like me," and feeling proud. But this is not always good for the child. It may sound nice to be the favorite, but it can be a heavy coat to wear, full of expectations to be perfect all the time.

On the other side, you have the scapegoat, the child who can't seem to do anything right. This child takes on all the blame, all the harsh words, and feels the heavy hand of unfair judgment. They are like a bucket where the mother dumps all her anger and bad feelings.

When she looks at the scapegoat, she doesn't really see her child; she sees a screen on which to project all her insecurities and problems. For the scapegoat, life in this family feels like being in a constant storm, with no shelter or rest.

These roles, however, are not set in stone. They can flip or change whenever the mother feels like it, often without warning. If the golden child suddenly starts speaking up or wanting to follow their own dreams, the mother might feel like she's losing control. They are no longer that perfect mirror but a rebel making their own mark. To a narcissistic mother, this can be very upsetting and she might decide to swap roles, making someone else the golden child to bring the former back in line.

This switching of roles only adds confusion and lack of trust among siblings. No one can feel safe or sure of their place, causing a feeling of always walking on eggshells.

Children who grow up with a narcissistic mother carrying these heavy roles can end up with deep scars. It's crucial for them to understand that these roles are not really who they are, but rather what their mother needed them to be. It's possible for them to heal and find their true selves away from their mother's shadow. But it takes hard work, often with help from friends, other family members, or a professional like a counselor. The first step on this journey to healing is to know and understand these roles and that they are not the child's fault.

THE PUPPETEER'S MOTIVES: WHY NARCISSISTIC MOTHERS ASSIGN ROLES

In a family guided by a narcissistic mother, life is like a play where each child is given a part. The reason behind handing out these roles goes much deeper than just a mom trying to keep her house in order. It's about staying in control. When a mother decides which child is the star and which one is the troublemaker, she's setting up a game where she is the sole ruler.

Now picture a balance scale, the kind with two sides you might see in old pictures. On one side, there's the golden child, lifted high, and on the other, the scapegoat, weighed down. By doing this, the mom keeps the upper hand. She becomes the person everyone in the family is trying to please. No one wants to upset her, because that might mean the roles could change, and they could lose their place.

When siblings are competing for their mom's attention, it's hard for them to stand together. Instead of being a team, they become rivals. This rivalry is especially sad because it doesn't come from the siblings themselves; it's a game crafted by their mother. This division ensures that the mom remains the one with power, as the kids are too busy sorting out their mixed feelings and confusion to notice that it's their mother pulling the strings.

Another secret reason for these roles is for the mom to deal with her own thoughts about herself. She might see herself as the best of the best, and to keep believing that, she makes one child the "golden" one. This child can do no wrong and is showered with love and praise. It's like the mom is cheering for herself through this child. But her fears and doubts about herself are real too. Instead of facing these, she throws them onto another child, the scapegoat, who can't seem to do anything right in her eyes. It's unfair and painful, but it helps the mom avoid looking at her own flaws.

Role changes are like curveballs, making sure the kids never feel completely safe. They are always trying, reaching for a love that shifts like the wind. It's a clever, if not cruel, way to keep everyone on their toes.

This twisted setup is sort of like a scary thing called "Stockholm Syndrome." This happens when someone is caught by another and starts to feel thankful for small bits of kindness, even though they're still trapped. For kids with a narcissistic mom, even a little praise feels like a big deal because they're so used to being unsure of where they stand. They can end up feeling grateful for any small sign of love, just like a captive might feel towards their captor.

It's a harsh reality, and it breaks the open, trusting bond that should be a part of every family. Growing up this way, children might not even realize there's another kind of love – the kind that's given freely and isn't used as a trick or a trap.

SCARS AND SHADOWS: THE IMPACT OF THESE ROLES ON CHILDREN

In a family, each person might find themselves labeled or stuck in a certain role. Parents might not mean to do it, but sometimes they praise one child a lot and might be tough on another. This can shape how kids see themselves in the big world and how they connect with others.

When a kid is always the star, or "the golden child," the family often thinks everything they do shines bright. This child gets lots of "Atta boys!" or "You're so smart!" This might sound great, but it can be tough too. This child might end up feeling a heavy weight, a guilt, because they think they have to be perfect all the time. They feel like they must keep proving they are worth all the praise. If they make mistakes, they might be scared, thinking they've let everyone down. Sometimes, they can start to think they are more important than others, which isn't a kind way to be.

Then there's the kid who seems to carry the blame, called "the scapegoat." When things go wrong, they're often the one who gets the frown. This can really hurt. That child might start to believe they're not as good as others, that they can't do anything right. This feeling, like a mean shadow, might stick with them, making it hard to believe in themselves. They might walk around feeling like nobody could really love them, because they've been taught to think they're the problem.

When these roles jump around, like a game of musical chairs, it confuses kids. Imagine one day you're the hero, the next day the villain. How are you supposed to know who you are? This makes it hard for them to feel steady and sure about themselves. It's like wearing glasses that make everything look fuzzy. They then carry this mixed-up feeling into making friends and finding love.

For instance, the always-praised child might grow up hunting for thumbs up in every corner of their life. They might worry a lot about what friends and partners think, always trying to show they're worthy, instead of knowing they're good enough just as they are. Now, think about the child who's been blamed for everything. They might be scared to let people get close because they think they'll just get the cold shoulder. They might think, "Why try if I'm just going to get pushed away?"

It's super important for kids to feel loved for who they are, not for being perfect or for taking the blame. They need to feel safe to make mistakes and learn from them, not to be scared of failing or to always think they're in the wrong. Grown-ups should help kids understand this, so children can grow up liking themselves and knowing how to be good friends and sweethearts. These early roles can leave a mark on a kid's heart, but with care and understanding, every child can learn that they are valuable, no matter what role they've been given.

THE HEALING PATH: OVERCOMING THE EFFECTS OF THE GOLDEN CHILD AND SCAPEGOAT ROLES

Acknowledging the roles that were given to you in your family is a big step in starting to heal. When a mother puts herself first in ways that hurt her family, this can shape her children into certain roles. Maybe you were the one who always tried to fix problems or perhaps you were the child who could do no right. Understanding these roles is important.

One way to work through these feelings is by writing in a journal. Putting your thoughts on paper can be a powerful way to see and accept what you've been through. Talking to someone you trust, like a good friend or a therapist, can also help a lot. Sharing your story with another person can make your feelings feel real and important.

It's very important to remember the roles you were stuck in are not true pictures of who you really are. They were twisted by your mother's own problems. You are worthy, no matter what roles you were made to play.

Doing things that make you feel good about yourself can help rebuild how you see yourself. Taking care of your own needs is a great first step. This can mean different things for everyone, from taking a walk to taking time to read a favorite book. Setting goals for yourself can also be a helpful way to grow your self-esteem. Maybe you want to learn a new skill or finish a project you've been putting off. Doing things you enjoy, like a hobby that makes you happy or helps you relax, is another way to love and accept yourself.

Sometimes, the hurt from having a mom who always put herself first is deep. Professional help, like therapy, can give you the tools to work through this pain. Therapists have special training to help with these tough feelings. There are different kinds of therapy that have helped many people who grew up like this. One kind is called Cognitive Behavioral Therapy (CBT). It helps you change the thoughts that bring you down. Another kind is Eye Movement Desensitization and Reprocessing (EMDR). It uses eye movements to help you process and let go of hard memories.

Finding a group of people who have been through similar experiences can also be a big comfort. Support groups, whether they meet in a room or online, let you share and learn with others who understand. They can make you feel like you're not alone.

There are places online, like the "Out of the FOG" forum, that offer support and information for people with family members who have hard personalities. Finding a community like this can be a part of your healing journey. It's a place where you can talk to others who really get what you're going through.

BREAKING FREE: STRATEGIES FOR ADULT DAUGHTERS OF NARCISSISTIC MOTHERS

Creating healthy limits—or boundaries—is like building a fence in our lives. This fence keeps us safe from being hurt by a mother who thinks mostly of herself, a kind of mother called 'narcissistic.' When you grow up with a mother like this, she often gives you a certain 'job,' a role you're supposed to play to make her happy. Maybe she wanted you to be perfect or to always take care of her needs before your own. Now, to heal, you need to step out of that role and protect yourself.

One way to set these boundaries is by choosing how much and when you talk to your mother. For example, maybe you decide you will only talk to her once a week on the phone for 30 minutes, or you'll only visit her once a month. You might also decide there are topics you will not talk about with her because they bring up bad feelings. In severe cases, it might be healthiest to stop talking to her completely. This is known as 'no contact,' and it might be the space you need to heal.

Learning about narcissism can also help you understand why you feel the way you do. Imagine finding a map after being lost in the woods for hours—it can give you that kind of "aha!" moment. There are clear reasons for your mother's behavior and how it has affected you. Reading books about daughters with mothers like yours can be a flashlight in the dark. "Will I Ever Be Good Enough?" by Dr. Karyl McBride is one book filled with stories that might sound like yours and ideas on how to get better.

As you read and learn, you start to build a stronger sense of who you are—your 'self.' Loving this self is so very important when breaking away from the role your mother put you in. Think of it like taking care of a garden inside you. You need to water it with good thoughts and pull out weeds of bad feelings. Doing things like paying attention to the present moment, quietly sitting and feeling your breath, or telling yourself kind things can act like sunshine and rain for your inner garden.

Still, healing is not something you have to do alone. Breaking free takes time, and sometimes the path is bumpy. It's smart and okay to ask for someone to walk with you, like a guide. This guide might be a therapist or a counselor—someone trained to help people who are struggling. They can offer you tools and support that make the journey toward healing a bit easier.

Setting boundaries is key. educate yourself, learn to love who you are, and always know you can reach out for help. this is your path to walk, but it's a path that can lead to a happier, healthier life, free from the unfair job your mother might have given you long ago.

5

THE NARCISSIST'S WEB: TRIANGULATION AND FLYING MONKEYS

In this game of life, it's tough when your own mother is playing the game unfairly. Sometimes, moms who love themselves more than anyone else use sneaky moves to keep everyone guessing and themselves in charge. This is especially true if you have a mom who thinks she's always got to be the star of the show. One of their favorite tricks is called triangulation, and it feels a whole lot like a never-ending game of chess, where unfortunately, you might be an unsuspecting pawn.

Imagine you have a sister, and you've always been close. But lately, there's tension, and you're not sure why. It could be because your mom whispered something not-so-nice in your sister's ear about you, painting you as the bad guy. Suddenly, there's a fight between you two and guess who's got control? Mom. She's managed to cause trouble while making herself look like she's just an innocent bystander.

But why do this? It's a clever way to shift attention. If everyone's busy with their own little dramas, they aren't focusing on what mom might be doing wrong. Plus, while everyone's busy picking sides and arguing over who said what, she's sitting back and reaping the rewards of the chaos she's created.

So, what can you do to get out of this chess game? First, you've got to understand that it's happening. If you notice fights popping up without good reason, or people miscommunicating all over the place, or even feeling like there's some kind of competition going on when there shouldn't be, those are big red flags. These are signs of triangulation at work.

Now, here's the hard part: don't just take information at face value, especially if it's coming from Mom. Check the facts yourself, and make sure you're not falling for her manipulations. It's like being a detective in your own family, trying to find the truth amid the stories.

The next steps aren't easy, but they're crucial for breaking free. It starts with talking openly, without mom in the middle. If something seems off, go straight to the person involved and have a heart-to-heart. Setting boundaries with Mom is another huge step. It means telling her what's okay and what's not, and sticking to those limits so she can't keep playing her games.

Lastly, and most importantly, look after yourself. This might mean talking to a counselor or joining a support group. Other people have been through the same thing, and they can help you heal from all the hurt and confusion that triangulation has caused. Remember, it's not about winning the game—it's about living your best life, free from the chessboard of manipulation.

FLYING MONKEYS: THE NARCISSIST'S UNWITTING ACCOMPLICES

In this chapter, we'll talk about a term that comes from a famous movie, "The Wizard of Oz." Some of you might remember the flying monkeys in the story. They're not just creatures from a tale but serve as a symbol for a certain kind of behavior in real life. In the world of personal relationships, especially when dealing with a narcissist, we sometimes encounter what we call "flying monkeys." This term describes people who have been tricked or convinced by the narcissist to do their dirty work for them.

Imagine this: a mother who loves to have everything her way is upset with her daughter. Instead of talking to her daughter directly, she talks to the son or a family friend, turning them against the daughter. She might say things that aren't true or only tell parts of the story that make the daughter look bad. This mother is using the son or family friend as her 'flying monkeys' to spread her messages and keep control without having to be the 'bad guy' herself.

This move is similar to something called triangulation. It's when someone doesn't deal with a problem face to face but uses others to control and twist the situation to their liking. To avoid being caught in such a trap, it's super important to identify these 'flying monkeys.' They might be harder to spot, especially if they are close friends or family members who start acting odd or take sides without hearing the whole story.

A big hint that someone might be a 'flying monkey' is if they change how they act around you suddenly. Maybe they only tell you what the narcissist says or they repeat negative things over and over, without any good reason. Understanding these signs helps you see who might be under the narcissist's influence.

It's critical to remember that those acting as 'flying monkeys' might not even know they're being used. They could be caught up in the manipulation as victims themselves. This is why dealing with them requires care.

One of the best ways to handle 'flying monkeys' is to set boundaries. This means deciding what behavior you will not accept and making it clear to others. If you tell someone firmly but nicely that you won't listen to bad words about someone without proof, they might think twice before coming to you with gossip.

Another helpful skill is practicing discernment—being wise about what is true and what's not. This helps you see through lies and stand strong in what you know is right.

Lastly, it's important to keep your feelings in check around the narcissist and their 'flying monkeys.' Don't let them drag you into an emotional mess. Staying calm and not letting them get to you will keep your mind clear and peaceful.

Understanding how 'flying monkeys' work gives you the power to keep your life free from the mess a narcissist tries to create. It protects your relationships and your wellbeing. Keep your eyes open and your heart steady, and you'll be able to recognize and deal with these situations wisely.

NAVIGATING THE NARCISSIST'S WEB: STRATEGIES FOR SURVIVAL

In a world where words can be woven into webs, it's vital to see the threads that can trap us. Daughters of mothers who focus only on themselves face a tricky task. These mothers can play games with their words and actions that can make us feel lost or turn us against those we love. It's like being caught in a spider's web without even knowing it.

What's important to grasp first is the trick called triangulation. This means your mother might try to pull another person into your chats or fights, to make them her sidekick. It's like she's got a game on the playground, and she doesn't want to play fair. We also need to spot the 'flying monkeys,' the people who might not even know they're being used to pass on hurtful messages or rumors. Like in the tale of Oz, these monkeys don't see the strings attached to their wings.

Knowing these sneaky moves gives us a kind of superpower. We can't be played like chess pieces if we watch the player's hands. We can see when she tries to drag our brothers, sisters, or friends into our business to take her side. When we catch these moves in action, we can keep our calm, hold onto our true friends, and protect our inner peace.

To stay on our feet in this web, we should draw clear lines that shouldn't be crossed. Tell the 'flying monkeys' we won't listen to hurtful whispers, and make it clear to our mothers where the limit lies. It's like telling someone they can't come into our yard without asking. It's about respecting ourselves.

Straight talk is the magic spell that can break the web's hold on us. If we all say what we mean to each other, without secret signals or hidden messages, the game falls apart. We protect our family ties by not letting sneaky words in between them.

Treating ourselves with kindness is our shield. We need to remember to breathe, rest, and do things that make us smile. Taking care of our heart, mind, and body helps us stay strong, no matter what the web may throw at us.

Sometimes, it helps to have a guide through this maze. A therapist who gets it, who knows how these mind games work, can be a guiding light. They can teach us how to untangle the threads without getting stuck.

We're not alone, either. We can find others who have walked this path in support groups. Websites like Psychology Today are like maps that mark where these groups meet.

In the digital world, there are places filled with people who understand. The subreddit r/raisedbynarcissists is one such nook where voices from around the globe gather to say, "I get it, I've been there too." Here, in this online family, the journey feels a bit less lonely.

By understanding the tricks, drawing our lines, talking openly, caring for ourselves, and maybe getting help from others, we can steer clear of the web's stickiest corners. It's about knowing the game and choosing not to play. That's how we turn the web into just a bunch of strings, easily brushed aside.

6

DECODING THE NARCISSIST: RECOGNIZING AND RESPONDING TO MANIPULATION

When you're dealing with a narcissistic mother, it's like living in a cloud of smoke; it's hard to see clearly, and you might end up choking on confusion. It begins subtly, but soon, you realize you're being led through a maze where right seems wrong and up feels down. That's gaslighting.

This tricky game is all about your mom making you doubt everything you trust, including your own memory and feelings. She might tell you that things you remember never happened. Imagine you know for sure that she didn't come to your school play — you scanned the room for her face and felt that pang in your heart when she wasn't there. But later, she swears she was in the back, clapping the loudest. This makes you question your truth. Was she really there? Why don't you remember seeing her? This is the essence of gaslighting: it challenges your reality.

The idea comes from an old movie, "Gaslight," where a man makes his wife believe she's losing her grip on what's real and what's not. He did sneaky things like dimming the house lights and then denying it was happening. That's the kind of twisted behavior that a narcissistic mother can display. She might do it to avoid blame or to keep you under her thumb.

Identifying gaslighting is tough because it's not always obvious. It's not like a cut on your arm where you see the harm right away. It's more like a slow-growing mold on bread — you might not notice until the whole loaf is bad.

Here's how you can spot the signs: if you often feel confused after talking with your mom, if she denies things you know happened, or if she accuses you of being too sensitive or making things up. Here's the twist – your mom probably won't do this just once; she'll do it again and again. Over time, this can make you feel like you're always wrong, like you can't trust your own brain. This is how your self-esteem starts to wear away like a rock under a waterfall, becoming smaller and smaller.

The outcome of constant gaslighting could be you feeling lost and anxious, always second-guessing yourself. It might even get to the point where you wonder if your memories are real, or if it's all in your head.

The first step toward clearing the smoke is recognizing that it's there. Understand that what you're experiencing isn't right and it isn't your fault. Gaslighting is a game of power, and the only way to win is not to play. Even when your path is smoky, hold onto your truths. Remember the events as you know them, keep a record if needed, and trust your feelings. They are valid and they are yours.

By spotting the signs of gaslighting, you take a critical step toward fresh air, toward reclaiming the control over your life that your mother's narcissistic ways have clouded.

THE PUPPETEER'S STRINGS: RECOGNIZING TRIANGULATION

Triangulation is like a game of keep-away, but not a fun one you might remember from being a kid. Imagine there are three people. Person A is the one who wants to be in charge or get their way, Person B is the one they are trying to control or make look bad, and Person C is the person they bring into the mix to help them do it. Often, Person C doesn't even know they're part of this game.

When dealing with a narcissistic mother, for example, she's often Person A in this game. Let's say you're the daughter, and in this case, you are Person B. Your mother goes to another family member—say, an aunt or uncle—and that person becomes Person C. Your mother might tell your aunt a story about something you did, but she changes the details. She paints herself as the one who's hurt or done wrong, and you as the person who is causing trouble.

Here's how it plays out; your mother tells your aunt, "You know, my daughter never has time for me. She's always too busy with friends. Makes me feel like she doesn't care." But what really happened is you spent the entire day helping her, and by evening, you were so tired that you cancelled plans with friends to go home and rest. The story your mom tells isn't the full truth.

The sad part is, the aunt, who is Person C, often believes your mother. The aunt doesn't have all the background, so she might take your mother's side and even talk to you about it. She might say, "Your mom feels really left out. Don't you think you should spend more time with her?" Now, the aunt, without meaning to, has joined your mother's side in this game of keep-away. You feel alone because it feels like your own family doesn't see what's really going on.

It's not just tough, it hurts, and it can make you feel really isolated, like you're on an island all by yourself. Even worse, it starts to make you doubt your own truth because now you have two people thinking something is wrong with you.

But there's a way to break out of this. The very first step is like turning on a light in a dark room. It's about recognizing that this game of keep-away, this triangulation, is actually happening. If you notice your mother constantly telling stories about you to others, and these stories make you seem bad or wrong, she might be playing this game.

Acknowledge it to yourself: "Okay, Mom is telling these tales to make me look bad. This isn't right." It won't fix everything right away, but knowing what you are up against is like planting your feet on the ground when you're ready to push back. It's the starting line for standing up for yourself and not getting lost in the game she's playing.

FLYING MONKEYS: RECOGNIZING THE NARCISSIST'S HELPERS

"Imagine you have a friend who likes to stir up trouble but never wants to get their hands dirty. They send others to do their bidding, spreading rumors or creating problems. In the story of 'The Wizard of Oz,' there's a wicked witch who sends her flying monkeys to create chaos. Now, in real life, these 'flying monkeys' don't have wings or furry coats, but they do resemble those creatures in a way. They're people who, maybe without knowing it, help someone—often called a narcissist—hurt others.

You see, when we talk about a narcissistic mother, we're talking about a person who is very focused on themselves. They think they are better than others and often don't care about other people's feelings. A mother like this might twist the truth to make herself look good or to get what she wants. And sometimes, she uses other people—just like the flying monkeys.

She might say things to your aunts, uncles, or your friends that make you look bad. These people, who could be close to you, might not even know the whole story. They only hear your mother's side, so they think they're helping. But really, they're just spreading the hurtful things your mother started.

It's like being in the middle of a game, but you don't know the rules. These 'flying monkeys'—the people your mother talks to—become part of that game. They carry her words and actions further, making it harder for you to feel safe and loved.

It's tough to see it happen. It's even tougher when you realize the people you care about might make things worse without meaning to do so. That's why it's important to understand who the 'flying monkeys' are and what they do. Once you know, you can start to protect yourself.

Protecting yourself might mean that you have to talk less to some of these people. I know it sounds hard. These could be folks you love and trust. But if they keep bringing your mother's hurtful words or doing things that upset you, it might be a good idea to keep a little distance. That way, you can stay away from more harm.

Sometimes, though, you can have real, honest talks with these people. If you think they will understand, you could explain how your mother's behavior is hurting you. It's not easy to share these things, but it might help them see the truth.

These 'flying monkeys' might not see what they're doing. they might think they're helping, not hurting. by knowing about them and finding ways to deal with them, you're taking steps to look after yourself. it's about creating a space where you can live without the chaos the 'flying monkeys' bring. and that's a big step towards peace and happiness."

COUNTERING THE CHESSMASTER: RESPONDING TO MANIPULATION

Recognizing manipulation is like spotting a sneaky cat—it's the first step before deciding what to do. It's the same when you're dealing with your narcissistic mother. It's one thing to see her tricky ways, but it's just as key to know how to handle them right.

Think of it like this: if someone is trying to make you feel all jumbled inside, take a step back. Keep your cool when talking to your mother. If she tells you something that's not true, don't dive into the deep end with emotions. Instead, stick to the facts. Imagine your mother saying she was at your big school show when you know she wasn't. Instead of getting upset, you might say, " let's talk about setting limits, which is like building a fence for your personal space. 'Flying monkeys' are people who might not realize it, but they're helping your mother by bringing her news about you, or the other way around. To keep things simple, don't give them too much info about your life. Or you might tell them firmly, "Please don't tell my mom about this." It's like saying no to someone asking to borrow something you value a lot.

It's really tough to face, but you can't make your mother change her ways. What you can do is choose how you react. If she starts playing mind games, maybe you decide that's your cue to end the chat, or you could talk to someone like a counselor to help sort through the tricky feelings.

Building a group of people who have your back is like planting a garden of friends and helpers outside your mother's shadow. These could be pals who get what you're going through, or maybe uncles, aunts, or cousins who cheer you on. It might even be a professional who listens and gives advice. They're your team, there to support you when the going gets tough.

Dealing with a narcissistic mother can be like walking through a maze. recognizing her schemes is your map. keeping your cool, stating what's real, setting clear borders, and knowing you can't change her—that's your compass. walking away from the games, getting help, and having buddies to lean on—that's like having a good pair of shoes to keep you moving forward. your journey might not be easy, but with the right tools and people by your side, you can make your way through stronger and wiser.

7
DRAWING THE LINE: NAVIGATING BOUNDARIES WITH NARCISSISTIC MOTHERS

Imagine you have a garden that is yours, full of flowers and plants you care about a lot. You want to keep it safe, so you put up a fence—the fence keeps things that might hurt your plants away, it's about care, not about anger at those on the other side. This is what setting boundaries is like.

A boundary is like that fence in your mind and heart. It tells others, "This is okay, but that is not." Boundaries are rules you set that show what you will allow and what you won't. They help keep you safe and show people how to treat you well. They are super important for everyone, but for those with a tough mom, they can be life-saving.

Psychology, which is the study of how we think, feel and act, tells us that boundaries are key for being okay inside. For daughters with mothers who tend to be all about themselves—those we call narcissistic—setting these limits is even more important. Why? Because these moms can often make you feel small, twist things to make you feel bad, or use tricky ways to control you. They might not see your needs as important as their own.

A boundary isn't about being mean to your mom; rather, it's taking care of yourself. It's saying, "Mom, when you call me names, I won't stay and listen," or, "Mom, I can't visit every day, but I can come on Sundays." It means if she crosses the line and hurts your feelings, or demands too much, you have the right to step back and say, "That's not okay with me."

Let's be real clear about this: It's not easy to put up these fences, especially with someone as close as a mom. You might feel guilty, bad, or scared in the beginning. These feelings are normal—it's tough to change how things have always been. But remember, even though you might feel these things, it doesn't mean setting the boundary is wrong. It takes strength, and over time, you'll see that the fences you put up are helping keep your inner garden happy and healthy.

Setting these boundaries is not a way to get back at your mom. it's not about her at all. it's about you feeling okay, being respected, and living a life without someone always making things hard for you.

With clear and kind boundaries, you can start to have better control over your life and emotions. It may take some time, and that's okay. Your peace of mind and well-being are worth the effort and patience. And every time you stay true to your boundaries, you're taking a step forward, making sure that beautiful garden of yours flourishes.

BOUNDARY VIOLATIONS: RECOGNIZING SIGNS FROM NARCISSISTIC MOTHERS

Recognizing the invisible lines that should not be crossed by others is key in understanding how our mothers may overstep. These lines are our boundaries. They are important because they help us to feel safe and respected. But sometimes, a mother can be different in a way that is not easy to handle. Some moms may think they always know best. They might even have a strong need to be the center of attention. We call this being narcissistic. When a mother is like this, she might not see or care about those invisible lines.

Imagine your life is like your own garden. You decide what flowers to grow and where to plant them. Your garden has a fence, which is like your boundary. A narcissist mother may not see this fence. She comes into your garden as she pleases, picks your flowers without asking, or tells you how to do your gardening. But this garden is yours, not hers.

She might walk right into your room without knocking first. Maybe she looks through your things or reads your diary. These are your private spaces, and she's stepping into them like they're her own. This can make you feel like you don't have your own special space. When you talk about your feelings or your thoughts, she might say they are wrong or silly. She may make you feel small for making choices she doesn't like.

For every choice you make, she might have a word to say. It can be about simple things like the clothes you wear. Sometimes, she also tries to pick who you should be friends with or what job you should have. It's like she's holding the paintbrush to the picture of your life. That can make you feel like you don't have the freedom you should.

To make things harder, she might use your love for her like a tool. She could say things that make you feel bad for her. These things are like traps to make you do what she wants. You want to be kind and loving, so sometimes you think you have to do as she says. But this is not a nice way to ask. It's called guilt-tripping.

Being aware of these actions is like turning on a light in a dark room. Now you see the lines she shouldn't cross. Knowing is the first, very important step. Once you see how she comes into your garden and what she does there, you can start to put up a stronger fence. This isn't mean or unloving. It's a way to care for your garden properly, so that you and your flowers can be healthy and grow. When you know your boundaries, you can start to teach others to see them, too. Even if that person is your mother.

DRAWING THE LINE: HOW TO SET BOUNDARIES WITH A NARCISSISTIC MOTHER

Setting boundaries with a person who always thinks about themselves, especially if that person is your mother, is a very hard thing to do. However, doing this is important for your own peace of mind. Here is what you can do step by step.

The first step is figuring out what parts of your life need these limits. Think about moments when you feel upset or stressed because of something your mother does. Maybe she enters your room without asking, calls you many times a day, or makes choices for you without your okay. It could be she talks about things you wish to keep to just yourself. These are areas where you need to say, "This is my space, and here are the rules for it."

Once you know where you need those lines, you have to talk to her about them. It's like drawing a line in the sand and saying, "You can come this far and no further." When you talk to her, use words that are kind but firm. Make it clear you're serious. You can say, "Mom, I love you, but I need to make my own decisions without you choosing for me."

But here's the thing, mothers who only think about themselves might not like hearing this. They might get angry or try to make you feel bad. This is where you must stand like a strong tree, even when the wind is pushing hard against you. Remember, you're doing this for your well-being, not to hurt her feelings. She might say, "You're being selfish," or "After all I've done for you," but that's just the wind. Be like that tree and stand still.

Have a plan for when she doesn't respect the boundaries. For example, if she comes into your room without asking, you might say,

"Mom, we talked about this. Please knock next time." If she keeps calling you non-stop, you might decide to only answer once a day or send a message saying, "I'll call you at this time." You've got to follow through every single time, or the lines you drew will fade away.

These steps aren't simple, and it may feel like you're climbing a steep hill. But every person needs their space to breathe and be themselves. When your mother starts to see the lines, and you keep showing her where they are, life becomes easier. You can then spend time with her without feeling like you're losing a piece of yourself.

STAYING FIRM: DEALING WITH THE FALLOUT OF SETTING BOUNDARIES

When you decide that it's time to set clear limits with a mother who shows signs of narcissism, it's like putting up a fence in your garden. That fence tells others where they can walk and helps keep your space safe and peaceful. This process, much like gardening, isn't easy. It can stir up big emotions in both you and your mom.

Imagine you tell your mother you can only talk on the phone once a week instead of every day. A mom who thinks a lot of herself may react in ways that seem very extreme. She might get very angry. Picture a teapot on the stove, steaming and whistling—that's anger. Her words might feel like hot steam coming out with no warning, saying that you're being mean or selfish. Her anger can be loud and scary, making you feel like you're doing something wrong simply by trying to take care of yourself.

Another way she might respond is by trying to make you feel guilty. Guilt-tripping is when someone tries to make you feel bad for your choices. Think of it as a backpack being filled with heavy rocks, each rock a word or an action meant to make you feel heavier with guilt. She might say things like, "After all I've done for you, you treat me like this?" or "A good child would want to talk to their mother." This can tug at your heart and make you question if you're being unkind.

Sometimes, a narcissistic mother might pull back her love. Emotional withdrawal is like the sun hiding behind clouds on a cold day. Where once her attention was warm and all on you, now there is only a chilly silence. She might not talk to you or show any caring, hoping this will force you to take down your fence and let things go back to how they were.

Knowing these reactions might happen helps brace yourself. Stay as firm as the ground during a storm. It's your right to have a peaceful garden. It may hurt when she gets mad, loads you up with guilt, or turns away. Yet remember, you're doing this for your well-being, planting your garden the way you need it to grow.

No one should tend to their garden alone. Look for help from friends you trust, members of your family who understand, or a therapist. They can be like a fence post, helping to hold the fence up when the ground gets shaky.

Every time you keep your boundaries in place, quietly but firmly, you're actually being kind to yourself. It's like giving yourself sun and water to grow strong and healthy. Each "no" you say to her, each choice you make to keep your limits, is a "yes" you say to yourself. It's an act of love and respect for you, which is always worth the hard work. Remember, the most beautiful gardens are those that have been carefully designed and well-protected.

THE POWER OF NO: ASSERTING YOUR RIGHT TO EMOTIONAL SAFETY

Maintaining healthy boundaries with a narcissistic mother is challenging, yet crucial for your well-being. These boundaries act like invisible fences that let you decide what you are okay with and what things cross the line. One of the simplest but most effective ways to enforce these boundaries is by saying "no." Though it's often easier said than done, mastering the ability to say "no" can be incredibly empowering.

Sometimes, your mom might ask you to do something you're not comfortable with, or she may demand you agree with her on everything. It's alright to refuse such requests or demands. This doesn't mean you don't love or respect your mom. It means you are taking care of your emotional health. Saying "no" is not only a sign of personal strength, but it is also necessary for sustaining a sense of respect and self-worth.

For a narcissistic mother, hearing "no" can be tough. She might see it as a sign you're not on her side, or even as a personal attack. But it's important to remember it's not about her in those moments—it's about you. You have the right to protect yourself from stress or activities that don't feel right. When your mom asks something of you that pushes your boundaries, stand firm. Your emotional safety must come first.

If saying "no" is hard for you, it might be because you're used to giving explanations. You may feel like you need to offer a good reason for your refusal. But remember this: "no" is a complete sentence all by itself. You don't owe anyone an essay on why you're not doing what they ask. You can say "no" without giving a reason. This can take practice, and it might feel strange at first, especially with your mom, but it's both powerful and liberating.

It can be helpful to practice saying "no" outside of stressful situations. Start with small things, like when someone offers you a coffee and you don't want it. Just say "no, thank you," without an explanation. Build up to saying "no" in more important situations. The more you practice, the easier it will become to use it when it really counts.

When you do say "no" to your mom, stay calm and firm. It might lead to an argument, but remember that you are not responsible for her reaction. Her response is her own. By saying "no," you are not fighting or being mean - you are simply taking care of yourself.

In essence, think of "no" as a shield. It can protect you from things that can crack your happiness or hurt your heart. Your mom might not like this shield much because it changes the way things have always been between you. But it's a shield you have every right to carry, for your peace and health. Keep practicing it, use it wisely, and let it give you the strength you need to maintain healthy boundaries in your relationship with your narcissistic mother.

NURTURING SELF-COMPASSION: OVERCOMING GUILT IN BOUNDARY SETTING

As you start to set limits with a narcissistic mother, you might notice a heavy feeling in your chest or stomach. That feeling has a name: guilt. Some people wear it like a backpack full of stones, and others might feel it only sometimes. But when dealing with a mother who thinks only of herself, that guilty whisper can become a shout.

Imagine your emotions like a garden. Each one is a different flower or plant. Guilt is like vines that can quickly wrap around all the others. But here's something not everyone knows: feeling guilty is pretty normal when you say "no" to a mother who is used to hearing "yes."

You see, a mother who loves herself too much uses tricks to keep you doing what she wants. She might make you believe that taking care of yourself is selfish. She can twist her words and actions to make it seem like you are doing something wrong by saying "no." But the truth is, she's the one playing with your feelings.

So, when guilt blooms like weeds in your emotional garden, remember to be kind to yourself. This is what we call self-compassion. Imagine talking to yourself like you would talk to a good friend. What would you say to a friend who feels bad for taking care of themselves? You would say, "You're doing the right thing," and "It's okay to put yourself first." Say these words to yourself.

Setting boundaries with your mother is a big step on the road to feeling better. Think of it as building a fence in your garden to keep the guilt vines away from your flowers. Boundaries are your rights, and they help you stay strong and true to yourself. It's not easy, but it's important for your recovery and self-respect.

Caring for yourself also means stepping outside the garden sometimes. Self-care means doing things that make you feel good and at peace. Perhaps you like to walk, read, or listen to calming music. Maybe you enjoy a hot bath or spending time with friends. These activities are like sunshine and rain for your emotional garden, helping the good plants to flourish.

Sometimes, though, those guilt vines are strong, and we need some extra help. Seeking support is like inviting a gardener who knows how to deal with tricky vines. Talking to a counselor, joining a group with people who understand, or chatting one-on-one with a trusted friend can provide new tools and support to work through the guilty feelings.

Setting boundaries is not about being mean or unkind to your mother. it's the opposite. it's about being kind to yourself, so you can maybe, one day, have a healthier relationship with her, even if from a distance. you deserve to feel good, happy, and free, just like everyone else. you're not doing anything wrong by taking care of your own emotional garden. keep those boundaries clear, and keep being kind to yourself.

8

BUILDING THE FENCE: YOUR GUIDE TO SETTING BOUNDARIES WITH A NARCISSIST

Understanding the importance of setting boundaries and how to establish and maintain them effectively with a narcissistic mother is a critical element for anyone in such a challenging relationship. To thrive and protect oneself, it's essential to comprehend the full power of setting these limits. Boundaries are like an invisible fence you build around yourself. They are rules or guidelines that you set to let other people know what you are okay with and what you are not.

Boundaries act as a protective shield, safeguarding your physical, emotional, and mental space. Imagine you are living in a home with a yard. The fence around your yard tells others where your property starts and ends. It also helps to keep things out that you don't want in your yard. Similarly, boundaries work in relationships. They help you keep out unwanted behaviors or treatment from others, especially from a mother with narcissistic tendencies.

In the context of a narcissistic mother-daughter relationship, boundaries help protect the daughter from further emotional abuse. A narcissistic mother may try to control your life or make everything about herself, often ignoring your feelings and needs. She may also be critical, manipulative, or demanding. Setting boundaries tells her that those behaviors are not okay with you, and it's your way of taking a stand for your own emotional health.

Boundaries can range from limiting conversations about certain topics to restricting the frequency of interactions. For example, you might decide that you will not tolerate being shouted at or insulted. So you create a boundary by calmly asserting that you will end the conversation if your mother starts to raise her voice or say hurtful things. Another boundary might be choosing to see her only in public places or only for a certain amount of time.

They are essential for maintaining self-respect and personal well-being. By setting boundaries, you assert your value, indicating that you won't tolerate disrespectful treatment. This action sends a clear message to your narcissistic mother that you respect yourself even if she has trouble respecting you. It helps you maintain control over your life and keeps you from being hurt by her unhealthy behavior.

Boundaries can reduce feelings of stress, anxiety, and helplessness, promoting a healthier mental state. When you know you have the power to say "no" to something that is not good for you, it can make you feel stronger and more at peace. Imagine holding the reins of your life firmly in your hands, steering clear of unnecessary turmoil.

To sum up, boundaries are not about pushing someone away or being mean. They are about taking good care of yourself. When dealing with a narcissistic mother, setting and upholding these boundaries can feel tough, but remember, you are entitled to respect, love, and a healthy mind and heart. By building this boundary blueprint, you learn to navigate the relationship in a way that protects you and encourages a mutually respectful dynamic as much as possible.

THE FINE LINE: IDENTIFYING YOUR PERSONAL BOUNDARIES

Identifying your personal boundaries is the first step to setting them. Imagine you have a special space around you that is just yours. This space keeps you comfy and safe. Think of boundaries as the invisible walls of this space. They let others know what is okay and what is not when they interact with you. To set these walls up, you need to be clear on where they should stand.

Take a moment to think back on times you've talked or spent time with your mom and wound up feeling upset or uneasy. Maybe there was a holiday dinner where she questioned your life choices in front of everyone, or a phone call where she insisted on giving advice you didn't ask for. These uncomfortable feelings are clues. They are like little red flags your heart waves to say, "Hey, something wasn't right about that!"

Now, let's look closer at those red flags. Picture those past moments like scenes from a movie. Pause at the parts that hurt. If you could step into that movie, what would you change? Maybe you would tell movie-you to say, "Mom, I appreciate your concern, but I'm really happy with how things are going." Or perhaps, "Let's talk about something else; I'm not comfortable discussing this now." The changes you imagine are the roots of the boundaries you need.

It's key to remember that the walls you set up around your space belong to you and you alone. They are built from your feelings, your comfort zone, and what you value. What's okay for one person might not feel okay to you, and that's perfectly fine. Your friend might not mind if their mom gives them a daily wake-up call, but if you're the kind who needs quiet mornings, having your mom call early might be a no-go in your book.

Your boundaries can be about anything that matters to you. They can cover how often you want to talk on the phone, the kind of advice you are open to, or what life choices are off-limits for discussions. Think of them as guidelines that help your relationship grow happier and healthier. Your boundaries are there to protect your well-being and to make sure your and your mother's relationship can be the best it can be.

As you think about your limits, consider your values, your peace of mind, and what you need to feel respected and heard. Maybe it's needing respect for your career choices, or wanting some parts of your life to be just yours. Every `no` you set means you are saying `yes` to your comfort and peace.

Identifying your boundaries doesn't mean you don't care about your mother. it's quite the opposite. by setting boundaries, you're making sure that the love between you two has room to grow without making you feel trapped or wrong. now that you've started thinking about your boundaries, the next step is learning how to communicate them firmly but kindly.

BUILDING THE WALL: HOW TO SET BOUNDARIES

Creating clear boundaries with those close to us can sometimes be a tough task, especially when it involves a narcissistic mother. However, setting these limits is a very important step in taking care of ourselves and our well-being. Let's talk about how to communicate those boundaries in a clear and self-assured way that still respects both you and the other person.

When you want to set a boundary, think about using "I" statements. These are phrases that begin with 'I' to express your feelings and needs without making the other person feel blamed or attacked. For example, if your mother often criticizes the choices you make, you might feel hurt or angry. In this situation, you could say something like, "I feel upset when you criticize my decisions. I need you to respect my choices." By saying it this way, you're explaining your side without pointing fingers, which can help prevent the other person from getting defensive.

Being firm yet fair is also key when you are drawing these lines. It's sort of like being a kind and reasonable boss who needs to make sure the rules are followed. You want to stand your ground because your needs are important. But you also want to avoid being too harsh or setting your expectations too high. Try to keep in mind that the other person may have feelings about the boundary you're setting, and that's okay. You can listen to those feelings, but still be clear that your boundaries need to be respected.

Now, it's not always going to be easy. When you're dealing with a narcissistic mother, she might not be too happy about these new limits you're setting. She could resist, or even pretend she didn't hear them at all. This is when you might feel like giving in, but it's actually a time to stand strong. Remember to stick to your boundaries and repeat them if you must. It's all about being consistent. Think of your boundaries like a fence you've built. If it gets knocked down, you have to put it back up to keep your yard safe.

Anticipate that your mom might try to cross your boundaries or make light of them. She might try to make you feel guilty or say things that make you question yourself. This is your cue to remember why you set these limits in the first place. It's for your peace of mind and to build a healthier relationship. Every time you reinforce your boundaries, you are reminding both of you that your feelings and needs are valid.

NAVIGATING THE MINEFIELD: DEALING WITH BACKLASH

Setting boundaries with a narcissistic mother is not an easy task. Such a mother often views boundaries as personal attacks, leading to a backlash that can take many forms. She may turn to guilt-tripping, making you feel like you're doing something wrong by asserting your own needs. Sentences that start with "After all I've done for you..." or "A good child would never..." are tools in her arsenal designed to make you doubt yourself.

Anger is another weapon she might use. This can be outright rage or subtle, passive-aggressive remarks designed to unsettle you. She might raise her voice, use harsh words, or even stop talking to you entirely to show her displeasure.

Alternatively, she might play the victim to resist the boundaries you set. She could cry, claim you don't love her, or suggest that she is ill or in distress because of your actions. This tactic is aimed at making you feel responsible for her emotions and manipulating you into backing down.

When you encounter these tactics, it's essential to stay calm. Engaging in arguments will only fuel the fire and can leave you feeling more drained than before. It may be helpful to rehearse calm responses in advance or even to have a script in mind. Phrases like, "I understand you're upset, but this boundary is important for my well-being" can be firm yet non-confrontational ways to maintain your stance.

Prioritizing your well-being is crucial. You might feel a natural urge to make peace or to prevent any discord, hoping that appeasing your mother will keep the relationship smooth. However, this comes at a cost to your mental health. Consistently setting aside your needs for another person, especially one who may never fully recognize or appreciate them, can lead to long-lasting feelings of resentment and unhappiness.

It's natural to want to avoid conflicts, especially with a person who raised you. Indeed, most of us have an inbuilt desire to seek approval from our parents. But this shouldn't be at the expense of your mental and emotional health. Boundary-setting is healthy and necessary, especially when dealing with someone who, knowingly or not, disregards your needs.

If maintaining the boundaries you need for your own peace leads to ongoing hostility from your mother, you might have to take a step back and seek external help. A therapist or counselor can provide a safe space for you to explore your feelings and experiences without judgment. They can also offer techniques and coping strategies to help you maintain your boundaries and handle any guilt or stress that comes with them.

Setting boundaries doesn't make you a bad child; it makes you an adult taking responsibility for your own life and happiness. with time, and perhaps professional guidance, you can learn to maintain these boundaries while navigating the complex relationship with a narcissistic mother. it's a journey that takes strength and self-care but one that can lead to a healthier, more balanced life.

MAINTAINING THE FENCE: ENSURING BOUNDARIES STICK

Boundaries are like invisible lines we draw around ourselves to keep safe and happy. When dealing with a mom who thinks mostly about herself, putting these lines in place is very important. But once these lines are drawn, we must keep them there, always the same, like the walls of our homes that don't move.

Imagine you tell your mom that she can't just come to your house without asking first. That's a boundary. But then, if one day she comes over without calling and you just let her in and act like it's fine, you've moved your boundary. If you do this, she may think, "these rules aren't so serious," and she'll keep doing what she wants.

It's like telling someone they can't take cookies from your cookie jar, but then when they do, you say nothing. They will keep taking cookies because they think you don't really mind. Be serious about your rules if you want them respected.

Sticking to your boundaries isn't easy, though. Sometimes you might feel alone or unsure. That's why friends and family who care about you are like stars on a dark night—they guide you and remind you that you're doing the right thing. Talk to them when you're feeling down or when you're wrestling with whether or not to let your mom cross a boundary. They can give you the push you need to stay firm.

For more support, you can turn to people online who have walked in your shoes. There are communities filled with people who grew up with moms or dads who loved themselves more than anyone else. A place like r/raisedbynarcissists can be a spot to share your story and to listen to others. Reading about people who are in the same boat can make you feel less alone, and their triumphs can be your lessons.

But sometimes, the challenge of dealing with a self-loving mom is too heavy, and the weight can make you feel like you're sinking. It's okay to ask for a helping hand. Think about meeting with a therapist or counselor who gets what it's like to deal with this. These are special helpers who listen to you and teach you tips and tricks to keep those boundaries standing tall, even when the winds blow hard.

Imagine you're learning to play soccer, but you've never tried to score a goal before. A coach can show you how to kick the ball just right to make that goal. In the same way, this professional can coach you through keeping your boundaries firm and dealing with any tricks your mom might try.

You can only hold up your boundaries if you don't let them shake or fall. friends and family can help, online buddies can share their stories, and if the storm gets too wild, a professional can stand with you. keep your lines clear and steady, and you'll have the best chance at a peaceful relationship with your mom.

9
THE ART OF BECOMING UNINTERESTING: MASTERING THE GRAY ROCK METHOD

In this part of the book, let's dive deep into the Gray Rock Method. Imagine you're sitting by a river, and you see all kinds of stones. Most of them just blend in, right? But once in a while, there's a stone that catches your eye because it shines or has a bright color. The Gray Rock Method is about being one of those stones that doesn't stand out—it's about being the dull, unnoticed rock that doesn't attract attention.

The idea here is simple, but powerful. When dealing with a mother who shows signs of narcissism, she may often try to start arguments, say things to upset you, or try to control you with her emotions. These are her ways of getting what she wants: your emotional response. It's your attention and reaction that she's after. But what if you could make yourself as emotionally uninteresting as that gray rock by the river? That's what this method is about.

A smart person named Skylar came up with the Gray Rock Method. Skylar had to handle someone who often tried to control and manipulate others and learned that being unresponsive was an effective defense. This method has since helped many people deal with difficult situations.

Here's how it works: You keep your talks short and sweet. When your mother tries to start a drama or says something to push your buttons, instead of reacting, you just give a simple, flat response. If she says something mean, instead of getting upset or defending yourself, you might just say "Okay" or "I see." You keep your tone of voice even and your face calm. You don't give her any signs that you're upset or excited. You're aiming to be as thrilling as watching paint dry.

Now, remember, this isn't about being mean or rude. It's not about giving the silent treatment or ignoring her completely, which can sometimes make things worse. It's about self-care and keeping your emotions safe. You still listen and respond, but you do it in a way that doesn't give her the reaction she's looking for.

It's like if someone wants to play a game where they throw a ball at you, trying to get you to throw it back. But instead of throwing it back, you just set the ball down gently. Soon, they'll realize the game isn't fun if you're not really playing along, and they may stop trying to involve you in that game.

The Gray Rock Method won't change your mother's behavior — that's not the goal. The goal is to keep yourself from being hurt by her actions. Over time, if you're consistent, she might learn that those old tricks don't work on you anymore and she might start interacting with you in a different way. But even if she doesn't, you'll be protecting your peace and well-being, and that's a big win.

THE RIGHT TIME TO USE THE GRAY ROCK METHOD

The Gray Rock Method is a way of dealing with people who seem to take your energy. Imagine someone like a narcissist – a person who may only think of themselves and not care much about others' feelings. They may try to make everything about them and leave you feeling tired or upset. The Gray Rock Method could be a lifesaver in those times, but it's not a fix for every problem. It's like a special tool in your toolbox – you only bring it out when you need it.

Let's say you're the grown-up daughter of a mom who often makes you feel this way. You love her, but sometimes, being around her feels too hard. Talking to her might leave you feeling worse, not better. When you can't, or don't want to, cut off contact completely – which we call 'No Contact' – the Gray Rock Method can be a powerful way to save your strength.

Here's how it works. Instead of being colorful and interesting like a bright red rock, you are calm and plain like a gray rock. You give short, simple answers to questions without showing much feeling. You don't share exciting stories or big news that might get the other person going. This way, they might start to see talking to you as not so interesting, and slowly, they may look somewhere else for attention.

But there's a big "if" here. If you still live with your mother, or you see her a lot, you can't always turn into a gray rock. It might make the situation tougher. In other words, if you go gray rock all the way, it might upset your mom more. She might try harder to get a reaction out of you, which can make things worse.

So what can you do? Think of it as being 'selectively Gray Rock.' It's like playing a smart game of hide and seek. You use the gray rock method only when you really need it. Let's say your mom asks you what you had for lunch. You might say, "I had a sandwich," with no extra details or emotions. But if she asks you something more important, like if you're feeling sick, you might choose to answer more fully because that's part of caring for each other.

In those moments, you're the judge. Ask yourself, "Do I need to share a lot here, or just enough?" The idea is to save your energy for the times and the people that fill you with joy instead of taking your strength away.

The gray rock method can be a bit like a dance. you step forward and back, using your best moves to keep your peace and balance. by using this method, you can take part in life with your mother when needed without letting it pull you down. you get to choose when and how to protect your heart, and that's a powerful thing.

THE HOW-TO GUIDE FOR IMPLEMENTING THE GRAY ROCK METHOD

When you're dealing with a tough situation, like when someone is trying very hard to pull your strings or push your buttons, staying calm and cool is the best way. This method we're talking about is called the Gray Rock Method. Think of it as you becoming like a gray rock: not catching anyone's eye, just there, steady, and most importantly, boring. But hold on, it's not about just sitting back and letting things happen. It's about being in charge by choosing not to give a big reaction.

So, let's start. The first thing you have to do is notice when these tricky times happen. Maybe it's your mother who, during your family's meal, chats about things that make everyone uneasy, or when you talk on the phone, she asks questions that are too personal, or when holidays come, and the pressure is on. Spot these times and get ready.

Once you see one of these moments coming, it's time to be that gray rock. Let's say your mother tosses a word grenade your way, trying to get you fired up or into an argument. Here's what you do: keep it short and dull. You might say, "Hmm, that's interesting," without letting your voice show any ups or downs. Or, "I'll think about it," and move on.

The key here is not to let on too much about what's going on in your life. If she doesn't know the details, she can't use them to stir up trouble. So, if she asks about your work or your friends, you might just say, "Everything's normal," and then talk about something boring, like the weather. It's like talking about paint drying. Who can argue about that?

You might be thinking, "Wait, aren't we supposed to connect with our family?" Sure, you are, but think of it this way: this is for those times when the cost of sharing feels too high, when what you share gets twisted and turned into something it's not. You're not being mean; you're just guarding your peace of mind.

So, the aim here isn't to make your mother upset. Far from it. You're doing this to protect yourself, your feelings, your heart. When you become the human version of a gray rock, you become less interesting to spar with. It's all about making yourself such a so-so target that the person who's trying to push your buttons just... loses interest.

This isn't easy, and it won't feel natural right away. It takes practice. Each time you respond like a gray rock, it's like a little workout for your patience. And the next time, it'll be a tiny bit easier. Give yourself permission to take it slow and remember that you're doing this for a good reason: to keep your boat steady on wavy seas.

NAVIGATING THE CHALLENGES OF THE GRAY ROCK METHOD

When you choose to use the Gray Rock Method, imagine it like putting on invisible armor to guard your feelings. Think of this armor as a cool, smooth stone that does not react no matter what happens around it.

However, using this method is not as easy as it might sound. It's a bit like jumping into the sea and keeping your balance against the waves. There will be troubles, and it's wise to know what they might be.

First off, you might feel a tug at your heart. This could be guilt knocking on your door, making you question if it's wrong to seem cold or distant, especially towards someone like your mom. But here's the thing—protecting yourself isn't mean or wrong. It's looking out for yourself so you can be healthy and happy. Remember, you're wearing the invisible armor for a very good reason.

Imagine the family gathering where your mom is used to getting a big reaction from you. But this time, you're the steady, calm rock. When she doesn't get the response she expects, she might turn up the volume on her actions. She might toss more words at you or act in ways to get you to break your calm. This is tough, for sure. In moments like these, hold on to your invisible armor tightly. Keep your answers as exciting as a gray pebble on the road—short, simple, and dull.

It's like when you play a game and stick to the rules no matter what happens. You wouldn't change the way you play just because the other players want you to. Stick to the 'rules' of the Gray Rock Method, and keep your cool at all costs.

But it's not just your mom you might have to think about. Other people in your family might not get what you are doing. They might say, "Why are you being so quiet?" or "Why don't you talk back when she says things like that?" They might not see the invisible armor you're wearing, and to them, you might come off as harsh or uncaring.

In situations like these, you can let them in on a snippet of your game plan. You might say, "I'm trying a new way to keep things peaceful." You don't have to spill all your secrets, just enough to let them know you have a plan. The goal here is to make your family time more smooth and less like a wild roller coaster ride.

Working with the Gray Rock Method is a bit like walking on a balance beam. You might sway a bit, and that's okay. The important thing is to stay on it and walk forward. By knowing what might shake your balance, you can stand firm and keep the peace within yourself and around others.

THE ROLE OF SELF-CARE IN THE GRAY ROCK METHOD

When you're using the Gray Rock method with a person who's making life hard, like a narcissistic mother, it's kind of like you're a gray rock by the river, not interesting or exciting. You blend in with the other rocks so that the rough waves, or the mean words and actions from your mom, just flow over you without picking you out as a target. But doing this – not reacting or showing much feeling – can make you feel very tired inside, even if it helps keep the peace outside.

Imagine that inside you, there's a cup that holds all your feelings and energy. Each time you have to act like a gray rock, it's like your cup spills a little. If you don't fill your cup back up, one day you'll find it empty, and you'll feel worn out and sad. So, it's super important to do things for yourself that make you feel good and full again.

Think of what makes you smile or feel calm. For some people, it could be curling up with a good book where stories take them to a happier place. Others might find that going for a walk outside, listening to the birds sing and feeling the sun on their skin, helps them fill their cup right up to the top. Or maybe sitting quietly and breathing deep, letting their thoughts come and go like clouds, can make them feel whole again. This quiet time could be meditation, and it helps to clear your head and ease your heart.

You might have your special way to care for yourself, and that's perfect. Whatever helps you unwind and feel at peace after being that gray rock, make sure you do it. Like putting on your favorite music and dancing around, or taking a long, warm bubble bath. These things are your self-care activities. They're like a charger for your spirit, giving you the energy to face another day.

But self-care isn't just about being alone. Humans, like birds flying together, feel stronger when they're with others who understand and help each other. Reach out to friends who really listen and have your back, ones who give you good feelings and not bad ones. There might be groups with people who have dealt with tough mothers too, where you can share your story and hear theirs. They can be like a mirror, showing you that you're not alone and giving you strength.

Some people might find it really helpful to talk to a therapist, someone who's like a guide in tough times. A therapist knows a lot about how words can hurt and can give you tools to protect your feelings, just like a good umbrella in a rainy storm.

Being a gray rock doesn't mean you never feel or that you push away your feelings. when you're away from your mom, let yourself feel all your feelings, like painting on a big canvas with all the colors. let them out in a safe place, so they don't get trapped inside. by taking good care of your own heart and head in these ways, you'll be able to keep being strong, even when things are tough.

10

CUTTING THE TIES THAT BIND: UNDERSTANDING NO CONTACT AND LOW CONTACT STRATEGIES

The act of disconnecting from someone who has a deep connection to our life, like a mother, feels unnatural. Yet, when dealing with a narcissistic mother, this step could be the path to healing. The 'No Contact' (NC) strategy means making a bold choice to stop all talks, messages, and meets with this person. We take this hard road when the hurt caused is so great that any small talk keeps the wound fresh, stopping it from getting better.

Starting the NC method is not easy. Often, we face people who don't understand, thinking it's just a fight that will pass. They might say, "But she's your mom," pushing us to question our choice. However, when a daughter has faced years of harm from a mother who should be her safe place, she must put her own peace first.

To stay true to this choice, it takes a heart of steel and a circle of friends who get it. These friends become like a safety net, catching you when emotions threaten to pull you down. Talking with experts like therapists or joining groups with folks who've walked your path can make a heavy load feel lighter. They remind us we're not alone and help us understand the whys and hows of what we're doing.

After starting NC, it's like a storm in the heart - a mix of feeling free, feeling bad for the choice, and missing what could have been. These feelings might crash over us like big waves. This is why letting ourselves feel these hard feelings is key. They're signs of the healing happening inside. If the storm feels too much, it's okay to reach out to a pro to help us ride the waves.

While we deal with this, loving ourselves and caring for our needs become the most important things. It's like putting on a seatbelt in this bumpy ride. We learn to hold ourselves kindly, do nice things for ourselves, and give ourselves the kind of love we missed.

THE BALANCING ACT: UNDERSTANDING THE LOW CONTACT STRATEGY

Low Contact, or LC for short, is like finding a middle road: you're not completely cutting off your narcissistic mother, but you're keeping her at a safe arm's length. Imagine you have a garden. You don't want to lock the gate forever, but you're not going to let in every bug and critter either. You choose what and how much you want to let in. That's what Low Contact is all about—managing what gets through the gate to your personal garden.

Sometimes, you can't just shut someone out of your life completely, or maybe you really don't want to. That's where LC steps in. It's like creating a bubble around yourself. It's not a wall, but it's a space where you can breathe easy because you have control over who steps into it and when. With LC, you're keeping just enough contact to acknowledge the relationship, yet not so much that it makes you feel bad or unsafe emotionally.

To make LC work, you need to lay down some clear lines in the sand —boundaries. Kind of like how a game has rules, boundaries help keep things running smoothly. And just like a captain on a ship, you have to stick to your course and not let the waves push you around. If you decide that talking to your mom only once a week is what feels okay for you, then hold tight to that plan.

Setting boundaries starts with figuring out what amount of contact doesn't stir things up too much for you. Maybe it's okay to talk on the phone but not to visit in person. Or perhaps you're fine with visits but don't want to chat about touchy subjects like your job or personal life. It's like knowing which ingredients work in a recipe and which ones will spoil the dish.

Following the LC path isn't all smooth sailing, though. You might have to face your mom's pushback when she hits the boundaries you've set. She might try to guilt you into crossing your own lines, or she might become mad or sad about the limits. That's tough, and it's normal to feel a bit guilty yourself. It can tug at your heartstrings to set limits with someone you're supposed to be close to.

But here's the thing to remember: those boundaries are like a life jacket keeping you afloat. You're doing this to keep your emotional world from getting stormy. You're looking out for yourself, and there's nothing wrong with that. It's about making sure you're in a healthy place, like taking an umbrella out into the rain.

When you're walking this LC path, it's a real help to have people in your corner. Talking to therapists or counselors can give you a good game plan and help you stick to it. Support groups are like cheer squads that understand exactly what you're going through because they're right there with you, and they can remind you why you're doing this when things get hard.

Lc isn't about closing doors; it's about choosing which ones you leave open and how wide. your emotional health is worth every step and every boundary, so take care of your garden and let it flourish in a way that's right for you.

THE FORK IN THE ROAD: CHOOSING BETWEEN NO CONTACT AND LOW CONTACT

When you're faced with a choice as big as deciding whether or not to stay in touch with a parent who has hurt you deeply, it's like standing at a crossroads with two different paths ahead. On one hand, you have the choice of 'No Contact' (NC), and on the other, there's 'Low Contact' (LC). Both these choices are tough and personal, because they reflect your unique experience and feelings.

Firstly, let's think about how bad the hurt has been. The harshness of the behavior you faced plays a big role in your choice. If the pain caused by your parent's actions or words feels much too heavy and hard to bear, then cutting off contact might feel like the only way to breathe and start healing.

Your emotional health matters most here. Are you feeling over-whelmed? Do you feel stronger or weaker after meeting or speaking to your parent? Your answers to these questions can guide your decision. Some people find that stepping away completely gives them the peace needed for their hearts to mend. It's like stepping out of a storm into a quiet space where you can dry off and warm up.

Others, however, might choose a different method to handle the situation. They might prefer the idea of LC—keeping their parent in their life, but only sometimes and only in small, controlled ways. This can mean setting firm boundaries, like only talking on the phone once a week or only at family gatherings, to limit the hurt but still keep a connection.

When you choose nc or lc, it's not about being harsh to your parent. it's about taking care of you. it's like when you're on an airplane and they tell you to put on your oxygen mask before helping someone else. you need to make sure that you can breathe first.

Creating a safe space for yourself is the main aim here. This space allows you to fix the wounds, learn more about who you are, and eventually, blossom. And just like a safety net beneath a high-wire walker, this decision can catch you if you slip, letting you know that your well-being is protected.

These decisions aren't written in stone. Life changes, feelings shift, and you might find what worked before doesn't fit anymore. That's okay. You can always rethink your choice and adjust your plan. There's a lot of power in understanding that you are not locked into any one path.

Through all of this, talking to a therapist or counselor can be a massive help. They are the guides that can help you map out your inner world and give you tools to navigate it. They'll listen without judging, offer comfort, and when you're ready, they can help you step forward, whether that's toward NC, LC, or a new path you hadn't even thought of yet.

Handling the emotional side of things after you've made the decision —be it NC or LC—is no small task, and a professional can make it a little bit easier by being there with you. They can help you understand your feelings, cope with the hard days, and celebrate every step forward you take. Remember, moving towards a happier life is a journey, and it's one you don't have to take alone.

NAVIGATING THE EMOTIONAL STORM: COPING WITH THE AFTERMATH OF NO CONTACT OR LOW CONTACT

When you make the hard choice to take some space from your mother, especially when she's used to having you close, things may get tough for a while. Implementing No Contact (NC) or Low Contact (LC) with a narcissistic mother isn't just about making a decision and walking away. It often starts a storm of emotions, both in you and in her.

If your mother leans toward narcissism, she may not see your need for space as something for your well-being. To her, it might feel like you're pulling away something that's hers – your attention and time. Get ready for different tactics she might use to bring you back. She might try to make you feel like you're wrong or selfish, using words that dig deep like, "After all I've done for you," or "You know I always want the best for you." This is called guilt-tripping. It's a way to poke at your feelings of responsibility and love, making you question your choice.

Sometimes, she might not stop at words. She could come at you with anger or actions that are meant to hurt. You might face mean messages, unexpected visits, or even hear from other people about how upset she is. This can feel like an emotional attack and is why you need to be ready with ways to handle it.

Just like getting ready for a storm, you have to build your shelter, stock up on what keeps you strong, and know who to call when you need help. The shelter is your new set of rules for contact with her – what you will and won't accept. Stock up by reminding yourself why you need this space and how it's helping you grow. The people you call for help, those are the friends, family, or a support group who know your story and stand by your decision.

But don't forget about the storm inside you. Choosing to take space can bring a mix of hard feelings. You may feel sad for the relationship you wish you had, guilty like you're doing something bad, or perhaps a sigh of relief because you've finally put your well-being first. It's okay to feel these things. They're honest feelings, and they need space, just like you do.

Writing in a journal can be a way to talk to yourself about these feelings. Find a quiet spot, take a pen, and let your thoughts flow onto paper. It's not about writing perfect sentences; it's about letting your heart speak without holding back.

Sometimes, speaking to someone like a therapist can shine a light on dark spots. They're like guides who've helped many others through the same storm. They can help you understand why you feel what you do and how to move forward.

And in all this, make sure you're not alone too much. Being alone with tough feelings can be like sitting in a dark room. Call someone who makes you laugh, invite a friend over for tea, or join a group where you can share your story.

Lastly, remember to take care of yourself in simple ways. Maybe start a new hobby, take walks, or learn something new. Small steps for you can make a big difference in getting through this tough time. It's about being kind to yourself and building a life where you are happy and strong.

UNLOCK THE POWER OF GENEROSITY
MAKE A DIFFERENCE WITH YOUR REVIEW

"Kindness, like a boomerang, always returns."

— UNKNOWN

Did you know? People who help others without expecting anything in return tend to lead more joyful and fulfilling lives. Now, isn't that something we all desire? I'm all in for spreading that joy, and I hope you are too.

So, I have a small favor to ask...

Would you be willing to light up someone's world, even if you'll never know whose life you brightened?

Imagine someone out there feeling lost and confused, just like you might have felt before finding support. They're searching for answers, seeking relief from their struggles, yet they don't know where to start.

Our goal is to spread awareness and understanding about the complex dynamics between narcissistic mothers and their daughters to as many people as possible. Everything we do is driven by this mission. But, to truly make an impact, we need to reach... everyone.

And this is where you come into the picture. People often decide whether to pick up a book based on its cover and, importantly, its reviews. So, on behalf of a fellow survivor who needs this book but hasn't found it yet, I'm asking for your help:

Please consider leaving a review for this book.

It doesn't cost you a thing, takes less than a minute, but could forever change someone's life. Your review might just be the beacon of hope for:

- Another daughter finding her way out of the fog of confusion.
- A woman rediscovering her self-worth and inner strength.
- An individual breaking free from the chains of manipulation.
- Someone finally understanding the dynamics of their toxic family relationships.
- A reader embarking on a journey towards self-love and healing.

Feeling that 'feel good' vibe and making a real difference is easy - just leave a review.

If the thought of helping someone in the shadows makes you smile, then you're exactly who I hoped to connect with. Welcome to the club - you're one of the good ones.

I can't wait to assist you in navigating through recovery, healing, and empowerment, quicker and more effectively than you imagined. The insights and strategies ahead are going to be transformative.

Thank you deeply for considering this request. Let's continue this journey together.

Your biggest cheerleader, Natalie M. Brooks

PS - Remember, sharing wisdom is one of the most powerful gifts you can offer. If you believe this book could light someone else's path, don't hesitate to pass it on. It's a wonderful way to spread kindness and support.

11

SELF-CARE: YOUR LIFELINE IN THE SEA OF NARCISSISM

Self-care. You might have heard of this word before, but what does it really mean, especially if you grew up with a mother who always put herself first? It's a way to look after your whole self, not just your body, but also your mind and your feelings.

Let's start with your body. Taking care of it means eating foods that make you feel good and strong. It's also about moving and using your body, like walking, dancing, or playing a sport. Remember to relax too. Your body needs sleep and rest just as much as it needs food and exercise.

Now, how about your mind? Keep it healthy by giving it some quiet time. Mindfulness is like giving your mind a break, watching your thoughts pass by like clouds in the sky. Writing in a journal can also help you see what's happening in your thoughts. For some, talking to a therapist can offer great help, like having a guide when you're lost.

Then comes your emotional health, which is all about how you feel. When you're sad or upset, it's okay to let those feelings out. You could cry, talk to a friend, or maybe write about it. You also need to be strong with your boundaries. If something doesn't feel right, say no. It's okay to put your needs first. Look for people who care about you and support your growth.

The truth is, self-care isn't just treating yourself to sweet treats or a long bath, though those moments are nice. It's the choices you make each day to keep yourself feeling well. These choices can be tough, especially when you have a lot on your plate. But even something small, like taking a deep breath when you're stressed, is a start.

Let's say someone asks you to do a big task when you're already very busy. You might feel like you should say yes, but self-care is recognizing that you've got enough going on and saying no. Or maybe you start each day by thinking of one thing you're thankful for, letting that gratitude push out some of the dark thoughts.

When things get really hard, and you feel like you can't manage on your own, reaching out for professional help is a strong form of self-care. It's not a sign of weakness; it's a sign you want to get better.

For daughters of moms who always looked out for themselves, learning self-care can be a big change. It means looking in the mirror and saying, "I'm important, too." It's not selfish to take care of yourself; it's necessary, like water or air. It's the tool you use to keep going, to heal, and to build a life you deserve, step by step.

THE IMPORTANCE OF SELF-CARE: WHY YOU CAN'T AFFORD TO NEGLECT IT

Taking care of oneself sounds simple, doesn't it? Like eating your greens, getting good sleep, or taking a nice, warm bath. But when you've grown up with a mom who only sees her own reflection in everything, caring for yourself becomes much more than that; it's vital for your own well-being.

If you are a daughter of a mother who is mostly wrapped up in her own world, your heart and mind often feel like they're in a rough sea. Each wave of her self-centered actions can push and pull you, making you struggle to keep your head above water. This is why regular self-care is like a lifeboat in those choppy waters.

Let's talk about why.

When you look after yourself – and I mean really make it a part of your daily life, it's like giving yourself a shield and a soft cushion all at once. A shield because it helps you deal with the hard, hurtful things she might say or do. A cushion because it reminds you that you deserve kindness, even if it's your own kindness, especially when the world around you seems harsh and unkind.

Creating a routine of self-care opens up a small piece of the world that's all yours. It's a place where the rules are not set by your mom's needs or moods. In this space, you can breathe. You can feel what it's like to be stable and calm, no matter what storm is brewing outside. It's like building a cozy fort with soft blankets and pillows where the chaos can't reach you. This fort is important because it's one place where you have control, and things can be predictable, easy, and soothing.

This isn't about fancy things. Self-care is no luxury. It's not selfish. It's as necessary as air. It's what sparks joy inside you – maybe it's a quiet cup of tea before everyone wakes up, a walk in a park, or just saying 'no' when you need to. Without it, your inner light dims, and that's when the darkness can creep in, bringing friends like sadness, worry, and a deep tiredness that doesn't go away with sleep.

When you forget to put yourself first, that's when the trouble brews. That's when the big waves can knock you down – burnout they call it, or its cousins depression and anxiety. They're like uninvited guests that don't know when to leave.

But when you make that choice – yes, it is a choice – to say 'I matter', you're picking up the pen and re-writing the old story. This new chapter stars a you that's stronger, brighter, and filled with a belief that's louder than the doubts your mom might have left on your doorstep. This is the story where you are the heroine, and you save the day with a magical tool called self-care.

By choosing to take that time, whether it's a few minutes or a few hours, you are telling yourself and the world, 'I am important.' And you are. You're carving out your own happiness in small slices until one day you look back and realize you've baked a whole, beautiful cake.

So remember, self-care is your birthright, not a treat. It's the first and best step toward a life where you feel strong, worthy, and completely, beautifully you.

THE BARRIERS TO SELF-CARE: WHY IT'S HARD AND HOW TO OVERCOME IT

Daughters of mothers who only think of themselves often find it hard to take care of their own needs. This trouble comes from different places, but it's something many face. Here's why it's hard for them and what they can do to get better at taking care of themselves.

First, they might feel that taking time for their needs is wrong or selfish. This thinking is something their mothers might have put into their heads. Maybe their mom taught them that what they wanted or needed wasn't important. It's a tough thought to shake off, but it isn't true. Taking care of yourself isn't selfish; it's necessary, just like eating food or breathing air.

Next, they might not feel they deserve to be treated well. If someone hears over and over that they aren't good enough, they might start to believe it. This happens a lot when a mother keeps saying mean or hurtful things to her daughter. These words can cut deep, and healing from them isn't easy, but it is possible.

Sometimes, daughters of such mothers don't even notice they're forgetting their own needs. They might be so used to putting their mom first that they don't know how to switch and care for themselves. This is like being in a dark room for a long time and then not knowing how to act when someone turns on the light.

But no matter how late it seems, it is never too late to start taking care of yourself. Each little step you take matters a lot. You can begin by looking at your thoughts about self-care. Ask yourself why you think it's wrong or why you don't deserve it. When you find those thoughts, question them, turn them around. Tell yourself you do deserve good things and caring for yourself is a good thing.

If you need a hand, there's no shame in asking for it. You could talk to friends who make you feel good about yourself, a family member who understands, or a professional who knows how to help people with these problems. Getting help is actually a form of self-care too.

Starting with small things can make a big difference. It could be as simple as setting aside time for a walk, taking a long bath, or choosing food that makes you feel good and healthy. When those small things start to feel normal, you can try to add more self-care habits. These can be bigger, like saying no to things that hurt you or spending time on a hobby that makes you happy.

Every small thing you add to your self-care routine is a step toward feeling better about yourself. It's a way to show yourself the love and care that you should have always had. It's not just important; it's your right. Remember, taking care of yourself helps you to be your best, and when you're at your best, you can give your best to the world too.

A PRACTICAL GUIDE TO SELF-CARE: STRATEGIES AND TIPS

Self-care means taking steps to look after yourself. It's like giving your body and mind the food and rest they need. Think of it like caring for a plant. A plant needs water, sunlight, and good soil to grow. We are the same: we need different kinds of care to feel our best.

Let's start with the body - physical self-care. It could be as simple as stretching your arms up high in the morning or dancing to your favorite song. Maybe you like to feel the wind on your face as you walk in the park, or you prefer to make a tasty lunch full of colors and fresh tastes. The big idea is to pick things that make you smile and feel full of energy. It's about listening to what your body is telling you. If you're tired, maybe it's a short nap you need. If you're full of energy, a bike ride might be perfect.

Moving on to our minds - mental self-care. Our thoughts can be busy like bees in a hive, buzzing around all day. To calm them, you might sit quietly and watch your breath, in and out, like the tide in the sea. You could lose yourself in a story, flipping through the pages of a book. Or, you could master a new skill, like playing a tune on a guitar or fixing a leaky tap. These things can make your mind quiet and clear, like water in a glass.

Now, let's talk about feelings - emotional self-care. Feelings are like the weather; sometimes sunny, sometimes stormy. To take care of them, you might scribble in a book everything you feel, without worrying if it's pretty or ugly. It just needs to be true. Or, you might make something - a drawing, a pot, or a scarf. Creating can help say the things words can't. And if the feelings are too heavy, talking with someone who listens well can be like a balm. Whether it's a wise friend or a person trained to help us understand our feelings, sharing can make our hearts feel lighter.

Taking care of yourself isn't the same for everybody. what works for your friend may not work for you, and that's okay. try different things. see what fills you with joy or peace. do more of that. it's like finding the right key for a lock. keep trying until it clicks.

Imagine your life is a garden. Self-care is like caring for this garden. Some days you'll pull out weeds (that's saying no to things that don't help you grow). Other days, you'll water the plants (that's doing things that make you feel strong). Each day, you tend to your garden a little, and over time, it blooms beautifully. That's the power of self-care.

CULTIVATING A REGULAR SELF-CARE ROUTINE: MAKING SELF-CARE A HABIT

Creating a positive self-care routine is like planting a garden. You sow the seeds of wellness and watch them bloom over time. It's all about taking care of yourself a little bit each day. If you wait until your spirit feels dry and wilted, it's much harder to bring it back to life. When self-care becomes as normal as brushing your teeth, you'll find your days a bit brighter, your energy a little higher, and your ability to deal with life's twists a whole lot stronger.

Consistency is your best friend here. Think about it like watering that garden. A little care each day can keep your internal flowers perky and vibrant. This is especially true if you have a mother whose moods and actions are like unpredictable weather. That routine can become your personal garden wall, protecting your growth and keeping your space peaceful.

But how do you make sure your self-care routine doesn't wilt? You start by crafting a simple plan. Take a pen and paper, and write down what helps you feel centered. Maybe it's stretching gently each morning, or taking ten quiet minutes with a cup of tea. Perhaps a walk in the fresh air is your sunshine, or reading a few pages of a book gives you roots. This plan doesn't have to be grand or complex. Simple is beautiful, because you're more likely to stick with it.

Once your self-care activities are chosen, decide when you'll do them. You could promise yourself a stretch every morning, tea every afternoon, a walk after work twice a week, and reading time each night before bed. These blocks of time are your investment in yourself. Be sensible about it though. You know your life and your limits. Don't pack your plan so tight that it's another source of stress. The goal is to make your days better, not busier.

This plan isn't written in stone. As time goes forward, you might find that certain activities don't suit you as well as you thought, or maybe your life changes a bit. That's when you sit down with yourself—like an old friend—and ask, "How are we doing?" Adjust your routine just like you adjust a picture on the wall. Tilt it to find the right angle, and don't get upset if it takes a few tries.

Finally—and this is important—celebrate every bit of progress. If you've managed to take your walk three times this week when before you took none, that's a win. It's a big deal. Every step you take towards caring for yourself is precious. Mark your victories, even if it's just a mental 'gold star'. Your wellbeing is important, and caring for it is worth a cheer and a smile, every single time.

In the garden of your life, self-care is the sunlight, water, and soil that helps you thrive, especially when the world outside that garden gets stormy. Keep tending to it, and watch how you grow.

12

REBUILDING FROM THE RUBBLE: CULTIVATING YOUR SELF-IDENTITY

Under the crushing presence of a narcissistic mother, daughters often find themselves hidden behind a mask they never chose. This mask has been molded and painted by the heavy hand of expectation, leaving little room for the true face beneath to emerge. Living in the shadow of a keenly self-focused parent, these daughters have become masters of appeasement and adaptation, often losing sight of where their mother's image ends and their own begins.

The narcissistic mother's influence is such that it can completely obscure her daughter's sense of self. A daughter in this situation might view herself merely as a reflection—a pale extension of someone else's brighter, more assertive identity. It's like being a mirror, constantly angling to reflect the preferred portrait of your mother's choosing rather than showing your own true picture.

Picture for a moment a garden. In this garden, a variety of plants grows: some tall, some small, each different in color, shape, and size. Now imagine if one large, pervasive plant started to spread, its vines reaching out to overshadow the others. This plant saps nutrients and blocks sunlight, causing the other plants to wither or alter their forms to survive. The narcissistic mother can be likened to this dominant plant, always expanding and seeking attention, while her daughter adjusts her growth to avoid the shadows, often forgetting the natural direction she was once reaching for.

For daughters of narcissistic mothers, understanding this loss is the first step toward recovery. They must start by recognizing the feelings they've buried deep beneath layers of expectation and self-denial. It might be a love for painting brushed aside in favor of more 'practical' pursuits, or a fondness for simple joys belittled as unworthy of attention. Perhaps it's a quiet voice of dissent that was silenced before it ever learned to speak up.

To unearth the mask means delving into the ignored corners of one's heart, exploring the uncharted inner landscapes with tenderness and patience, seeking out the passions and opinions that were suppressed. It requires rigorous honesty to identify the protective coloring that has served as camouflage for so long.

Discovering these hidden facets of identity can evoke a wide spectrum of emotions, from anger at lost time to sorrow for the unacknowledged self. It's crucial, however, not to wallow in these feelings but to own them and use them as stepping stones toward authentic self-embrace. It's about recognizing that the lost self was never truly gone, just buried, awaiting recognition and revitalization.

Becoming one's authentic self involves learning to appreciate the unique voice within, to take pleasure in one's own thoughts and company, and to ascertain personal values separated from the maternal shadow. This journey of self-discovery isn't a single moment of revelation but a gentle and persistent flowering, a process that may require support from friends, counselors, or support groups.

Reconnecting with the buried self is the ultimate act of self-love. It is an acknowledgment that even amidst the tangled vines of a narcissistic mother's overbearing garden, there's a singular, beautiful plant —a true self—that's resilient and ready to reclaim its place in the sun. And when it does, it will flourish, not as an extension of the narcissistic mother's grand design, but as its own, distinct and vibrant being.

THE MIRROR MAZE: RECOGNIZING DISTORTED SELF-PERCEPTIONS

Self-perception is how we see and think about ourselves. It's like looking into a mirror and figuring out who we are. But imagine if that mirror doesn't show the real you. Instead, it's a bit like a funhouse mirror at a carnival, twisting your reflection in strange ways. For daughters of narcissistic mothers, their mirror of self-perception is often just like this — distorted.

Narcissistic mothers are often very focused on themselves. They might want to be the center of attention or need others to say how great they are. They can also be unhappy with anything that takes the spotlight off them, including their daughters' achievements and unique qualities. As a result, growing up with a mother like this can make it hard for daughters to see themselves clearly.

Daughters in this situation may feel like they're never good enough. They might work very hard and succeed, but inside they feel like they haven't done well at all. They might think, "I'm not smart," when they are. Or maybe they believe they must be perfect to earn love, which isn't true. These feelings are signs of feeling inadequate. It's like trying to fill a bucket with water, but the bucket has holes in it. No matter how much water you pour in, it never feels full.

Guilt is another feeling daughters of narcissistic mothers often know too well. They grow up hearing they are the reason for their mother's bad moods or problems. If mom is upset, they think it must be their fault. This guilt sticks to them like sticky syrup, hard to wash off, even when they become adults.

And perhaps the hardest part of all this is the deep-down worry that maybe they're unlovable or unworthy of care and affection. Imagine feeling like a tiny, forgettable gray pebble on a huge beach. It can make it hard to believe people could love or even see the real person inside.

These wrong self-perceptions are like thorns on a rose bush — they can hurt and make it hard to see the lovely flower they're attached to. They can make daughters doubtful and less confident in both friendships and work. They may have trouble making friends because they're afraid of being let down. At work, they might not ask for a deserved raise or promotion. They feel uneasy or sure that they'll fail even before they try.

Breaking free from these distorted self-perceptions is like using a pair of garden shears to snip off those thorns, so the rose — their true self — can be seen and enjoyed. It's not easy, but understanding where those wrong ideas come from is the first step. By recognizing that these thoughts aren't truths but reflections from a twisted mirror, it's possible to begin changing the image, little by little. Eventually, one can polish a new mirror, one that reflects the real, lovable person they have always been.

LAYING THE FOUNDATION: EMBRACING SELF-COMPASSION

When you were a child, your mom might have often told you what was not right about you. From tiny mistakes on your schoolwork to the way you combed your hair, she pointed out what she didn't like. You may have grown up feeling you were never quite good enough.

As an adult, these hard memories can stick with you like a shadow, shaping the way you see yourself and the world.

Now more than ever, it's time for you to learn about self-compassion. This is like giving yourself a warm embrace, telling yourself: "It's okay, you're doing your best, and that is enough." Think of self-compassion as that close friend who always has the right words and the kindest heart. Self-compassion is about being as nice to yourself as you would be to that dear friend.

Self-compassion involves three big ideas.

First, it's understanding that you really do matter. Just like every person in this big world, you have incredible value. Imagine you're looking at your reflection in a mirror, not just seeing the outside, but also realizing that inside is a person full of wonderful qualities. Remind yourself of this: "I am worth a lot."

Second, it's okay to be imperfect. Everyone makes mistakes and messes up now and then – it's part of being human. Instead of getting upset over slip-ups, give yourself the space to learn and grow. When things don't go as planned, instead of being hard on yourself, try to say: "It's fine. I can try again." Remember, every person has flaws, and that doesn't take away from who they are.

Third, speak gently and kindly to yourself. On rough days when everything feels upside down, speak to yourself like you would comfort a friend. Use soft, loving words, not mean or harsh ones. When you mess up, instead of saying, "I can't do anything right," say, "It's hard now, but I'm doing my best."

Why are these three steps so important? Because the tough words and harsh ideas your narcissistic mother shared might have built a wall around you, making you believe you weren't smart or good. This can lead you to be unkind to yourself and feel bad a lot.

As you practice self-compassion, it's like taking that wall apart, brick by brick. You'll start seeing that a lot of the bad stuff you thought about yourself isn't true. With each kind thought and soft word you give yourself, you grow stronger, and the shadow of those old memories gets a little lighter. It's not a quick fix – sometimes it takes a while. But every bit of kindness you show yourself is like a sunbeam breaking through a cloud, lighting up your own self-worth.

CONSTRUCTING THE PILLARS: IDENTIFYING PERSONAL VALUES AND BELIEFS

When we talk about figuring out who we are, a giant piece of that puzzle is what we stand for. Think of your values and beliefs as a hidden map inside you that helps guide the choices you make every day. They're the big, bold letters written across your heart that say what you think is good, right, and important. These inner truths are your secret code for walking through life.

Now, this can be trickier than it sounds. A lot of what we believe comes from our moms. When you were a kid, it was easy to nod along with her words. If mom said sharing is good, you shared. If she said to be kind to animals, you were gentle with every four-legged friend. That's all part of growing up. Your mom's voice was like a comfy blanket wrapped around your thoughts, keeping them safe and snug.

But here's where the adventure starts. You're not a little kid anymore. It's time to hike up your grown-up pants and dig deep to find your own voice. Ask yourself, what makes your heart beat faster because it feels so right? Maybe you get that special buzz in your belly when you help strangers. Or perhaps honesty lights up your world brighter than a fireworks show. That's all you, not your mom, not anyone else, just you.

Your values, those champions you choose for yourself, are really your life's compass. They're not just fancy ideas sitting on a shelf collecting dust. They're the north star in your night sky when you're lost in the dark. Let's say you believe kindness is king. When you meet someone new and a choice tap-dances up to you, whether to be friendly or not, your kindness value will whisper, "Go on, flash a smile." That simple, right?

These values aren't sleepy passengers in the backseat. They're up front, buckled in, and steering the wheel, especially in the tricky turns of life. When you're at a crossroads, wondering if you should take the job that pays buckets of money but steps on your belief of fairness, guess who's going to tap you on the shoulder? That's right, your values, asking whether this is really the right direction.

And let's not forget about relationships, the ties we have with other humans. Our values are like invisible threads that can pull us towards people or sometimes push us away. If you value honesty to the moon and back, you're going to drift towards folks who speak the truth, just like you do. You might even find that friends who play hide-and-seek with the truth don't fit as snugly in your circle. It's all part of the dance, and your values are the music setting the beat.

To put it simply, figuring out the values and beliefs that are truly yours, not your mom's echo, is like drawing your own map. This map doesn't show you the roads to cities or hidden treasure. Nope, this map shows you the way to be the you that only you can be. It's the one with all the right turns and stops that make you feel at home with yourself. And once you've got that map, the journey through life gets a bit more clear, a tad bit easier to navigate, because you've got the best guide there is—your own true north.

BLUEPRINT OF THE SELF: EXPLORING PERSONAL INTERESTS AND PASSIONS

When you were little, you might have liked certain things a lot. Maybe you loved painting, kicking a soccer ball, or watching the stars at night. As we grow up, sometimes we forget about these simple joys. But they are like hidden treasures that can help you find out who you really are.

Imagine you have a garden inside you. This garden is where all the things you love grow. Every hobby or activity you enjoy is like a special flower or plant in this garden. Some people have gardens filled with music notes from their love of singing. Others have gardens blooming with colors because they like to paint or draw. When you spend time doing what you love, it's like watering these plants. They grow stronger and so does your sense of who you are.

Exploring your personal interests and passions is a wonderful journey. It's like walking through your inner garden and discovering what's there. Maybe you have a passion for cooking, and every time you try a new recipe, it feels like you're adding a new plant to your garden. Or perhaps you love to build things, and every project adds a strong tree in your space. These activities make you feel good because they are a true part of you.

These hobbies aren't just for fun, though. They have a power that goes beyond just passing the time. When you find an activity that makes your heart happy, you are tapping into something very important. It's like meeting your real self, the person you are deep down below all the busyness of daily life. As you spend more time with your interests, you learn more about this person. You become friends with yourself.

Enjoying your hobbies brings another gift: a feeling of success. Each time you finish a painting, score a goal, or see a plant you've grown bloom, you feel proud. You did that. It's like giving yourself a gold star. This feeling, this sense of achievement, is a big hug for your self-identity. It whispers to you, "This is me. I did something great." It makes your inner garden thrive.

Your unique interests shape who you are. Like a fingerprint, no one else has the same combination of joys and passions as you. When you make time in your life for these interests, you honor your true self. Not only that, but you also show the world the special person you are. Every hobby you dive into, every passion you pursue, draws a more detailed picture of you, both inside and out.

In the end, it's these personal interests that carve out the statue that is you. They chisel away at the stone, revealing the beautiful figure inside. When you follow your passions, you give life to your unique identity. And like a strong tree in your garden, your self-identity stands tall, rooted deeply in what brings you joy and fulfillment.

BUILDING RESILIENCE: DEVELOPING HEALTHY COPING MECHANISMS

Developing healthy coping mechanisms is a game-changer when it comes to dealing with the rough patches that life sometimes throws our way. This is especially key when you're dealing with someone as challenging as a narcissistic mother. Your self-identity, that core sense of who you are, needs to stay strong and protected, even when it feels like you're up against a storm.

Now, you might be wondering, what are these healthy coping tools? and even though the waves are wild, you're totally focused on steering your vessel. Practicing mindfulness could be as simple as paying close attention to your breath. Imagine each breath is like a wave on the shore, coming in and out. When you're feeling over-whelmed, take a few minutes to just breathe. This simple act can anchor you back to the here and now, and stop those waves of stress from tossing you around.

Next on our list is journaling. Think of your journal as a loyal friend that's always there to listen. It doesn't judge, it doesn't interrupt, and it doesn't offer unwanted advice. It's just there for you to spill your thoughts onto the page. Whenever you're tangled up in emotions or stressed by your mom's behavior, write it down. Getting those thoughts out of your head and onto paper can make them seem less scary and more manageable. It's also a record of your journey, so you can look back and see how far you've come.

Finally, we have assertive communication. This is all about being clear and confident in how you talk to others, especially when you need to set boundaries. It's not about being aggressive or starting a fight; it's about respecting yourself and the person you're talking to. For instance, if your narcissistic mother criticizes you or tries to make you feel small, you can respond calmly and firmly. You might say something like, "I hear what you're saying, but I don't agree, and I'd like you to stop." Being assertive is like building a protective fence around your mental garden. It keeps the good stuff in and the unhelpful stuff out.

Using tools like mindfulness, journaling, and assertive communication won't change who your mother is, but they will change how you respond to her. And the best part is, these tools aren't just for dealing with her. They're for dealing with any sort of trouble that life throws at you. Employing these mechanisms can help you maintain your balance no matter the challenge, ensuring your self-identity remains strong and steady, rooted in your own well-being.

ADORNING THE STRUCTURE: CELEBRATING ACHIEVEMENTS AND STRENGTHS

Embracing your achievements and strengths is not just a feel-good exercise, it's a crucial step in understanding who you are and building a strong sense of self. This part of the chapter is all about the importance of recognizing the things you do well and celebrating your wins, no matter their size.

Imagine your life as a garden and every accomplishment, big or small, is like a flower blooming. Just as you would admire and take care of the flowers, you should treat your achievements with the same respect and attention. You might think some of your successes are too tiny to matter, like maybe you mastered a new recipe, or you finally organized that cluttered desk of yours. These aren't earth-shaking wins, but they are wins nonetheless and they add vibrancy to your garden. Even the smallest flower makes your garden more beautiful.

Now, think about the times when you've found things a little easier than others, or the moments when friends or family have come to you for help because they know you've got the knack for something. These are your strengths, your natural talents. Whether it's being a good listener, having a knack for making people laugh, or being able to put together furniture without breaking a sweat, these strengths are threads in the fabric of your being.

Understanding and embracing your strengths is like shining a light on the path of your potential. When you see clearly what you are good at, you can walk that path with confidence. Let's say you are great at organizing - that's a strength! You could use that strength to better not only your life but the lives of those around you. Maybe you could help a friend sort out their closet or assist a local community group in setting up for an event.

Acknowledging your strengths does another thing - it feeds your self-confidence. Every time you see yourself using a strength, it's like giving yourself a pat on the back. And with each pat on the back, you stand a little taller. You start to see that you can do many things, and do them well. Realizing your potential is like looking at a map and seeing all the roads open to you. Knowing your strengths allows you to choose your journey wisely.

It's vital to take time to reflect on what you have accomplished and the strengths you possess. Set aside a quiet moment, perhaps at the end of the day or week, to think about what you achieved. Maybe write it down in a notebook or share it with a friend or family member.

In celebrating your achievements and strengths, you paint a picture of yourself that is full of talent, ability, and potential. It's a picture that you should look at often, to remind yourself that you are capable of wonderful things. As you do this, you'll find that your self-identity becomes clearer and sharper, leaving no doubt about the unique and capable person you truly are.

FINAL TOUCHES: SEEKING PROFESSIONAL HELP

When you feel lost, unsure about who you are, or what you want in life, asking for help from a professional can be a smart step. This part of the journey to find your true self can be made smoother with some guidance from those who have studied the path of human thoughts and emotions: therapists or counselors.

Therapists or counselors are like guides in the world of our minds. Imagine you're in a thick forest, and the paths are all tangled up. You're not sure which way to go. That's when these experts come in. They have the map and the compass to help you find the clear path. They can sit with you and listen to your stories, your fears, and your dreams. They can help you peel back the layers, much like removing the outer shells of an onion, to reveal what's at the very heart of you: your true identity.

These professionals are trained to give you the tools and strategies to understand your emotions better. They can teach you how to handle the big storms of feelings that might seem scary or overwhelming. It's like learning to sail. At first, the waves and the wind might push you around, but with the right techniques, you can steer your boat even when the sea gets rough. Therapists can show you these techniques, teaching you how to use the sails and rudder to navigate through your sea of emotions.

But therapy doesn't always mean going through it alone. There's another kind of help that brings people together: group therapy or support groups. In these groups, people who might feel just as lost or confused as you do come together. Everyone shares what they're going through, and because of that sharing, you might start to feel less alone. It's like finding friends around a campfire, all sharing stories. You see the sparks fly up and light each other's faces, and you realize that everyone has their own struggles, just like you. This shared experience creates a sense of community, a circle of support that can hold you up when you're finding it hard to stand.

This circle isn't just about sharing the hard stuff, though. It's also a place for little victories and moments of joy. When you speak your worries out loud and someone else nods, saying, "I understand, I've been there too," it's a reminder that your journey is a shared human one. There is comfort in knowing you are not the only one trying to find your way back to yourself.

So if you're feeling stuck, think about reaching out. Whether it's one-on-one with a therapist or counselor, or in a group with others, asking for help is a brave and important step. Your story matters, and finding the right people to help you tell it can bring the pieces of your puzzle back together. In the end, you're piecing together the most beautiful picture of all: the true you.

MAINTAINING THE EDIFICE: CONTINUOUS SELF-EXPLORATION AND GROWTH

In the journey of self-identity, think of yourself as a traveler moving through the wide, open road of life. Your destination isn't a place, but rather a deep understanding of who you are. This road doesn't have an end. It twists and turns, with new scenes and sights appearing as you go along. Each day brings a fresh chance to learn more about yourself, to update the map you follow, and to grow in new, exciting ways.

Imagine you're walking through a forest that represents you. With each step, you're invited to check in with yourself. How do you feel? What do you like? What seems important to you? Over time, the trees might change colors, the paths might shift, and you might find new parts of the forest to explore. Just as the forest changes with the seasons, you also change as life goes on. Checking in with yourself is like sitting down on a bench in that forest and taking a moment to look around and see what has changed and what has stayed the same. It's about knowing that it's okay if the things you liked or believed in before are different now.

Your beliefs and values are like seeds you plant in the ground of this forest. Some grow for a long time and become big, strong trees. Others might only last for a season before they wither away. As you grow, some of your beliefs will stay with you, giving you shade and comfort. Others will change as you learn and experience more, and it's important to nurture these new seeds with care, allowing them to take root in your forest if they feel right.

Your interests and passions are the beautiful flowers and plants that fill your forest with color and life. They are what make your journey a joyous one. Maybe you love making art, helping others, solving puzzles, or cooking delicious meals. It is important to give these interests the light and space they need to flourish. Never let the fear of trying something new stop you from planting a fresh batch of flowers in your garden. Like a gardener tending to their plants, you must nurture your interests with patience and love.

Changing and evolving is a part of being human. it is completely okay for you to shift and grow. each of us is like a book that writes itself a little bit every day. some chapters might be about learning new skills, while others might be about saying goodbye to old habits. embrace the person you are becoming with each passing day, knowing that your journey is unique and beautiful.

So keep walking along that endless road, taking turns and detours as they come, always ready to explore the next part of your forest. Celebrate your growth and treasure your journey, for it makes you who you are, a special person with a story all your own.

13
HEALING THE INVISIBLE SCARS: UNDERSTANDING AND OVERCOMING EMOTIONAL INCEST

Emotional incest is a hidden form of abuse that often goes unnoticed but leaves deep marks on those who experience it. Imagine a parent turning to their child for comfort and support in ways that are not appropriate for a child's role. This happens more often than we think in families where a mom might care only about herself and her feelings.

In these situations, the lines that should separate the responsibilities and emotions of a parent and their child become mixed up. Instead of the parent being the strong one, providing love and guidance, the child is put in a place where they must take care of their parent's emotional needs. It's not easy to spot this kind of abuse, because there are no physical signs—no bruises or scars to see. But just because it's not seen doesn't mean it doesn't hurt.

Especially with daughters who have mothers that only think about themselves, this problem is all too common. Such a mother might look to her daughter to be a friend, confidante, or even a partner in an emotional sense. These moms might share secrets or speak badly about other family members, expecting the daughter to take their side. They might lean so heavily on their daughters for support that the daughters feel like they're carrying a weight too heavy for them.

It's a form of abuse because it puts pressure on the daughter to fill a space that is not hers to fill. She grows up feeling responsible for her mom's happiness and emotional well-being. These daughters might feel guilty or ashamed for wanting to live their own lives because they're so used to putting their mom's needs before their own.

If you found yourself nodding as you read this, you might have experienced emotional incest. You're not alone, and it's important to know that what happened was not your fault. It's also important to understand that recovery is possible. Healing starts with recognizing the signs and seeing the relationship for what it was—an unfair responsibility put on you as a child.

Some common signs of emotional incest include a sense of responsibility for your mom's happiness, feeling used or drained by her emotional demands, and difficulty setting boundaries in relationships. You might also find it tough to know your own needs and wants because you're so used to looking out for your mom's feelings first.

Once you recognize these patterns, you can start to work through them. Therapy can be a huge help in unpacking these experiences and learning how to set healthy boundaries. Books and support groups can also offer guidance and show you that others have walked the same path and found their way through.

Recognizing and healing from emotional incest is key to your personal growth. it's a journey worth taking, and on the other side, you might find a newfound sense of freedom and self-discovery. your past doesn't have to define your future. you have the power to create a life that is yours and not a reflection of your mom's emotional needs.

THE IMPACT OF EMOTIONAL INCEST: LIVING IN THE NARCISSIST'S EMOTIONAL WEB

When a daughter grows up in a home where emotional incest is happening, the weight of her mother's emotional world often falls on her shoulders. Emotional incest, unlike the physical kind, is less about touch and more about a mom leaning too much on her child for support, treating her not as a kid but more like a partner or best friend. The daughter becomes the listening ear for all the mom's troubles, from grown-up worries to personal, intimate details that are too heavy for a young heart to handle.

This burden can lead the daughter to feel like she must always be there to keep her mom feeling okay, creating a fierce sense of guilt whenever she lives her own life. She might think, "If I'm not there for Mom, who will be?" This constant stress can turn into a heavy, invisible backpack of worries that the daughter carries everywhere, squeezing her heart a bit tighter every day, making it hard to breathe and be herself.

As this girl grows up, this bag of worries doesn't just disappear. She might walk into a room full of people and feel like she's supposed to take care of everyone's feelings, always saying 'yes' when she really wants to say 'no'. The thought of making someone else unhappy, especially a boyfriend or close friend, might scare her, because deep down, she's been trained to put her own needs last.

Now, let's talk about how this impacts her relationships. A daughter who's gone through emotional incest often doesn't know what 'normal' looks like when it comes to love and friendships. She may say 'yes' when she's not comfortable, or 'no' when she wants to say 'yes', because her understanding of boundaries has become all mixed up. She might find herself in a friendship or a romantic relationship where it feels like her partner needs her in the same overwhelming way her mother did—something familiar, but definitely not healthy.

Another harsh truth is that these daughters might feel like they can't breathe freely, like they're always being watched and controlled, even when they're all grown up. They may have trouble making decisions for themselves because they're so used to their mom making all the calls. Speaking up for what they want or need becomes a battle inside. That little voice saying, "What will Mom think?" can make it really hard to live their own life instead of the one their mom wants for them.

Freedom and the courage to set out on their own path can be really challenging for these daughters. Breaking away from the grip of their mother's needs, they have to unlearn the idea that love means carrying someone else's emotional baggage. They need to understand that it's okay to have their own space, to make their own choices, and to take care of themselves first. Learning that giving yourself permission to be happy and free doesn't mean you are letting your loved ones down is a tough, but necessary lesson for these daughters to live a healthier, more independent life.

THE HEALING JOURNEY: BREAKING FREE FROM EMOTIONAL INCEST

In the path to recovery from emotional incest, understanding the steps crucially guides and supports the healing process. Now, let's navigate these steps like walking through a quiet, serene garden that leads to a place of peace and well-being.

The voyage begins with a tough but vital step: acknowledging the abuse, like finding the hidden key to the garden's gate. Emotional incest is confusing because it doesn't leave physical marks; instead, it's an invisible wound on your heart and mind. This kind of hurt happens when a parent, instead of providing a safe space, leans too heavily on a child for emotional support, treating them more like a partner than their kid. Recognizing this is not easy. You might feel like you're being ungrateful or misjudging your parents who loved you, after all. But here's the truth – love should feel good, not heavy or suffocating. So, when you realize that what happened was not normal or healthy, you're taking the first brave step into the garden of recovery. It might sting like a scratch from a thorny rose, but it is the start of healing.

As you wander deeper into the garden, you reach the stage of acceptance. This is where you sit on a bench under a sturdy oak tree and let the truth soak in – none of what happened is your fault. Blame has no place in this garden. You were the child; the grown-ups should've known better. Your feelings, whatever mix they are – sadness, anger, confusion – they're as valid as the colors of the flowers around you. Sometimes, sharing your story with someone who understands can be like a gentle rain that nurtures the garden of your heart. It could be a close friend who listens and that is a powerful realization that helps acceptance grow strong roots.

Venturing onward, you start to actively recover. This is the part of the journey where you roll up your sleeves and plant seeds for a future of well-being. Therapy can be like the gardener that helps you sort out the weeds from the plants. A therapist is trained to guide you gently and offer tools for understanding and coping. Self-care practices are your daily gardening – simple things like eating and perhaps exercising, all of which help strengthen you from the inside out. Establishing boundaries is crucial, too. Imagine putting a pretty fence around your garden. This is your space, and you decide who gets in and how much they can water your plants. Lastly, educating yourself about what healthy relationships look like can be likened to learning about plants – knowing which are good for your garden and which might harm it helps you choose who and what you let into your life.

This detailed look at the healing process is like wandering through a garden that's being brought back to life. With every step of recognition, acceptance, and active recovery, you nurture your inner garden, bringing it back to health, ready to bloom in ways you've always deserved.

THERAPEUTIC APPROACHES: NAVIGATING THE ROAD TO RECOVERY

Therapy stands as a mighty helping hand in mending hearts and minds hurt by emotional incest. This trouble, where a parent or close family member treats a child as a partner or confidant, can leave deep marks on someone's spirit. It can shape the way a person thinks about themselves and the world around them, often in ways that bear down on them like a heavy load.

One kind of therapy that has shown promise for healing from such wounds is cognitive-behavioral therapy, or CBT for short. This therapy looks closely at how what we think and what we do work together. People who have been through emotional incest might carry certain thoughts that don't help them—like thinking they must always make others happy, or that they are to blame for their family's troubles. These thoughts are like seeds that can grow into actions that don't help them live the life they want.

CBT works to find these thoughts and to question them. It's a bit like a gardener pulling out weeds so the plants you want can grow. By talking with a therapist, a person can learn to see these thoughts for what they are and to change them into ideas that are more helpful and true. This change doesn't happen all at once, but with time and practice, a person can build new ways of thinking that make them feel stronger and more free.

Another therapy that's been helpful for people with this kind of hurt is called Eye Movement Desensitization and Reprocessing, or EMDR. This therapy is like a special dance for the mind that helps it heal from trauma. Trauma is a kind of hurt that can happen when something very bad, scary, or sad occurs. With EMDR, people remember these hard things while doing a specific eye movement, or sometimes while tapping their hands or hearing certain sounds. This might sound strange, but what it does is help the brain work through these memories smoothly, like untangling a knot. For someone dealing with the aftermath of emotional incest, EMDR can bring relief and help them heal.

Lastly, therapy offers a place where feelings can unfold like a map—a map that shows where a person has been and where they want to go. In this safe place, they don't have to carry their feelings alone. They share them with someone who listens and helps them understand these feelings better. Alongside, they learn new ways to cope with life's challenges—like learning to take deep breaths when feeling overwhelmed or practicing how to set healthy boundaries with others.

Therapy is a place of learning, too. Learning about oneself and about the tools to navigate life more effectively. Whether through CBT, EMDR, or other therapy forms, the journey of healing from emotional incest is one of rewriting the story of one's life. It's about moving from a place of hurt to one of hope and strength. For many, therapy is the bridge on that journey, a place where change begins and grows, leading to a fuller, freer life.

BUILDING EMOTIONAL BOUNDARIES: YOUR DEFENSE AGAINST EMOTIONAL INCEST

In the journey of finding peace from the effects of having a narcissistic mother, setting up and keeping strong emotional boundaries is like building a safe fence around your heart and mind. Emotional boundaries are rules we make for ourselves that guide what is okay and what is not okay when it comes to our feelings and how other people, including our mothers, can affect us.

Think of it like this: when you were a child, you could tell the difference between your toys and someone else's. The same goes for feelings - your emotions are yours, and your mother's feelings are her own, separate from yours. When you have a narcissistic mother, she might act in ways where it seems like her feelings should be the most important in the room. She might get mad, sad, or upset and expect you to make her feel better. But it's not your job to fix her feelings. Your job is to take care of your own feelings.

Drawing the line might mean you have to say "no" more often. Perhaps your mother asks you to do things that make you uncomfortable – things that are more about what she wants than what is good for you. Saying no might be hard, but it's a big part of keeping your feelings safe.

There will be times when you'll need to tell her about what you need and how you feel. It can be scary to speak up for yourself, especially if you're not used to it or if you're worried about making her unhappy. Remember, though, that expressing your feelings honestly is healthy. It's not mean or rude; it's taking care of yourself.

Sometimes, setting emotional boundaries may mean you need to step back and not see or talk to your mother as much. If being around her makes you feel bad, gives you a stomachache, or makes your heart race, it might be a sign that you need some space to heal. Taking a break from her does not mean you don't love her; it means you are loving yourself more by giving yourself a chance to heal from the inside out.

Maintaining boundaries can feel selfish at first. But keep in mind that it is not selfish to take care of yourself. Think of emotional boundaries like putting on your oxygen mask first in an airplane emergency; you're no good to anyone else if you can't breathe yourself. By taking care of your emotions, you are making sure you can live a healthier, happier life. And that's not just good for you, it's good for the people around you who care about you and want you to be well.

CULTIVATING SELF-CARE: NURTURING YOUR EMOTIONAL HEALTH

Self-care is a key part of your journey to feeling better. It's like putting on your own oxygen mask before helping others, as they say on airplanes. When you take good care of yourself, you're not being selfish; you're making sure you have the energy and health to live your life well.

Think of stress as a heavy backpack you carry all day. It makes you tired and can hurt your back. Self-care helps you put that backpack down for a while. It gives you a break, so when you pick that backpack up again, it feels a little lighter. Self-care can also fix some of the hurt that stress causes your feelings and body.

Self-care activities are like mini-vacations for your heart and mind. They can make you feel happy, rest your brain, and remind you that you are special. Perhaps you like to fold into cozy yoga poses or sit quietly and let your thoughts float away like clouds during meditation. These physical activities are great because they help you to breathe deeply and relax your body, which can make your mind feel clearer and calmer.

But self-care isn't just about being still or quiet. It can also be about making or doing things that let your heart sing. If you write down your thoughts in a journal or swirl colors on a canvas when you paint, you're letting your inner self come out to play. This isn't about being a good writer or artist; it's about letting your feelings out in a healthy way.

Maybe you love to bake, take long walks, read books, or listen to music. These things are self-care too. They are like gifts you give to yourself because they make you smile and feel at ease. When you enjoy these gifts, even simple ones like watching a sunset or hugging a pet, you are taking care of yourself.

By doing these things often, you remind yourself that you matter. Your needs and feelings are important, just like everyone else's. When you believe that, you begin to treat yourself better naturally. You might start eating healthier foods, sleeping better, or saying no to things that hurt you.

Self-care helps you stand strong and say, "I am worth it! I deserve to feel good!" The truth is, everyone deserves to feel loved and happy, including you. So when you take time for self-care, you're not just healing now; you're also building a path to a brighter, healthier future.

Self-care isn't something extra you do when you find time. it's as necessary as eating and sleeping. make self-care a regular part of your life, and watch how you begin to bloom, like a plant that's been watered and cared for. you need that too. you deserve to feel good, to laugh, play, rest, and heal. that's what self-care is all about.

EMPOWERING YOURSELF: BREAKING FREE FROM THE EMOTIONAL WEB

Overcoming emotional incest is like slowly walking a path out of a thick forest into an open, sunny field. It's a journey, one that could be tough, but in the end, it leads to a place where you can stand tall and feel the warmth of the sun – your true self.

This process is about finding out who you are, apart from your mother's feelings and what she needs from you. For a long time, you might have felt like you're an extension of her, like a branch on a tree that can't stand alone. But that's not true. You're your own person, with your own heart and dreams.

So, how do you begin this change? not because it's someone else's favorite. You learn to listen to your own heart.

Next, it's about caring for your heart's well-being just like you'd care for a close friend. You wouldn't let a friend get caught in the rain without an umbrella, right? So you shouldn't let your own feelings get hurt or ignored either. Tell yourself it's okay to put up an umbrella to protect your emotions.

Soon, as you get better at knowing and looking after your feelings, it's like you've built a little fortress around your heart—a strong and healthy one, not one that keeps the good stuff out, but one that guards against the not-so-good stuff. Now, you're ready to connect with others in a new way.

Breaking free from emotional incest means you're no longer tied up in knots, worrying if your choices will upset your mother. Instead, you stand on your own, making decisions because they're what's best for you. And from this new standing point, you can reach out and form relationships that are balanced and healthy.

These new connections are like bridges. In the past, a bridge might have been wobbly or full of holes because it was built on the shaky ground of your mother's needs. Now, you're building bridges on solid ground—your ground. You're fair to yourself, and you treat others the same way. You give love, and you allow yourself to receive love without feeling guilty or owing something back.

In the end, this journey of growth does more than just free you; it transforms you. You're no longer a leaf blowing in the wind of someone else's emotions. You're like a tree with deep roots and strong branches that can weather any storm.

Taking this path isn't easy, and it takes time, but every step is worth it. Each step is a step towards a brighter, stronger you—a you that loves and knows love without strings attached. That's the ultimate reward of breaking free. It's a journey of becoming empowered with every move you make towards your own happiness and peace.

14

CUTTING THE INVISIBLE STRINGS: OVERCOMING CODEPENDENCY

THE PUPPET SHOW: UNDERSTANDING CODEPENDENCY IN NARCISSISTIC RELATIONSHIPS

When we think of a puppet show, we can almost see the strings controlling the puppet's every move. This is not too different from what happens in a relationship filled with codependency, especially when one person grows up with a narcissistic mom or dad. A child living with a parent like this often learns to put their parent's wishes above everything else, even their own needs and feelings. It's like the child becomes a puppet, dancing to the tune their parent plays.

Let's be very clear about one thing: Codependency doesn't just appear out of nowhere. It grows in the shadows of a relationship where balance and fairness are missing. Imagine a scale that is always tipped in one direction, the side where the caring parent should be is always up in the air because the other side is weighed down by the parent's unending demands for attention and admiration—a parent who may often act more like a child.

For many daughters, having a narcissistic mom means they've been taught, since they were very small, to ignore what they want and feel. Their mom might have shown them that pleasing her is what's important, and it's the only way to get love. What an imbalanced way to grow up, where a little one's needs are seen as less important than those of an adult who should know better. By the time these daughters become adults themselves, they might not even realize they've been stuck in this unfair dance.

However, this issue goes beyond the walls of the family home. Often, without realizing it, these daughters might find themselves drawn to other relationships later on—friends, partners, even bosses—who take and take, just like their narcissistic parent did. There they are, once again, playing the role of the ever-giving, ever-patient partner or friend, holding up the other person's world while their own needs sit quietly in the background.

If this sounds like a difficult knot to untie, that's because it is. This pattern of codependency is carved deeply into the paths we walk every day, making it hard to even see, let alone change. But by understanding where it started—in these twisted parent-child relationships—we begin to pull back the curtain on our own puppet show.

The key takeaway here is this: by recognizing the patterns—the endless giving without ever feeling filled up in return, the habit of saying 'yes' when we want to say 'no,' the quiet voice inside us that we've learned to silence—we can start to see the strings that have been pulling us along. When we understand that these habits began as survival tactics in the face of an impossible kind of love, we can begin to learn new ways of being.

These new ways might feel awkward at first, like taking off shoes that are too tight and learning to walk without them. But in time, they can lead us to a place where we stand firm on our own two feet, holding the strings of our own lives in our hands.

THE ECHO'S CRY: IMPACT OF CODEPENDENCY

Living in the shadow of codependency can weigh heavy on a person, often in ways they don't even see at first. It's like carrying a backpack filled with stones—one for every time you put someone else's needs before your own. Soon, the weight can grow so much that it starts to change how you feel about yourself and the world around you.

At the start, you might not notice much. You might think it's completely normal to always be the one giving in or saying sorry. But over time, keeping your true feelings tucked away can start to hurt. You might wake up one day feeling like there's a dark cloud of frustration hanging over you because you're not really getting what you need. It's like you're on a constant loop of doing things for others without a moment to breathe or ask, "What about what I want?"

This kind of living can nibble away at how you see yourself. When you're always the cheerleader for others, you might forget how to cheer for yourself. It's like you've lost the megaphone for your own voice. Your heart starts to whisper doubts, making you feel smaller and less important. That's when things like self-esteem, the feeling of being strong and good about yourself, start to slip away.

But it doesn't stop there. When your mind is in a constant hustle to make someone else happy, it's like feeding a garden but never getting to enjoy the flowers. You might start to feel tense, worried, or even find yourself feeling down more often. These feelings could grow into bigger problems like anxiety or depression, and that's tough stuff. It's as if your inner light dims a bit more each day, harder and harder to brighten up again.

And just like a plant that doesn't get enough sun can't grow right, your relationships can't bloom the way they should either. If you're codependent, you might find yourself in friendships or love where you're almost invisible, where the other person's wishes and wants take up all the space. You might imagine you're the perfect partner because you're so giving, but deep down, the seesaw of give-and-take is stuck, and you're always on the ground.

This off-balance dance can twist up the way you act too. Maybe you start to get sneaky with your unhappiness, letting it peek out in small, sideways actions. Suddenly, you're saying 'Everything's fine' with a tight smile, but inside, you're a boiling pot ready to whistle in protest.

Avoidance becomes a friend you didn't ask for, as you start to side-step anything that feels like it could make waves. Before you know it, the way you relate to others feels like a knotted-up ball of yarn, hard to straighten out and smooth again.

Breaking the chains of codependency isn't easy, but once you recognize the weight it piles on your shoulders, you can start to gently place those stones down, one by one. And maybe, piece by piece, you can rebuild that garden, this time with enough sunshine for yourself, and flowers that bloom just as well for you as they do for everyone else.

UNRAVELING THE KNOT: BREAKING FREE FROM CODEPENDENCY

Taking the first step to break away from codependency is like finding a hidden door in a room you've been in for a long time. It's realizing that you've been stuck in a pattern where you give too much of yourself to others and forget to take care of you. To start this journey, it's important to see this pattern for what it is.

Taking a good look at yourself is not always easy, but it's a mighty tool when trying to understand your relationships better. Think about the people you've been close with, both in the past and now. If you notice you often put their needs before yours or feel uneasy when you're not helping them, these could be signs of codependent behavior.

One really helpful way to dig into your thoughts and feelings is by keeping a journal. Writing things down can be like talking to a friend who never interrupts or judges. In the quiet space of your journal, you can ask yourself questions like, "When did I last do something just for me?" or "How did I feel the last time someone I care about was upset?" This practice can shine a light on moments where you may have leaned toward codependent actions.

Just as you might decide what's okay to let into your home and what's not, setting boundaries is like drawing a line to protect your emotional space. Boundaries let others know that you respect yourself and expect the same from them. It's about knowing that it's okay to say "no," to ask for help, and not to carry the weight of others' feelings all the time.

If you're the daughter of a mother who's always put herself first, it can be really tough to start setting these boundaries. It feels foreign and maybe a bit scary. But like learning anything new, it gets easier with time. Little by little, as you practice saying what's okay and what's not for you, it starts to fit into your life more naturally and becomes a way you stand strong in your relationships.

Sometimes the push you need to get past codependency can't be done alone, and that's perfectly okay. Therapists or counselors know a lot about how tough it can be when someone close to you, like a mother, thinks mostly of themselves. They can guide you, give you new ways to approach situations, and offer the kind of support that makes you feel not so alone.

Another way to feel that you're not by yourself in this is to join a support group. Whether it's face to face or on the internet, being able to talk about what's been going on with you and hearing other people share can make a huge difference. It's like finding out that not only do others understand, but they've been where you are, you're part of a group that's all working toward feeling better about themselves and their relationships. It's a place where you're not giving but receiving, learning, and growing.

THE PATH TO INDEPENDENCE: BUILDING HEALTHY RELATIONSHIPS

Overcoming codependency is a journey of building healthy relationships that are based on mutual respect, a fair share of giving and receiving, and clear ways of talking to each other. In these relationships, you understand that everyone, including you, has the right to their own feelings and needs. Sharing these feelings and needs in a direct and nice way is a big part of making a relationship healthy.

When you start to care for yourself and love yourself, you take a very important step on this journey. This is especially true for daughters who have grown up with mothers who think about themselves too much. These daughters often forget their own needs and feelings because they are so busy trying to make their mothers happy. Putting your own care first can help change this.

Taking part in things like quiet moments of thinking, yoga, or setting time aside for things you love to do are ways to take care of yourself. When you give time to your hobbies or interests, you are saying that what you enjoy and what makes you feel good is important. This is one of the first ways to start loving yourself.

Another big step in getting over codependency is building up your self-esteem. If you often feel like you're not enough or value yourself too little, this could be a sign that you depend too much on others. The good thing is you can work on feeling better about yourself. By saying nice things to yourself regularly, reaching small goals you set, and not letting bad thoughts about yourself take over, you can start to feel stronger and more sure of yourself.

Let's say you tell yourself, "I am a smart and kind person" every day. This is a good thing to say to yourself because those words can help you start to believe it's true. If you try setting a small goal, like taking a walk everyday or reading a book by the end of the month, and then you do it, you can feel proud. This pride helps you understand that you can set goals and reach them, making you stronger.

Turning negative self-talk around is also a powerful way to build self-esteem. If you catch yourself saying, "I'm no good at this," pause for a moment. Ask yourself, "Is this really true?" Often it's not, and you can work on changing that thought into something more positive, like, "I'm still learning, and it's okay to make mistakes."

Changing codependent habits doesn't happen overnight. it might feel hard at first. but by working to build healthy relationships, practicing self-care, and loving yourself a little more each day, you can make great changes. you will start to feel like you are enough, and you can enjoy life with others without losing who you are.

15
FROM WOUNDS TO WISDOM: A JOURNEY THROUGH TRAUMA RECOVERY

At the heart of this story is a wound that can't be seen but is very real — the deep, lasting harm from a special kind of mistreatment known as narcissistic abuse. When a person with a lot of self-love in a bad way—a narcissist—hurts another, it creates a unique kind of damage. It's like a poison that spreads slowly through the mind, causing much pain and confusion.

This type of hurt often comes from someone very close, like a parent. When that parent thinks only of themselves and not of their child's feelings or needs, the child can carry this heavy burden into their grown-up years. They may feel a deep sadness, fear things without knowing why, and jump at sudden sounds, carrying unseen scars that change how they see themselves and the world around them.

A study looking into the harm caused by emotional hurt showed that if your mom or dad cared more about themselves than you, it can make you carry a tough load. Even when you get older, you might feel this weight as a wound in your mind, making each day harder than it should be.

Though we cannot see this wound with our eyes, its effects are powerful. Imagine a recording that plays in your head, telling you that you are not enough, that the world is not safe, and that others cannot be trusted. That's the kind of message that keeps playing for people who have felt the sting of narcissistic hurt. It's a harsh voice that never quite goes away, often causing a storm of negative feelings inside.

Those feelings can take the shape of an always-present worry, a deep sadness that feels like a heavy coat, or a feeling that the past is always right there, too close for comfort. Your ability to see yourself in a good light and believe in a kind, safe world can get lost in the fog of this pain.

Experts, like those at the American Psychological Association, tell us that when you're hurt by a narcissist—especially by your own parent—it shakes the very ground you stand on. Your image of who you are can get twisted, and you may start to see the world not as a place of hope and warmth but as a dark, cold place where hurt lurks around every corner.

For daughters with moms who could not give the right kind of love, this wound often shows up as a heavy doubt about whether they are ever good enough, a feeling of not deserving love, and trouble connecting with others in a good, strong way. They carry invisible chains that make it hard to walk freely in life, to love themselves, and to build a world filled with trust and happiness.

This is the shadow of narcissistic abuse—a dark spot on the soul that needs light and care to heal. And while the hurt is deep, the good news is that healing is within reach. With understanding and the right kind of help, there is a path forward, away from the pain and into a brighter, kinder world.

HEALING TOOLS: THERAPEUTIC APPROACHES TO TRAUMA RECOVERY

Eye Movement Desensitization and Reprocessing, or EMDR for short, is a special way for people to work through very tough events they've lived through. Imagine your brain as a busy office where memories are sorted and filed away. Trauma, which is the name for really bad experiences that hurt inside, can mess up this filing system. EMDR helps by fixing the way these memories are stored in your brain, making them less painful.

Now, think about when you watch a scary movie, and how your heart might beat faster. Your eyes also move a lot as you watch. In EMDR, you think about the tough memory while your eyes follow a therapist's moving hand or light. This helps your brain work through the memory. Doctors did a study that shows how this can make people with PTSD, which stands for the fear and hurt that stays after trauma, feel better. That's pretty amazing.

For women healing from narcissistic abuse, which means they were treated very badly by someone who only cared about themselves, EMDR can be like a special tool. It can help them understand their memories in new ways and start feeling better about themselves.

But that's not the only way to heal. There's also something called trauma-sensitive yoga. It's like regular yoga with stretching and breathing, but it's extra gentle for people with trauma. When bad things happen, people sometimes feel like they can't control what happens to their own bodies. Trauma-sensitive yoga helps them feel in charge again.

A group of smart people wrote a paper where they found out that this kind of yoga helps people with complex trauma, which means really deep and long-lasting hurts, to feel less stressed and have healthier minds. For daughters of women who didn't take care of their feelings, this type of yoga can make them feel strong and kind to themselves.

Next up is Cognitive Behavioral Therapy, or CBT. It's like having a coach for your thoughts. Sometimes, your thoughts can be like a broken record, saying mean things to you over and over. CBT helps you press stop on that record and play a new song, one that's kinder and truer to who you are.

Lots of studies, like one in this big library of medical info called The Cochrane Database, say that CBT really does help people with trauma heal. It helps them fight back against the tough things they've learned to believe about themselves because of how they were treated by their mothers who only thought about themselves.

This can be really hard, but important work – changing those thoughts is a big step towards a happier life. It's like cleaning out a backpack full of rocks, so it's lighter to carry. And every woman who has been through that kind of hurt deserves to walk freely, not weighed down by the past.

THE POWER OF PROFESSIONAL HELP: FINDING THE RIGHT THERAPIST

Taking the steps towards healing after dealing with a narcissistic mother can be tough, but finding the right therapist is like finding a guide who knows the way through a dark forest. This person isn't just any guide, though. They need to really get what you've been through. It's like they need a special map—the kind that shows all the tricky spots where someone with a heart heavy from narcissistic abuse might get stuck.

The good news is there's a group called the International Society for the Study of Trauma and Dissociation. They're like the mapmakers for finding this guide. They offer resources to help you find a therapist who knows all about trauma and can approach your experience with the care it deserves. This isn't just any therapist we're talking about, but one who understands the deeply hurtful things a narcissistic mother can do and say, and how those things echo inside a daughter's heart and mind for years.

If you're a daughter who grew up with a mother like this, working with a therapist who truly grasps the gravity of your experience is like finding someone who can speak your heart's language. They can help create personalized plans for healing, steps that make sense for you because they are made just for you.

Now, the therapy room itself can become a kind of safe harbor, a place very different from what you might have known. There, you find the care, belief in your worth, and respect that you might have missed out on before. When your therapist shows empathy and validates your feelings and experiences, it's like they're handing you pieces of a puzzle you've been trying to solve without a picture to guide you. This can help fix or "correct" those bad emotional memories by replacing them with new, good ones.

A study in a journal called "Psychotherapy Research" even found that this kind of relationship between you and your therapist is super important for success in therapy. Why? Because when you're with someone who is kind, listens you begin to see how a healthy relationship feels. For a person who's been through the confusing and painful ways of a narcissistic mother, experiencing this kind of positive relationship is like a light in the dark, showing the healing path ahead.

For women whose feelings were often pushed aside or trampled on by their narcissistic moms, being in a therapy relationship that uplifts and honors their voice can be life-changing. It can stir something good inside them, starting a healing process that reaches deep down to heal old wounds. And that's something truly powerful—a kind of medicine for the soul that can start the journey towards a brighter, healthier tomorrow.

SELF-HELP AND SELF-CARE IN TRAUMA RECOVERY

When going through tough times, getting help from experts like therapists or counselors is very important. They can guide you in ways that are hard to find on your own. However, there are simple things you can do yourself to make things better. These actions are like helping hands that work with therapy to heal your heart and mind.

Think about when you feel sick. Yes, you might see a doctor, but you also rest, drink tea, and take it easy. That's a bit like what you do for your mind with self-help methods and taking care of yourself.

A smart group of people wrote in the Journal of Mental Health and Clinical Psychology about ways to help yourself. They talked about writing down your thoughts, paying attention to the present moment, and being kind to yourself can all make you feel better if you've been through tough times. If you've grown up with a mom who only thought about herself, these small steps can make a big difference every day. They help you understand your feelings, treat yourself with love, and keep your emotions balanced.

Now, think about self-care. Self-care means doing things to look after both your body and your mind. Eating good food, getting enough sleep, and finding ways to relax are like giving gifts to yourself. These gifts can cheer you up and make stress feel smaller.

In the Journal of Clinical Psychology, smart people again found out that self-care is really important for keeping your mind healthy. It helps you bounce back and grow stronger after hard times. Let's imagine you're coming back from a long, rough journey. Self-care is like coming home to a cozy, warm house where you feel safe and loved.

For a woman who grew up with a mother who only looked out for herself, taking care of herself is a big deal. It's like saying "I matter" in a world where she was told she didn't. It's a strong way to fight back against feeling unimportant and forgotten.

Taking care of yourself might look different for everyone. It could be making time for a hobby you love, going for a walk, or just saying "no" when you need a break. It is about listening to what you need and saying yes to it. It's okay to put yourself first sometimes, especially when you've always been asked to put yourself last.

Let's remember that self-help tools and self-care are part of a puzzle. They fit in with help from others and make the picture of healing whole. Writing your thoughts, being kind to yourself, paying attention to now, eating healthily, sleeping you create a complete and beautiful picture of recovery.

THE JOURNEY AHEAD: NAVIGATING THE UPS AND DOWNS OF TRAUMA RECOVERY

If you're the daughter of a mother who always seemed to care more about herself than about you, your path to feeling better might look like a twisty road rather than a straight line. This isn't just okay; it's totally normal. Some days you'll feel strong, like you've taken a big leap forward. Other days, it might seem like you've slipped a few steps back. This dance of healing isn't neat and tidy, but it's still a dance moving you toward a happier life.

A smart group of people who study how folks feel after scary or hurtful events found something important. They wrote down in the Journal of Anxiety Disorders that getting over trauma doesn't just go in one direction. Sometimes, people press on ahead. Then, at other times, it might be like they're walking backwards. It's a tricky thing because when scary things happen to us, it can really mess with our heads. And that's true even if the hurt didn't come from a stranger or an accident but from your own mom, who was supposed to be your shelter. So, it's really okay to have tough times, even when you've been working hard to feel better. Those hard days don't erase the good ones.

For daughters who grew up with a mom always looking in the mirror, always needing praise, and never giving much warmth, the journey to heal is yours alone. You can't compare it with anyone else's. There isn't a rule book that says how fast you should get better or which path you need to take. It's about finding your own steps, your own way, and giving yourself the time you need. The American Counseling Association, a big circle of caring professionals, tells us that healing from hard memories and feelings comes down to a lot of different things like how strong you are inside, who's there to help you, and the tools you have in your heart and mind.

If you're reading this and you're that daughter, I want to tell you something. Go as slow as you need to. Healing doesn't come with a stopwatch. Your small steps are huge. Each tiny bit of ground you gain is a victory. When you're learning to live without the heavy weight of your mom's needs on your shoulders, even little things like saying no to something you don't want or taking time for yourself are big deals. They're signs that you're on your way to a life where you're the star, not an extra in your mom's show.

Every smile you manage, every tear you let fall, they're all part of patching up your heart and finding the joy that's been hidden away. Every time you recognize your mom's voice in your head and choose not to listen, you're taking back power. It's not about speed; it's about just moving, in whatever way you can, towards the sun and away from the shadows. That's the dance of healing—sometimes slow, sometimes stumbling, but always, always beautiful.

16

GENTLE WAVES OF CHANGE: THE JOURNEY TO MINDFUL PARENTING

Mindful parenting can be a soothing way to care for children when compared to the harsher ways some parents might act. It's a kind way to raise kids that helps them feel heard and loved. Dr. Jon Kabat-Zinn, who knows a lot about being mindful, shared this idea with the world, and it has caught on because it makes the relationship between parents and kids better.

When parents pay close attention and listen to what their kids are saying without judging them, kids feel respected. This is very different from the way of parenting that's all about the parent's needs, where parents might pay more attention to what they want rather than what their children need. Mindful parenting means parents give their kids steady love and try to understand their kids' feelings. When parents do this, their kids learn to trust them, and the bond between them grows stronger.

For instance, if a child is having a tough time and begins to cry or yell, this is a moment for mindful parenting to shine. Instead of the parent reacting quickly with anger or annoyance, a mindful parent would stop for a moment and breathe deeply. This pause helps the parent remain calm and think clearly. Then, with kindness, the parent can understand why their child is upset and respond in a helpful way. Maybe the child needs a hug or an explanation about why they can't have what they want. This way, the child learns that it's okay to have strong feelings, and there are good ways to handle them.

This approach can also lead to fewer fights between parents and kids because there's more understanding and less anger. When a home feels peaceful, everyone can be happier and get along better.

It's also about being fair and clear with rules. Mindful parenting doesn't mean there are no rules. Instead, it's about finding the right balance. Parents still need to be in charge, but they do it with care. Let's say a child wants to play before doing homework. Instead of a parent saying, "Do as I say now!" without listening to the child, they could say, "I know you want to play, and you will have plenty of time to do that after your homework is done. Doing your work first is important because it helps you learn and grow."

In this way, the child understands why the rule is there in the first place. They feel their parent is guiding them, not just bossing them around. Mindful parenting is all about finding ways to show kids that you love them, you're listening to them, and you're there for them, but also teaching them about the world in a caring way. It's the opposite of a parenting style that only thinks about what the parent wants, and it gives kids the chance to grow up knowing how to handle their feelings and understand others better.

THE HEALING POTENTIAL OF MINDFUL PARENTING: BREAKING THE NARCISSISTIC CYCLE

When we talk about being a good parent, it's like being a gardener tending to a beautiful, growing plant. For those who grew up with a parent who was too focused on themselves, it might seem hard to know how to care for this little plant the right way. But that's where mindful parenting comes in, like sunshine and water for the garden. It's a way to make sure you don't repeat the cycle, to check that you're not too focused on yourself when your child needs you.

To be a mindful parent means to really pay attention, like noticing the small changes in your plant as it grows. You become more aware of your own habits, especially the ones that are about thinking of yourself first, which you might have picked up from how you were raised. By seeing these habits, you can make a choice to act differently. Like making sure to listen carefully when your child is talking instead of thinking about what you'll say next.

Sometimes, having a parent who was always thinking about themselves can leave deep marks, like scars on the bark of an old tree. Mindful parenting is like the gentle work of healing these marks. It takes time and care, but as you get better at understanding and dealing with these old wounds, you grow stronger. And just as a tree with healed scars can still grow tall and strong, so can you.

If you've ever watched kids playing, you'll know their feelings are like the weather—constantly changing from sunny to stormy! Being a mindful parent is like being a wise guide who shows them the ropes of this weather. When a child feels sad or mad, instead of just letting that storm rage, a mindful parent will sit with them, helping them name their feelings like clouds in the sky and teaching them how to let those clouds pass by without any rain. This helps them when they face tough times later because they know how to handle the storms themselves.

Now, this is important—the bond between a parent and child is like the roots of a tree. Strong roots make for a healthy tree. Through mindful parenting, these roots get deep and strong because the child feels safe and loved no matter what. This love helps the child to stand tall and sure, with a heart full of confidence rather than worry.

Remember that garden? It needs protection, too, against things like pests or weeds that could harm it. Just like in the garden, a child who has a secure bond and knows how to work through their feelings can spot when someone else is too caught up in themselves and might hurt them. They have their own protection, just like a plant that can withstand a few bugs.

Mindful parenting isn't always easy. It's like learning a completely new way of gardening. But every bit of effort you put in is worth it. It means you are giving your child tools for life—a heart that knows love, a mind that can cope with storms, and a bond that is as strong as the oldest tree in the forest. This is the gift of breaking the cycle—one mindful moment at a time.

EMBARKING ON THE MINDFUL PARENTING JOURNEY: NAVIGATING CALM AND STORMY SEAS

Starting your journey to becoming a mindful parent takes some work on yourself first. Mindfulness is about being awake and knowing what's happening right now. You're not lost in thoughts about the past or worries about the future. To be a parent who's there in the moment with your kids, you first have to learn how to be there for yourself.

One way you can start is by sitting quietly and paying attention to your breath. This is called meditation. It isn't complicated, but it takes practice. Find a quiet spot in your home, sit down, and just focus on how you breathe in and breathe out. Do this for a few minutes each day, and you might feel a change. Your mind could become clearer, and your heart could become calmer.

Another practice is yoga, which combines movement with breathing. It helps you get to know your body and mind better. Moving through yoga poses with attention can help make your body feel good and ease your thoughts. It's not about getting fit, although that might happen too—it's about being kind to yourself.

Journaling can be mindful too. It's like having a conversation with yourself on paper. Write about what you're grateful for, what's bugging you, or anything that's in your head. This can help you understand your thoughts and feelings better.

As you get more used to these ways of being mindful, you can naturally start bringing them into how you raise your kids. Maybe you'll find yourself taking a deep breath before you answer when they test your patience. Or perhaps you'll be better at really listening when they tell you about their day.

Sure, there will be tough times. Moments will come when you react without thinking, the way you always have. Maybe you get angry fast, or maybe you start to worry too much. But these moments are not failures—they're chances to learn and to grow stronger.

You don't have to do this all alone. You can find workshops for parents, where people learn and practice being mindful together. Or look for others on the internet who are trying to raise their kids this way too. You can find advice, stories, and support from books on mindful parenting, like "The Mindful Parent" by Charlotte Peterson.

This journey you're on, it's not about being a perfect parent. That's not what your kids need. What they need is a parent who's "good enough," which means being there for them, messing up sometimes, and making sure they know they're loved and safe. This idea comes from a smart guy named Donald Winnicott. He taught that it's better for kids when their parents are real—flaws and all.

Most of all, remember the pressure you feel to do everything just right, especially if you had a mom who was really tough on you— that's not what being a good parent is about. Take a breath, and know that every day, you're doing your best. That's more than enough.

17

CULTIVATING EMOTIONAL INTELLIGENCE: A LIFELINE FOR YOUR CHILD'S FUTURE

In the heart of real-life challenges, emotional intelligence stands out as a mighty tool that can not just change the way kids act, but also the way they look at the world and handle tough times—like when they have a grandparent with a very big ego who thinks only of themselves, which we often call narcissistic.

Let's dive into the real meaning of emotional intelligence, or EI, and why it's a game-changer. You might think it's all about knowing if you're happy or sad. But it's more. It's like being the captain of your emotions' ship. You know where your feelings are leading you, and you can steer them to make your day better, not worse.

This power we're talking about is made up of five things. First up, it's knowing what you're feeling inside, which is what we call self-awareness. Imagine you're a detective, and your job is to figure out what your own heart is saying. That's self-awareness.

Next comes self-regulation. Picture yourself being able to hit the brakes before you say something mean when you're mad. Or pushing the pause button on actions that could mess things up.

Then there's motivation. That's like your inner coach pepping you up to keep going, even when things feel tough or boring.

The fourth piece is empathy, which is like having superpowers to feel what someone else is feeling. It's seeing the world with their eyes and understanding why they might be sad or glad.

Last but not least, social skills help you get along with others, like the right words to make a friend feel better or knowing the fair way to share your toys.

Now, let's talk about kids and how this EI stuff plays out for them. Kids with strong emotional smarts can better handle it when life throws curveballs. They can talk things out instead of throwing a fit. This means in school, they can work well with others, which could even make their grades better.

There's this group that checked out schools where they teach EI. They said that the kids in those schools did way better than other kids—11% better, which is a lot.

Plus, when tough times hit, like dealing with a grandparent who's always talking about themselves and doesn't really listen, EI helps kids get through it. They don't fall apart; they got the skills to stay strong.

This is why understanding emotional intelligence is so important. It's like giving kids a shield to protect them from the not-so-nice stuff. And the good news? Emotional intelligence can be learned and grown, kind of like planting a seed and watching it turn into a big, beautiful tree. With a bit of help and the right tools, every child can grow their emotional understanding and become awesome at dealing with life, no matter what comes their way.

LAYING THE FOUNDATION: BUILDING EMOTIONAL INTELLIGENCE IN EARLY CHILDHOOD

Emotional intelligence is like a garden in our hearts that needs care from the earliest days of life. As a parent, you hold the watering can and the tools to nurture this garden, helping your child's emotional intelligence grow strong and vibrant.

Imagine your child comes home, shoulders slumped, a frown painting their usually bright face. They've lost a game they played at school, and they carry the weight of that loss. This moment, though small, is fertile soil for teaching. Sit down with them, look into their eyes, and open a conversation about the tumble of feelings tumbling inside them. "Disappointment feels like a heavy stone in our hearts, doesn't it?" you might say. "And frustration is like trying to push a mountain that just won't move." By putting words to their feelings, you're showing them the map of their inner world.

When your child starts to speak, let their words flow without interrupting. Nod, smile, and frown with them. Show them that this space between you is safe and their emotions are as real and important as the stars in the night sky. Encouragement to talk strengthens their ability to understand and steer their own feelings, like a captain navigating a ship through stormy seas.

Another treasure of emotional intelligence is empathy, that magic ability to walk in another's shoes. Say your child sees a classmate teased by others, their face turning as red as an autumn leaf. Bring this to a quiet conversation and explore what that classmate might be feeling. "Do you think they felt alone, like a tree in a wide, empty field?" Teaching them to stretch their hearts towards others lays bricks of kindness and connection in their growing garden.

Stories in books and movies are like windows into different worlds filled with emotions. When you read a tale of adventure or watch a hero's journey, pause and reflect with your child. Ask, "How do you think the rabbit felt when it got lost? Scared, maybe? Like when we can't see our house anymore?" This opens doors to understand that everyone has storms and sunshine in their hearts, just like they do.

Expression is a rainbow bridge from inside out, and children paint their emotions in a million colors if given the chance. Supply them with paper, crayons, clay, and instruments. Let their fingers dance, their voices sing, and their stories unfold. This is not just play—it's them speaking in the language of emotion that doesn't always use words.

Lastly, always, always practice active listening. When your child weaves their feelings into words, listen like it's the most important story you've ever heard. This tells them their feelings are worthy of attention and respect.

Thus, in these everyday chapters of life, you gently water and tend to your child's emotional intelligence, nurturing a garden that will one day flourish with understanding, empathy, and heartfelt connection to the world around them.

CULTIVATING EMOTIONAL INTELLIGENCE IN ADOLESCENCE: NAVIGATING THE EMOTIONAL ROLLERCOASTER

Adolescence is a rollercoaster of many changes, and with it comes a sea of emotions that can often feel like too much to handle. If you're a parent with a teenager at home, you've got a special role to play. You can help your teenager ride these emotional waves and learn how to understand and control their feelings better. This is what we call developing emotional intelligence.

Now, even though your kid has hit their teen years, it doesn't mean they've stopped watching you. They might act like they don't care or like they know everything, but they're paying close attention to how you handle your own feelings. You've got to show them how it's done. When you're feeling mad or upset, let them see you taking deep breaths or stepping away from a problem until you're feeling calmer. This is showing them, not just telling them, how to manage their feelings in a healthy way.

Communication is super important. Teens have a lot on their minds, but they might not always want to talk about it. Make sure they know that when they're ready to chat, you're there to listen without being quick to judge or criticize. When they do open up, listen to what they're feeling and thinking. Conversation is a two-way street; it should feel easy and safe for them to say what's on their mind.

Friends and other people in your teenager's life play a huge part too. It's key for your teen to know what a healthy relationship looks like. Keep the door open to discuss the importance of respect, being honest, and really listening to others. Show them that true friends will treat them right and make them feel good about themselves.

As they grow, they'll need to figure out how to work well with people. Getting your teenager into clubs, teams, or volunteer work can teach them valuable lessons about getting along and understanding others. These activities teach them to cooperate, which is a big deal in the world of emotional smarts.

Next up is helping them master self-regulation. It's a fancy term, but it's all about controlling their impulses, managing stress, and making smart choices. Start by teaching them some stress-busting tools like taking a moment to be mindful or doing some deep breathing exercises. Back in 2010, smart folks from the University of California, Los Angeles, found that being mindful can really help teens with managing their emotions.

Goals, those are important too. Chat with your teenager about what they want to achieve—could be a skill, a grade, or even a personal project—and help them lay out the steps to get there. Having something to work towards can keep them pumped and focused.

Helping your teen develop emotional intelligence isn't about one big talk or a miracle solution. It's about everyday actions, honest talks about feelings, guiding by example, and supporting them through all the ups and downs. Remember, even though they may seem all grown-up, they're still learning how to deal with life's big emotions. And you, you're their guidebook.

THE ROLE OF EMOTIONAL INTELLIGENCE IN PROTECTING AGAINST NARCISSISTIC ABUSE

Raising a child to be strong on the inside is a big job, especially when they need to deal with tough situations. If their grandpa or grandma is a person with a narcissistic personality, it means they often think they're the most important and might not treat others nicely. This can be hard for kids to understand and make them feel many different feelings.

To help kids get through this, teaching them about emotional smarts – or emotional intelligence – can be like giving them a special shield. It's not a real shield, but it's a way for them to understand and handle the tricky emotions that might pop up when they're with a narcissistic person.

A kid who knows a lot about emotions will see it when someone tries to trick them with mind games. These games can make kids question what's true or feel bad for no reason. Narcissistic people often use these tricks, like saying something didn't happen when it did, or making someone feel guilty to get what they want.

When kids are smart about emotions, they can tell when someone's trying to twist the truth. They learn to know what they're feeling and why. This helps them to stay calm and not react in a way that'll make things worse. Think of it like knowing when to walk away from a game that isn't fair.

Having emotional smarts also teaches kids to get back up again when things get them down. Everyone falls, but not everyone gets up quickly. In 2017, people who study how teens grow up found that those who really understand their feelings can handle stress much better. This means they don't stay sad for long and can bounce back like a ball after being pushed.

By helping your child learn about emotions, you're not just keeping them safe from hurtful words or actions; you're stopping a bad pattern. Kids who are good with feelings are nice to others and don't copy the unkind ways of narcissistic people. They listen, care, and share, making friends and not hurting them.

In a home where someone has faced tough times because of a person with narcissistic ways, growing a child's emotional smarts is good for them and a big step toward healing. It's kind of like planting a garden of kindness where only harshness grew before. As a parent, this is something powerful you can do. It gives your child what they need to grow up healthy in their heart and mind, and it starts to change things for the better.

18

BOUNCING BACK: CULTIVATING RESILIENCE IN CHILDREN TO DEFY THE NARCISSIST'S LEGACY

In a world where families often face tough challenges, resilience emerges as a hidden strength, a kind of secret armor that protects children, especially those growing up with a narcissistic parent. What exactly is resilience? stronger than ever, after a hard fall. It's like being a bendy tree in a mighty storm - the tree sways but doesn't break.

When experts talk about resilience, the American Psychological Association shines a light on it as a kind of superpower to roll with the punches. They say it's the process of doing okay even when things around you are not okay, like when bad things happen, or you're dealing with a lot—like a parent who's always thinking of themselves first. This isn't about hiding from tough times; it's about learning to dance in the rain.

So, can resilience help kids who live with a parent that seems to care more about themselves than anyone else? Absolutely. This super-power acts like an invisible shield, guarding them against the hurt that comes from a parent's self-centered ways. And the good news? This shield, resilience, isn't something you're born with - it's a skill.

Just like riding a bike, it can take some practice, but eventually, you get the hang of it.

A smart and caring expert, Dr. Ann Masten, who knows a lot about how we deal with tough times, tells us a really important truth: resilience isn't just for a few 'chosen ones'. It's actually pretty common and most people have what it takes to be resilient. The idea that resilience is only for the lucky few is just a make-believe story.

Now, why does this matter when talking about kids and a parent who shows narcissism? Because growing up with such a parent can be like walking through a minefield. You never know when an explosion of self-interest will happen next. Kids may feel like they're always second best, or they might even believe it's their fault when things go wrong.

But when kids learn resilience, they start to see that it's not about them - it's about the parent's challenges. They understand that everyone faces hard times, but they don't have to let those hard times dictate who they are or who they'll become. They can learn to keep going, to adapt, and to find joy even when it's hard.

So, think of resilience as this incredible, learnable skill that helps kids navigate through life with a narcissistic parent. Like a compass in a storm, resilience won't stop the rain, but it will help them find their way through it. And as they grow, this resilience will be like a trusty friend, always there to help them become strong, thoughtful, and emotionally healthy adults. Let's help our kids find and polish this secret armor - their resilience - to protect them and help them thrive in any weather.

THE ROLE OF RESILIENCE IN THWARTING NARCISSISTIC INFLUENCE

In a world where families can be tricky, children sometimes face tough times. When a parent, like a mom, thinks only about themselves more than usual, it can create a home filled with stress and worry for a kid. This self-centered way is often called being narcissistic. Kids can feel like they're in a twisty maze, trying to keep their mom happy all the time. But here's a tool that's like a flashlight in that maze: resilience.

Resilience is when you can handle hard feelings and bounce back from rough spots. It's like being a sturdy tree that bends in a strong wind but doesn't break. When a kid has a narcissistic mom who tries to pull their strings like a puppet, it can make them feel small. But a resilient child can see what's going on. They know it's like a game, and they don't have to play it. Instead of getting upset, they keep their cool and remember their worth.

Imagine standing on a beach when waves keep knocking you over. If you stand up each time, that's resilience. A narcissistic mom may try over and over to push her child into feeling unsure or less important. Resilience helps the child stand back up, not letting the waves drag them down. This power keeps their heart strong, stopping mean words from sticking.

Now, let's talk science. The National Institute of Mental Health, a big group of brain experts, have found out that resilience is more than just a good feeling. It's like a shield for your mind. Kids with this shield can dodge the arrows of sadness and worry that come from living with someone who's always thinking of themselves. It saves them from feeling stuck in a dark cloud of bad thoughts, allowing them to enjoy the sunshine of good days.

But resilience doesn't just protect a kid; it also opens doors to new worlds. Children can step outside the shadows of a tough home life and make friends. Real friends understand give-and-take, not like the one-way street at home with a narcissistic mom. Here's where resilience is the key. It lets a child know what a true, kind friendship looks like.

Having this key, a resilient child looks for friends who share, who listen, and who care – friends who treat them as a team member, not an extra. These friendships are like cozy blankets, keeping children warm against the cold they might feel from a parent who's not very giving.

Resilience is a superpower, one that every kid can grow inside themselves. It lets them lift their head high in a storm and find others who will walk with them in the rain. So no matter how much a narcissistic mom might try to make them doubt, a strong, determined, and resilient child will know the truth: they are good enough, and they always have been.

FOSTERING RESILIENCE: STRATEGIES AND TECHNIQUES

In a home where one parent has a very strong personality, like someone with narcissistic traits, kids sometimes don't feel heard. They might keep their thoughts and feelings locked up inside because they worry about what might happen if they share them. But what's really important is this: every child should know they can talk about whatever's on their mind and in their heart without being scared of getting into trouble or being laughed at.

Start by sitting down with your child regularly, maybe at the dinner table, and ask them to tell you about their day. Tell them you want to hear the good stuff and the tough stuff, too. When they open up about what's happening, especially things related to the other parent, listen closely. Let them know you understand, and that it's okay to feel upset, happy, confused, or any mix of feelings. Say something like, "I get why you'd feel that way," to show you really hear them. And don't forget to remind your child that it's great they're sharing what's going on inside them because their feelings are really important.

When things get tricky, whether it's a hard math problem or a friendship that's making them feel twisted up inside, it's super good for kids to know they can come up with solutions themselves. You can help them learn this step by step. For example, if they're stuck on that math problem, sit down with them. Ask simple questions to help them think it through, like "What have you tried so far?" or "What could you try next?" Teach them to tackle problems piece by piece, so they don't get overwhelmed.

It's also great for kids to try new things, even if they're a little nervous about it. Maybe there's a sport they've never played or a subject at school they find tough. If they're afraid of making mistakes, you can tell them that even the biggest stars in sports or the smartest people in the world had to start somewhere—and they definitely made mistakes along the way. Mistakes aren't bad; they're part of how we learn. Tell your kid it's awesome to take healthy chances. When they see they can try, mess up, and still be okay, it gives them confidence.

Speaking of confidence, it's like a muscle. The more kids use it, the stronger it gets. Help your child see how great they are by pointing out the good stuff they do. Maybe they shared their toy with their little sister, or they got an "A" on a spelling test. Tell them you're proud, and remind them to feel proud too. When they start to believe in themselves, that's their confidence growing.

Growing up with a narcissistic parent is really rough. but by making sure your child knows their voice counts, teaching them to solve their own problems, letting them take chances, and helping them see their own worth, you're giving them tools to build a happy life, no matter what.

RESILIENCE IN ACTION: CASE STUDIES

In the book of life, we come across people who face great challenges. They seem to bend like strong trees in the wind but never break. Their stories teach us that no mountain is too high to climb if we hold on to resilience.

Let's dive into the story of a brave girl, Malala Yousafzai. Malala comes from a country where, for some, the idea of girls going to school wasn't welcomed. But Malala had a spark in her. She believed that all girls had the right to learn just as much as boys. She spoke up, even though it was dangerous. One day, those who didn't like what she was saying hurt her badly. But guess what? Malala didn't give up. Her spirit was stronger than ever. She got better and stood up taller than before. She traveled across the world, telling her story and fighting for girls' education. Malala's resilience showed the world that standing up for what's right could change things.

Now, let's bounce the ball to another story, that of Michael Jordan. Michael loved basketball. But when he tried out for his high school team, he didn't make it. Imagine how sad that would feel. However, Michael didn't let that stop him. He practiced, worked hard, and believed in himself. Eventually, he became one of the best basketball players ever! Michael's resilience shows us that sometimes, a 'no' can lead to a bigger 'yes' if we don't give up.

In our regular lives, we meet challenges that need resilience, too. Think about dealing with a difficult parent. A narcissistic mother might not understand or value your feelings. This can hurt deep down inside. Now, imagine you are in a situation where your mother says something unkind, and you feel like your feelings don't matter.

A resilient person in this case might take a breath and remember their worth. They know their feelings are important, even if someone else doesn't see it. They might say, "I know what I feel, and it's okay to feel this way." They find people who do understand to talk to, like friends or perhaps a counselor. And maybe, with time, they try to explain to their mother how her words make them feel, without expecting her to change right away. The resilient person takes care of their own heart, even when others don't seem to.

These real-life heroes and everyday resilience teach us a powerful lesson. Whether you are standing up for a big cause like Malala, aiming for your dreams like Michael, or facing daily challenges with family, resilience is your shield and sword. It's about knowing that you are strong, that your voice matters, and that no matter how many times you fall, you can, and will, rise again.

THE PATH AHEAD: CULTIVATING RESILIENCE FOR A HEALTHY FUTURE

When we think about resilience, like the strength that lets a bendy tree sway in a strong wind but not break, it's helpful to see it not as a single point you arrive at, but more like a path you walk along every day. This journey doesn't have flat roads or straight paths. It winds, it goes up and down hills, and it sometimes loops back on itself. Reminding your child of this journey is a way to encourage them to keep stepping forward, even when the road gets tough.

As your child learns and grows, the tricks and ways they handle the thoughts and feelings that come from having a mother who might not always think about others' feelings, might change too. Something that seemed to help yesterday might not do the trick today, and that's perfectly fine. The important thing is to keep an open mind and try new things, knowing that what's important is the learning and growing, not just sticking to one way because it worked before.

Now, imagine resilience like a toolbox. In this toolbox, you have different tools for different jobs—no single tool does it all. You should regularly check in with your child and go over the "tools" they've learned for dealing with tough times. This is reinforcing, kind of like practice for a sport or an instrument. When you practice, you get better, and the tunes and moves become a part of you. For your child, regularly talking about how to stand up to hard feelings, say kind things to themselves, or remember the good times, means these skills will become second nature, ready for when they really need them.

But just as a toolbox might sometimes not have the right tool for a very special job, there are times when kids—and adults too—need an expert's help to make or find that unique tool. If your child struggles a lot with their feelings because of the way their mother acts and speaks, it might be time to find someone who knows a whole lot about feelings and resilience. Therapists and counselors who understand what it's like to have a parent who always seems to put themselves first can give extra help and show your child new ways to manage their emotions and keep growing strong.

To sum it up, resilience against the rough weather brought by a narcissistic mother is something you can help your child build up over time. It's a mix of self-discovery, practice, and sometimes, a helping hand from someone who knows. Each step your child takes is a step towards them becoming their truest, most strong self, able to handle whatever comes with courage and hope.

19
CULTIVATING HEALTHY CONNECTIONS: TEACHING THE NEXT GENERATION

In the journey of growing up, one of the greatest gifts we can give to our children is the wisdom to create and maintain healthy relationships. As they step out into the world, the bonds they form with others will shape their lives in profound ways. That's why understanding the foundation of healthy relationships is crucial.

At the core of such relationships are mutual respect, understanding, trust, and equality. Let's imagine a see-saw in a playground, perfectly balanced, with a child seated at each end. They are having fun because they're both contributing equally to this balance. Healthy relationships share that balance. Like in a strong friendship, each person should have an equal say. They listen to one another, are considerate of the other's personal space, and lift each other up when times are hard.

Sometimes, though, relationships can be like a see-saw with one side stuck in the mud. In this picture, one person is doing all the holding up. The other is sitting heavy and not budging. This is what an unhealthy relationship can look like. It might be a friendship where one person is making all the decisions, not caring about the other's thought or feelings, or maybe one person is always doing the talking and never doing any listening.

By talking to our children about the tell-tale signs of a healthy relationship, they begin to understand what they should expect from others and themselves. If a child knows, for instance, that a true buddy is someone who cares about their feelings, they are more likely to walk away from a so-called friend who hurts their feelings or makes fun of them often.

Where do children get their first lessons on relationships? From watching and interacting with the grown-ups in their lives. They look at their parents, their aunts, uncles, and teachers. They notice whether the adults speak kindly to each other, if they listen and share, or if they shout and take control. Every action you show acts like a piece of a puzzle, helping your child understand how people should treat one another.

It's not enough to just tell children about the importance of healthy relationships; they need to see them in action. That's why showing healthy relationships through our own behavior becomes a powerful teaching tool. When we treat our partners and colleagues with respect and fairness, we are demonstrating to our children how they should expect to be treated, and how they should treat others.

The lesson here is clear: Fostering healthy relationships in children is not only about guiding them in their interactions. It's equally important to be a living example of what good relationships look like. Equip them with this knowledge, and they will have the tools to navigate social interactions and stay clear of the toxic grip of unhealthy ones. They'll learn not just to balance on the see-saw of relationships but to ensure everyone involved gets to enjoy the ride.

RESPECT: THE BUILDING BLOCK OF HEALTHY RELATIONSHIPS

Respect is like glue in any friendship or bond between people. It's the thing that sticks things together, making sure everyone is treated well and feels good. When we talk about respect, we often think of how we treat each other in day-to-day life. It's like the rules for a game where everyone can win. One key rule is to listen carefully when someone else is talking. It means you keep your ears open and your mouth shut when it is not your turn. This shows the other person you think their words are important.

Imagine you are chatting with a friend, and they start talking about a book they love. If you listen without interrupting, you're giving them respect. It shows you care about what they feel. But, let's turn the page. If you're the one talking about your favorite book, you deserve the same attention. If someone butts in or doesn't listen, it's as if they are saying your thoughts don't matter, which isn't fair. It's okay to remind them, in kind words, that you were not finished and would like to be heard.

Teaching respect isn't just about words; it's about understanding boundaries too. Boundaries are like invisible lines around all of us that we don't want others to cross. They help keep us safe and happy. Children especially should know that it's alright to have their own space, and it's just as alright to let others have theirs.

For instance, every now and then, someone might have a secret they don't wish to share, and that's okay. Even if it's a best friend, respecting their choice not to tell is part of being respectful. Just imagine it's a treasure chest they want to keep closed. You can be curious, but you know the chest is theirs, not yours. When we respect someone's wish for privacy, we show that we value their feelings as much as we value our own.

The colors of respect also paint how we see and celebrate what makes us all different. No two people are the same, and that's a wonderful thing. Everyone has their own stories, their own ways of looking at the world, their own likes and dislikes. When children learn that it's great to have such variety in the world, they begin to see that every person is a new chapter, full of surprises and things to learn.

Teaching respect for differences can stitch together friendships that might have never happened. It can open doors to new ideas and experiences. It encourages children to not only accept but also enjoy the fact that not everyone has to like the same ice cream flavor or have the same hobbies.

Through respect, the world gets a little brighter, a little kinder, and a whole lot more interesting. It's something we can all give, and in return, we create a place where everyone gets a chance to be who they are, to be listened to, and to feel valued. And the best part? It doesn't cost a thing.

COMMUNICATION: THE BRIDGE IN RELATIONSHIPS

Communicating well is like having keys to open many doors to friendship and understanding. To build healthy relationships, it's key to talk about what we think and how we feel in a clear and honest way. This isn't just something for kids to learn; it's a tool adults use every day to make their friendships and relationships stronger.

Imagine a young person is having a tough time with a buddy. Perhaps their buddy chose another friend to be on his team first, and this made the young person feel sad and left out. It's better for them to say, "I felt sad when I wasn't picked for the team," rather than not talking or acting grumpy. This openness can help friends understand each other's feelings. The buddy might not have meant to hurt feelings and, knowing this, might make better choices next time.

However, talking isn't the only part of good communication. Being a good listener is just as important. That means paying close attention and trying to feel what the other person feels. Suppose a friend is sad because their pet is sick. If a child listens with their heart, not just their ears, they won't be quick to say, "Don't be sad, you can get another pet!" Instead, they show they get how much their friend loves their pet by saying, "That's really hard. I am here for you." This empathy makes both friends feel closer because one is sharing and the other is truly understanding.

But what if friends don't agree? Sometimes, disagreements happen, and that's okay. But how those disagreements are handled—that's what's key. When conflict comes up, it's better to talk it out in a way that's fair and calm, not mean or hard-headed. For instance, if two kids want to play different games, they should talk to find a game they both like instead of getting mad or yelling. And they shouldn't say things that hurt on purpose. Personal attacks, like "You never let me pick the game because you're selfish," make things worse. Instead, they can say, "I feel like we always play your game. Can we try mine today?"

Teaching kids these communication skills is like giving them a toolkit. A toolkit they can carry into adulthood, where they'll keep building on those skills for even stronger connections with others. It might start with learning to share toys and move on to sharing thoughts and feelings in a way everyone can grasp. And just like fixing a wobbly table or a squeaky door, adults also need to keep their communication tools in good shape to maintain good relationships. Whether we're kids or grown-ups, talking things through and really listening can turn a tough situation into a chance for learning and growing together. That's the real magic of talking and listening

—it's the path to understanding each other and living happier with our friends, families, and everyone else we care about.

EMOTIONAL INTELLIGENCE: THE HEART OF HEALTHY RELATIONSHIPS

Emotional intelligence is like having a super tool for dealing with feelings – your own and others'. It's a big part of making friends and getting along with people. Just think about a puzzle. If we can figure out where our own feelings fit and understand where other people's feelings fit too, we make the whole picture of getting along much clearer.

Let's think about a time when you were a child. Imagine you wanted to play with a toy, but someone else was playing with it, and you got really mad. If you had a chance to learn about emotional intelligence when you were that young, you might have understood that feeling. You'd realize, "Hey, I'm mad right now because I really wanted a turn with that toy." Recognizing that feeling is the first big step.

Now, think about how you would say that today. Instead of just being upset and maybe yelling or grabbing the toy, children with high emotional intelligence can use their words. They could say, "I'm feeling frustrated because I didn't get a turn to play." See how that's better? It's like giving a name to the feeling and also saying why it's happening. That's a really smart way to deal with a tough feeling.

But there's more to emotional intelligence than just knowing about your own feelings. It's also about looking at your friends and family and understanding what they feel. This part is called empathy. Imagine you see your friend sitting alone and looking sad. Empathy is like giving you special glasses to see why they're sad. Maybe they didn't get a turn to play either, or perhaps they're just having a bad day.

Teaching children about empathy is like giving them a key to unlock more friendships and build strong ones. When kids understand why their friends are sad, they can help or just be there for them. This is how they show they care. And when we show we care, our friendships grow.

So, how do you teach this? It's simple and hard at the same time. When your child is playing with others, watch them closely. If they seem upset or their friend does, take a quiet moment together. You can ask, "How do you think your friend feels?" or "What can we do to make things better?" This will help them start to use those empathy glasses we talked about.

A child with a good grip on emotional intelligence is like a little superhero. They can make their own bad feelings less powerful and help make others feel better too. It gives them superpowers like patience, kindness, and understanding. And guess what? These superpowers work for grown-ups, too! The more we all practice understanding our feelings and the feelings of others, the better we all get along. And that makes everything a little bit nicer, just like finishing that puzzle we started, one piece of understanding at a time.

BREAKING THE CYCLE: THE POWER OF HEALTHY RELATIONSHIPS

In our world today, we see people who act like they're the center of everything. They think mostly about themselves and sometimes treat others as if their feelings don't matter. This is called narcissism, and it's a big word for when someone loves themselves so much that they forget to care properly for the people around them. However, if we step in early and teach our children about sharing, kindness, and understanding others, we can help prevent this from becoming a pattern in their lives.

See, children are like sponges, soaking up everything they see and hear. When we show them how a good relationship looks and feels, they learn what is okay and what is not okay. They learn that it's not right for someone to always take control, ignore other people's thoughts, or be mean. Instead, they learn to love themselves without being unkind or unfair to others.

When children grasp the idea of what a healthy relationship is, they become smart about their choices. They steer clear of friendships and bonds where they feel pushed down or unimportant. If someone tries to make them feel small, they'll say, "This isn't how friends should act," and they'll look for better, healthier connections.

Moreover, when kids grow up knowing that respect and caring for others' feelings are essential, they are less likely to act in ways that hurt others. They won't feel the need to make everything about themselves because they realize that everyone is important. This is how we stop them from maybe becoming people who could hurt others without realizing it. Teaching them to put themselves in someone else's shoes helps them understand the impact their actions have.

It's not just about stopping bad things from happening. It's also about making sure good things happen in their lives. For instance, when a child understands that it's nice to listen, share, and help, they make friends who appreciate and respect them. They learn to give and take, which are essential parts of any excellent and loving bond with others. These kinds of healthy habits can make them happier and more content in life.

By guiding children with these life lessons today, they'll grow up to be adults who value and nurture good relationships. They'll aim to do well by others, knowing that when everyone feels heard and respected, life is nicer for all. In this way, they'll spread kindness and understanding instead of selfishness and unfairness. They'll build a world where we can count on each other and grow together, which is a powerful way to keep everyone's heart full and happy.

And that's why playing our part in teaching the young ones about love, support, and empathy is not just a small thing. It could help change the world into a kinder, more thoughtful place – one child's heart at a time.

20

THERAPY: THE COMPASS GUIDING YOU OUT OF THE NARCISSIST'S MAZE

Navigating the choppy waters of recovery after enduring the tumultuous relationship with a narcissistic mother is akin to finding your way through a thick, confusing fog. Therapy acts like a beacon of light in that fog, guiding you to a clearer understanding of your past and illuminating the path to a healthier future. This portion of the chapter delves into how therapy can be a cornerstone in rebuilding your life after narcissistic abuse.

UNDERSTANDING THE ROLE OF THERAPY

Imagine carrying a heavy suitcase everywhere you go, filled to the brim with all kinds of emotions and memories from your time spent under the shadow of a narcissistic mother. Therapy provides a safe place where you can set down this suitcase, open it up, and sort through its contents one by one. This process is not merely about unpacking but about understanding each piece, figuring out what to hold onto, and what to let go of.

In this safe space, therapists act as skilled guides. They are trained to listen without judgment and offer helpful advice without the bias that often comes from friends or family members. With a therapist, there is an assurance that your feelings are valid and important. Unlike interactions with a narcissistic mother, where your emotions might have been dismissed or ridiculed, therapy offers a warm environment where you are heard and your feelings are acknowledged.

As you wade deeper into the counseling process, you will discover that therapy does much more than just offer a shoulder to lean on. Professional therapists possess a keen understanding of how individuals like you may be entangled in a complex web of emotions and experiences. Through their expertise, therapists can help you recognize the often-subtle patterns of narcissistic abuse and their deep impact on your life. This recognition can be a powerful force, giving you the knowledge and confidence to make sense of your past experiences.

Armed with this newfound insight, you can begin to work with your therapist to develop strategies and tools that are tailored to help you cope with the effects of narcissistic abuse. Whether these effects manifest as lingering anxiety, struggles with self-esteem, or difficulty trusting others, your therapist can provide advice on practical techniques to combat these challenges. For instance, you might learn breathing exercises to calm anxiety when it arises or practice affirmations to bolster your self-worth.

What's more, your therapist can coach you on how to interact with your narcissistic mother, should you choose to maintain contact. Together, you can create a plan that might include setting firm boundaries or finding safe topics for discussion. This kind of preparation is invaluable; it puts you back in control and equips you with a sense of agency, helping to prevent old patterns from reemerging.

In essence, therapy holds a mirror up to your life, allowing you to see both the scars and the strengths. It is about more than speaking and being heard; it is about learning, growing, and emerging more resilient than before. As you close this chapter and reflect on the integral role therapy can play in your recovery, remember that reaching out for professional help is not a sign of weakness, but rather a brave step towards healing and wholeness.

EXPLORING THERAPEUTIC APPROACHES

Cognitive Behavioral Therapy, or CBT for short, is a way to help people who have gone through tough times because someone close made them feel bad about themselves, like daughters who had mothers who only thought of themselves and not of their children. CBT is like having a guide for your thoughts. It helps you see the paths your mind goes down, especially the gloomy ones that lead you to feel bad about yourself. Then, it gives you tools to build new paths towards good and strong thoughts.

Imagine your mind like a garden. Negative thoughts can be like weeds that were planted by a narcissistic mother, making you feel like you're not enough or like you carry the blame for her unhappiness. CBT is like gardening; it helps you pull out those weeds and plant new seeds of positive thoughts. You learn to tell yourself, "I am good enough," and to understand that you don't have to carry someone else's hurt.

Next, there is this special way of healing called Eye Movement Desensitization and Reprocessing, or EMDR. This can sound complex, but think of it as a way to clean out old, painful memories, kind of like washing stains out of your favorite shirt so you can wear it without remembering how it got dirty. EMDR uses your own eye movements to help you sort through and clean these memories. People who've been hurt by someone's harsh words or actions, like with narcissistic abuse, can find peace through EMDR. It's like after you clean up those stains, your shirt feels comfy again, and you can enjoy wearing it without thinking of the bad stuff.

Lastly, there's a therapy known as Dialectical Behavior Therapy, or DBT. This is like going to school for your emotions. It teaches you ways to stay calm and handle feelings that run high or change a lot, which can happen when you have a mother who always thought she was the only one who mattered. DBT has four main skills: being present in the moment (mindfulness), getting through tough times without falling apart (distress tolerance), handling your feelings smoothly (emotional regulation), and talking to people in a way that works out well (interpersonal effectiveness).

For daughters of mothers who made everything about themselves, these skills are a big deal. They are like learning how to sail your boat on a wavy sea. You learn to notice the water around you (mindfulness), to ride the waves even when they're scary (distress tolerance), to keep your balance in the boat (emotional regulation), and to ask for help from other boats if needed (interpersonal effectiveness).

Using CBT, EMDR, and DBT, daughters of mothers who were too caught up in themselves can find their way back to feeling strong and valued. They can learn to quiet those old, harsh voices and replace them with their own kind and powerful words.

CHOOSING THE RIGHT THERAPIST

When you've faced hurt from someone who thinks too highly of themselves, finding the right person to help can make a huge difference. It's like needing a special key to unlock a tricky door. Therapists who really know about this type of hurt are like having a master key. They get what you've been through and know just the right ways to help you find your strength again.

Imagine trying to explain a very specific problem with your car to a mechanic who has never worked on your car's model. It might be frustrating, wouldn't it? It's the same when talking about the hurt from someone with too much self-love. A therapist who focuses on this knows just what tools and parts you need to start feeling better. They won't make you feel small or misunderstood. They've seen it all before, and they're ready to help you heal.

Now, you might wonder, "How do I find such a person?" One good place to start is the internet. There are websites, like Psychology Today, where you can find lists of therapists. They let you search for therapists who have the right skills to help with the kind of pain you're dealing with. You can even look for professionals close to where you live. It's a bit like having a map that shows you where all the helpers are located.

It's essential, though, that whoever you choose to talk to makes you feel safe and heard. Trust me, this feeling is as important as finding someone with the right skills. Just like any friendship or team, you want to feel a sense of connection. If, for some reason, the first therapist you meet doesn't quite fit what you need, it's okay to look for another. It's your journey, and you have to travel with someone who makes the trip better, not harder.

Sometimes, words of mouth is more trusted than what we read online. Ask around. Maybe a friend, a doctor, or someone else you trust knows just the right person to talk to. Reviews left by other people can also guide you to a therapist that makes you think, "Yes, that's who I need!"

Now, don't forget the day-to-day stuff—when and where is this person available? Does their fee fit within your budget? And the big one: Can you use your health insurance? These things matter because they make getting help more doable for you.

Times are changing, and so are ways to get support. Online therapy is a new door that's opened up. With platforms like Talkspace or BetterHelp, getting support is as simple as sending a message from your phone or computer. You can chat with a therapist from the comfort of your home, which can be super convenient, especially when you can't leave your place or prefer not to.

The best helper is one who knows the path you're on and walks beside you with the right map, gear, and encouragement to keep you moving forward.

NAVIGATING THERAPY: WHAT TO EXPECT

When you first meet with a therapist to talk about the tough times with a narcissistic mother, it's like opening the first page of a book that's been closed for many years. The beginning of therapy, or the initial sessions as they're known, is where the story of you starts to unfold. You sit down, maybe feeling nervous or hopeful, and the therapist starts a kind of detective work that will help them know you better.

The therapist will start by asking about your life story - from when you were a little kid to where you are now. They'll want to know about how it's been growing up, how you get along with your mom, and the things that are hard for you today. It's as if they are gathering puzzle pieces to understand the full picture of your world. It's not nosy; it's necessary, because every bit of history you share helps them see where you're coming from and where you want to go.

This chat helps the therapist make a plan just for you, like a personalized roadmap to feeling better. It won't be just any plan, but one that's crafted with care, taking into account everything you've been through and where you hope to be.

Therapy isn't just about talking, though. It's also about doing and learning. In sessions, you'll dive deep into your memories and feelings. It's a bit like being a detective in your own life, hunting for clues about why you feel what you feel, and how to make it better. You'll learn about tools and tricks to help you cope, like a builder learning to use new tools to make a stronger house.

And there's homework, too - but not the boring kind you might remember from school. This homework is about using those new tools in your daily life. Maybe you'll write down your thoughts in a journal or practice ways to keep calm when things are tough. This keeps your therapy muscles strong, even when you're not in the session.

Now, healing and getting better doesn't happen overnight. Think about it like planting a garden. You can't just put seeds in the ground and expect flowers the next day. It's the same with therapy. Sometimes, the progress is so slow that you might not notice it at first. But every tiny step is like a new sprout in that garden. Maybe today you stood up for yourself in a small way, or you felt a bit more at peace than yesterday. And that's worth celebrating!

You have to have patience on this journey, and know that every little win is a part of the big change that's happening inside you. Like sunlight slowly rising at dawn, the small victories add up, and before you know it, you've come a long way from where you started.

COMBINING SELF-HELP STRATEGIES WITH PROFESSIONAL HELP

In the journey of healing, professional therapy shines as a beacon of hope and transformation. It offers a safe path, guided by experts who understand the struggles you face when dealing with a family member shaped by narcissism. Yet the path doesn't end at the therapist's door. It stretches into daily life through self-help strategies that complement therapy's deep healing.

Imagine your life as a garden that you tend daily. Therapy is like the season of rain that nourishes the soil profoundly, but self-help is the everyday watering and care that keeps the garden thriving. Journaling is one such tool, a simple way to water your garden. It's like talking to a friend who never judges, always listens. By writing down your thoughts and feelings, you become more aware of your internal world, uncovering patterns and acknowledging feelings that may hide beneath the surface.

Mindfulness is another strategy, it's like the sun nurturing your garden, helping to grow and flourish. It's about living right now, in this moment, not lost in the past or anxious about the future. Simple practices like breathing deeply or noticing the play of sunlight on leaves can center your thoughts and calm your mind.

Moreover, self-care is the fertile soil for your well-being. It's the kindness you serve yourself through activities that bring you joy and relaxation—be it taking a walk, enjoying a warm bath, or reading a book. It's paramount to remember that caring for yourself is not selfish. It's essential.

And when you feel adrift, discovering new insights and strategies through books and online resources can be like finding a map. Websites such as Out of the FOG provide valuable instructions and forums that act like a compass, guiding you through the fog of confusion that often surrounds life with a narcissistic family member.

A sense of community is like the trellis that supports plants as they grow. Support groups are this trellis, giving you a structure to lean on. Here, you realize you're not alone. Connecting with others on similar paths provides relief, understanding, and validation. It's a powerful feeling to be heard and to listen, to share your story and recognize it in others.

In this age of digital connection, even when you're alone, community is a click away. Platforms like Reddit host active communities such as r/raisedbynarcissists. Here, in these groups, people come together over shared experiences. You can seek advice, offer support, or simply soak in the understanding that comes from knowing others are facing battles similar to yours.

While threading together the fabric of therapy and self-help strategies, it's vital to remember that one does not replace the other. Each has its place in the tapestry of healing. Self-help strategies offer everyday tools for immediate relief and empowerment. Meanwhile, therapy dives deep, addressing the roots of emotional turmoil and guiding personalized change.

Employing both creates a layered approach to your healing journey. It strengthens resilience and fosters a more complete recovery, letting you nurture your life's garden into a place of beauty and peace.

CONCLUSION

As we close the final pages of this important book, let's take a moment to revisit the purpose that has guided our exploration together. We embarked on this journey to shine a light on the often-hidden challenges faced by daughters of narcissistic mothers. Our goal, from the start, has been to understand, navigate, heal, and grow from the unique struggles that arise within this dynamic. Now, standing on the cusp of new beginnings, it's time to summarize the path we've walked and prepare for the steps ahead.

In Part 1, "Understanding Narcissism and Its Impact," we laid the foundation by unpacking the complex world of narcissism. We dove into the mother-daughter bond, looking closely at how a narcissist bends this connection to her will, often using sharp tools of manipulation that can leave deep marks. Recognizing these tactics is the first critical step in the healing process.

Moving to Part 2, "Navigating the Narcissistic Landscape," we shared strategies to confront the stormy weather of life with a narcissistic mother. Here, the talk turned to tactics like setting firm boundaries and adopting the Gray Rock Method—an approach of becoming unreactive to avoid feeding the narcissistic cycle.

We then journeyed through Part 3, "Healing and Personal Growth." It's in these chapters that we learned to embrace the gentle arts of self-care and started to rebuild our personal identities, brick by brick. We recognized the chains of codependency and took our first steps towards freedom and self-reliance.

In Part 4, "Breaking the Cycle," we accepted the weighty, yet rewarding, responsibility of ensuring our future families flourish in a healthier environment. We explored nurturing the seeds of emotional intelligence in our children and the immense value of seeking expert guidance to help us through the most tangled paths.

Let's reflect on our key takeaways: understanding the thick shadow of narcissism, the liberation found in setting boundaries, and the light that healing and growth cast on our lives. Above all, we learned the unshakable truth that breaking the cycle is the ultimate act of courage and love.

Now, with the map in your hands, I encourage you—you brave, resilient soul—to begin your healing journey. Utilize the tools and directions this book has provided, and do not hesitate to reach out for professional anchors when the waves grow large.

I extend my deepest thanks to you for your commitment to forging a healthier, happier life. It's okay to take small steps. It's fine to move at a pace that feels right to you. Healing isn't a race; it's a personal voyage with the most worthwhile of destinations: a harbor of self-love, inner peace, and nourishing relationships.

So take that step, embrace the change, and remember: teaching our children empathy plants the roots for a future of understanding and kindness. Your journey might be challenging, but your courage and determination are powerful. They have brought you this far, and they will carry you through to a life no longer in the shadow of narcissism, but in the warmth of your own, well-earned light.

LIFE BEYOND THE NARCISSIST - THEIR DARK PSYCHOLOGY, GASLIGHTING AND MANIPULATION EXPLAINED

IDENTIFY NARCISSISTIC ABUSE & LEAVE TOXIC RELATIONSHIPS (CODEPENDENCY RECOVERY)

INTRODUCTION

WHY THIS BOOK MATTERS: UNVEILING THE MASK OF NARCISSISM

Emma stood quaking, the phone still warm in her trembling hand. Her best friend had finally said what no one else dared to: "You're trapped in a maze built by someone who only loves themselves." Until that moment, Emma hadn't seen the trap that love had disguised, the daily mind games that left her doubting her memories, thoughts, and worth. She'd become invisible in her own life, all because she didn't understand the shadow that loomed behind his charming smile—narcissism.

Emma's story is not unique. Countless people suffer in the shadows of relationships where their reality is constantly questioned, where they are undermined by someone using them as a mere stage for their own performance—the narcissist. Books and movies often show narcissists as just self-loving or arrogant, but rarely touch on the deep hurt they can cause. As a result, the sharp edges of dark psychology, gaslighting, and manipulation remain shrouded in mystery. Without the keys to recognize these patterns, many remain locked in confusion and pain.

This book's heartbeat is to cut through the fog surrounding these tactics. To reveal them not through complex jargon that confounds but through simple, direct communication that connects. Understanding is the first step toward freedom, and this book aspires to be that guiding light for the lost.

You may wonder, why am I the voice raising the alarm? I've spent years listening to and aiding those shadowed by narcissism's touch. My tools? Practical, real-world advice and a passionate belief in empowerment. I have tackled the labyrinth of manipulation and now offer a map to all who seek to find their way out.

As we delve into the chapters of this book, we'll peel back layer after layer of narcissistic behavior. We'll lay bare the tactics of gaslighting, show how to spot manipulative behavior, and provide solid ground to stand on when the world tilts. We'll then look ahead, to healing and regaining strength. It's not just a book, but a journey from confusion to clarity, from hurt to hope.

This journey is for everyone who has felt the sting of a narcissist's bite and for those around them seeking to help—friends, family, and healthcare professionals. My words stand with you, an offered hand for those ready to step out of the shadow and into the light.

Throughout, I'll be right beside you, offering words that feel like a friend's comforting hand on your shoulder. We'll talk plainly, candidly, and with a passion inspired by countless stories like Emma's. With each page, you'll grow stronger, more informed, and more capable of reclaiming the life that is rightfully yours.

So, take this first step with me. Discover the signs and strategies to dismantle narcissism's disguise and rekindle your inner light. This isn't just another book; it's a promise that with knowledge comes power—the power to heal, to grow, and to be whole once more. Welcome to a journey of truth and transformation. Together, let's unveil the mask of narcissism.

1

UNMASKING NARCISSISM: TRAITS, TYPES, AND ORIGINS

Narcissism is a word you may have heard thrown around to describe someone who seems full of themselves or acts like they're more important than others. But there's much more to it than that. It's not just having confidence or taking pride in your accomplishments. Narcissism, at its core, is a way some people act and feel that can cause serious problems for themselves and the people around them.

To really understand narcissism, think of it as a condition where a person has a very high opinion of themselves—so high, in fact, that they often fail to care about how others feel. They usually want others to look at them and say, "Wow, you are amazing!" They crave this kind of attention like a flower needs the sun to grow. However, unlike the flower that quietly blooms, a person with narcissism may go out of their way to be noticed, bragging about themselves and their accomplishments to make sure everyone knows just how great they are.

But it's important to separate narcissism from just feeling good about oneself. We all like a pat on the back when we do even when they haven't done anything to earn it. And if they don't get it, they might react with anger or become really sad. Their mood and happiness often depend on getting flattery and approval from others.

This need for constant admiration can lead to problems in relationships. It's hard to be friends with or work with someone who never thinks about your feelings or needs, isn't it? People with severe narcissism might struggle to think about other people's perspectives. This lack of empathy is like not finding a friend to help carry a heavy box—it leaves others feeling alone and unsupported.

Though, that narcissism isn't black and white. there's a whole range of behaviors from a little bit self-centered all the way to what doctors call narcissistic personality disorder, or npd. this disorder is when the characteristics of narcissism become so intense that they interfere with a person's life and cause a lot of distress.

The numbers say that about 6 out of every 100 people might be dealing with NPD, and it happens more often in men than women. That might not sound like many, but the effects of being around someone with severe narcissism can ripple out and touch the lives of many others.

So now you see, narcissism is more than just loving the person you see in the mirror. It's a complex way of being that affects people's minds, their behaviors, and their hearts. It's like a tangled knot that's hard to undo, and it takes a lot of work, sometimes with the help of a doctor or therapist, to sort it all out. Understanding this can help us be more kind and patient to those struggling with such a challenging condition.

UNVEILING THE TRAITS: THE NARCISSIST'S MODUS OPERANDI

Narcissists are a special kind of person, and you can usually tell if you're dealing with one by the way they act. They behave as if they're the most important person in the room, always looking for others to look up to them and shower them with kind words. It's like they're on a stage with bright lights shining down, expecting the crowd to clap and cheer just for them, all the time.

They walk around with their heads held high, thinking they deserve the best of everything without waiting a turn. They want your attention, your respect, and all of your compliments without giving much back. These people can be very good at winning you over though, with their smiles and smooth talk. At first, you might not see the real them. They can be the star of the show and make you feel like you're part of an exciting event. But watch out, because their charm often hides what they're really up to.

Have you ever known someone who always has to be in charge and seems to use friends like tools? That's a typical move for narcissists. They have a plan, and they'll twist words and situations to get what they want. They're like puppet masters trying to pull the strings to make everyone dance around them. Because they're so focused on their goals, they'll often ignore how other people feel. It's like they can't see or don't care about anyone else's pain or needs.

Take Steve Jobs, for example. He was a visionary, sure, but stories say he could also be cold and didn't always care about others' feelings. His eyes were on Apple's future, his future, and he often brushed aside the concerns of his colleagues or friends if they didn't match his goals. A lot of people admired him, but that doesn't mean his way of treating people was okay.

It's also common for narcissists to feel jealous or think that everyone else is jealous of them. They dream of endless wins and fame, believing they're the smartest or most beautiful people out there. Remember Billy McFarland, the guy who created the Fyre Festival? He sold people a dream of a luxury music event that turned out to be a disaster. He promised more than he could give and didn't seem to care about the people he let down. His story shows how believing you can do anything without working out the details and thinking of others can lead to a big fall.

Understanding these traits helps us recognize when we might be dealing with a narcissist. It's important for us to know that it's not about us – it's all about them and their need to feel on top of the world. It's good to be kind, but we should also look after ourselves and not get caught up in their games.

TYPES OF NARCISSISTS: THE MANY FACES OF NARCISSISM

Understanding narcissism is like trying to spot different birds in a vast forest. They all have wings and feathers, but once you look closer, you begin to see the unique patterns and colors. Narcissists, much like those birds, come in different kinds.

Many of us think of the loud, braggy sort when we hear the word "narcissist." That's the overt narcissist. Picture someone who walks into a room like they own the place, talks mostly about their great life and all they have achieved, and seems to care little about what anyone else says or feels. They love the spotlight, and boy, do they shine there. But it's not a warm light; it's like a spotlight in a cold, dark theater.

However, not all narcissists shout their presence. Meet the covert narcissist, quieter than their showy cousins. They don't make a big scene, but they still believe they are very, very important. These folks may seem shy or even say that they're the unlucky ones. It might look like they're just down on their luck, but deep down, they think they're owed the good stuff just as much – maybe even more. They want your sympathy, your praise, but for how tough they have it, not how great they are.

Then there is the communal narcissist. They seem kinder and are harder to spot. They're the ones lending a helping hand, always in the middle of good works. You might see them at charity events more often than a cat is seen napping. But watch close, and you'll spot the signs. They're doing good things to hear "Wow, you're amazing," not because they care so much about the cause. Even when they're doing something nice, it's all about them.

Let's take a real-life example to understand this better. Bill Cosby was once a beloved public figure, known for his humor and seen as a model of good values. Behind this kind mask, a different story lurked. When the truth came out about the bad things he had done, it was clear that his public image was just a cover for the respect and admiration he craved. This fall from grace showed a stark contrast between the good-guy image and the not-so-good actions, highlighting the communal narcissist's ability to hide behind a curtain of supposed virtue and kindness.

It's important to understand that under all these types of narcissism is a common thread—a deep need for attention and a feeling that the world owes them something. These folks just have different ways of trying to fill that need. Knowing the different faces of narcissism can help us spot the signs and deal with them sensibly. Remember, even if they seem as different as can be, at the heart, they're dealing with the same struggles.

DIGGING DEEPER: THE ORIGINS OF NARCISSISM

When we dive into the roots of narcissism, we look at two main ingredients that mix together to form the characteristics we know: what's born into us (genetic factors) and what we go through as we grow (environmental factors). To put it simply, the way someone turns out to be a narcissist is like making a recipe, where both what they naturally have and what they experience play big parts.

Studies show that narcissism is somewhat passed down in families, which means if your parents or grandparents might have had these traits, there's a chance you might too. Scientists say that narcissism can be moderately inherited. This does not mean that if your parent is a narcissist, you will definitely be one too. Rather, it just suggests that your family line might have a trend, a pattern of such personality traits.

However, just because there might be a genetic side to the story doesn't mean you'll actually end up being a narcissist. This is where the environment steps into the picture. The way a child is brought up has an enormous impact on how these traits come into play or stay hidden. Take parenting styles, for example. How mom and dad behave and treat their child can tip the scales.

Some parents may swing too far to one end of the pendulum by giving too much praise, treating their kids as if they can do no wrong. This can sound nice at first, but when a child gets used to always being in the spotlight, they may grow into adults who expect that same special treatment everywhere. This might lead them to become self-centered and to believe they are more important than others – key signs of narcissism.

The other side of the coin can be just as tricky. If a child does not get enough attention, love, or care - which can be just as harmful as getting hurt physically or emotionally - they might create a mask of narcissism to protect themselves. They may pretend to feel better than others or more important to cover up the pain of feeling forgotten or neglected.

It's critical to understand that pinpointing the source of narcissism is not about finding one single cause. It's a web of many factors woven together, and each narcissistic person has their unique story of how they became who they are. This complexity is what makes dealing with and healing from narcissism a challenging task. Recognizing the mix of genetic and environmental influences is a key step in figuring out how to help someone with these traits to possibly lead a more balanced and empathetic life.

2

UNMASKING THE SHADOW: A DEEP DIVE INTO DARK PSYCHOLOGY

Dark psychology is something we might not always notice, but it's happening around us more often than we'd like to admit. When we talk about dark psychology, we're shining a light on a part of being human that isn't very nice to talk about. It's all about how some people use sneaky ways to make others do what they want.

When we define dark psychology, we're looking at the tricks and hidden paths some people take to get what they want from others. Imagine you've got a friend who always seems to make you do things you didn't plan to do. Maybe they make you feel like you'd be a bad friend if you didn't help them out, or they might twist the truth so that the story seems a little bit different than it actually is. These are all examples of someone using dark psychology to pull your strings like a puppet.

The scary part is that it's not just the "bad guys" in movies who do this; it can be anyone. It could be a person you work with, a friend, or sometimes, although we don't like to admit it, it might even be us. It's important to understand this because knowing about it can help us spot when someone's trying to use these tricks on us. And if we're really honest, it might help us realize when we're tempted to use them, too.

Now, not everyone who uses dark psychology is doing something really terrible. Sometimes people don't even realize they're doing it. You might hear someone say, "You wouldn't understand, it's an adult thing," to make you feel left out and more likely to agree with them. Or, have you ever seen a commercial where they say, "Hurry, offer ends soon!" even though it's been the same offer for a long time? That's dark psychology at work, too. It pushes you to act quickly in fear of missing out.

One of the most known faces of dark psychology is when someone shows narcissistic behavior. This means they think they are the most important person and they want everyone else to agree. They might make everything about themselves and ignore what other people need or want. They can be charming at first, which they use to hide their selfish tricks. They love to be in control, and they're really good at manipulating the story to make that happen.

In the end, dark psychology is a powerful and sometimes hidden influence. It's a tricky part of human behavior that can make people play unfair games to get ahead. But the more we know about it, the better we can protect ourselves from being fooled and stop ourselves from using it in the wrong way. It's a tough lesson, but it's really important for keeping our relationships honest and healthy.

THE DARK NEXUS: LINK BETWEEN DARK PSYCHOLOGY AND NARCISSISM

In the shadowy corners of human behavior, two troubling traits often walk side by side: dark psychology and narcissism. When they join forces, they can create a cycle that's hard to break, trapping people in a web of manipulation and control that's tough to escape.

First, let's unwrap what we mean by narcissism. Picture in your mind a person who thinks very highly of themselves, so much that they believe they sit above everyone else. This person doesn't just love a mirror because they like what they see. They genuinely feel they're better than others, and as such, they deserve special treatment. Where normal folks might share and take turns, a narcissist takes first and gives later, if at all. They often don't feel or show care for others' feelings — this is what we call a lack of empathy.

Now, how about we shed some light on dark psychology? It may sound like something from a spooky tale, but it's very real. Dark psychology involves the methods some individuals use to get what they want from others in sneaky, often harmful ways. We're talking about tricks and mind games that can make someone else do things without realizing they're being pushed around.

When someone who loves themselves more than anything uses dark psychology, they become like puppet masters pulling strings. These narcissists can twist situations and conversations so subtly that the other person may feel they're the ones in the wrong. They know just what to say or do to make others doubt themselves or feel less important.

So, let's think about how this connection plays out and why it's crucial to understand it. If you learn the signs, you can spot when a narcissist is using these sly tricks. It could be a friend who always turns the talk to themselves, no matter what. Maybe it's a boss who makes you feel always just one step behind, thankful for the tiniest hint of praise. They may twist your words, or play on your fears and hopes, to keep you under their thumb.

By seeing these patterns, you put on a kind of armor. You start to recognize the games for what they are— just tricks and traps. You can imagine a shield around yourself, keeping you safe from such mind games. The armor doesn't make you cold or rude, it just helps you stay strong and not be pushed around. You learn to set boundaries, saying no when something doesn't feel right, and sticking to it.

In the same way, shining a light on these dark behaviors makes them less powerful. Knowledge is a powerful tool. By knowing how narcissists can use dark psychology to manipulate, you're better prepared to protect your well-being. It's like knowing the rules of a game – once you understand how it's played, you're less likely to be caught off guard and more likely to stay in control of your own actions. This understanding isn't just helpful; it's a safeguard for your emotional health.

THE MASTER PUPPETEER: DARK PSYCHOLOGY IN ACTION

At the heart of human interactions, there's a constant exchange of influence and control, often subtle and unseen. Dark psychology dives into the shadowy side of these exchanges, where some individuals wield psychological tools to twist the will and behavior of others for personal gain. This isn't just something you'd find in a textbook—it happens in the streets, in offices, and even in homes.

Consider this familiar figure: the charming con artist. They might come across as your new best friend or a trusted advisor. They have a gift for making you feel special and understood. But their ultimate aim is to part you from your hard-earned money through clever tricks and deceit. The con artist doesn't use force; they use a set of psychological tactics to lower your guard and exploit trust. They play on emotions, build false connections, and before you know it, you're caught in their web and swindled clean.

Or, picture the charismatic cult leader, brimming with passion and seemingly profound insights. They offer a sense of belonging, a chance to be part of something bigger than oneself. Slowly, the leader begins to demand more—money, loyalty, and above all, obedience. Their tactics can involve isolating followers from friends and family, instilling beliefs that outsiders are threats, and presenting themselves as the only reliable source of knowledge and security. Before long, followers may surrender their autonomy entirely, not through force, but through the manipulative use of dark psychology.

But there's hope, and awareness is the first step. By learning about these dark tactics, you can develop a shield against manipulation. Recognizing the signs—excessive flattery, too-good-to-be-true promises, pressure to make quick decisions, or attempts to isolate you from loved ones—is key to keeping the manipulators at bay.

To defend yourself and those you care about, nurturing a healthy skepticism can be beneficial. Not all that glitters is gold, and not everyone with a smile seeks to be a true friend. Always take your time in forming relationships and making decisions, especially when there are significant consequences at stake.

In essence, dark psychology is a very real game of mental chess being played every day. It's played by those who have something to gain from controlling others. But knowledge in this game can fortify your mind, helping you spot a potential move against you. Learning about these psychological techniques doesn't make you paranoid; it makes you prepared. So, as you move through the world, keep both your heart and your eyes wide open—so that you can love and trust, but also be clear-headed and cautious when the situation demands it.

BREAKING THE CHAINS: COUNTERACTING DARK PSYCHOLOGICAL TACTICS

As we journey through life, we often come across people who may not have our best interests at heart. Some of these individuals can use sneaky tricks that touch our minds and emotions in a way that can control or change how we act. It's like being a puppet on strings, with someone else pulling them. Knowing how to cut those strings is so important to stand strong and not let anyone twist your thoughts or feelings.

At first, setting boundaries might sound formal, like something from a business meeting. But really, it's about knowing where your personal 'no-go' zones are. Imagine you have a yard with a fence around it. Now think of that fence as a line that shows people what's okay and what's not. It's not about being mean; it's more like, saying, "Hey, this is my space, and I decide what happens here." In a relationship, this could be choosing when to say yes to helping and when to take time for yourself. Setting boundaries tells the other person that you respect yourself, and you expect the same from them.

Sometimes, though, even with boundaries, people will try to use their dark tricks to get what they want. Another tool for your toolbox is learning how to not let your heart lead all the time. This doesn't mean you turn into a robot with no feelings. It means you give your head some time to think things through. For instance, if someone always makes you feel bad to get their way, you start to notice that pattern. You might tell yourself, "I see what's happening here," and instead of feeling sad or hurt, you take a step back. It's like watching a movie instead of being in one—you see the big picture and don't get all tangled up in the drama.

But sometimes, these steps are tough to do alone, especially if the situation is really tricky or you're not sure how to handle it. This is where a pro can step in — a counselor or therapist. These are folks trained to listen and give advice without judging you. They've got the skills to help you understand your own mind and feelings better. They can offer you new ways to deal with difficult situations or people. It's kind of like having a coach who helps you play your life game better.

So, remember, having tools like clear fences (boundaries), keeping your feelings a tiny bit at arm's length (emotional detachment), and getting a helping hand from the experts (professional help) can make a world of difference. It's about taking charge of your life, keeping your mind and heart safe from those who might not play fair. It's empowering to stand up for yourself and say, "I'm in control. My life, my rules."

THE PATH TO EMPOWERMENT: RISING ABOVE DARK PSYCHOLOGICAL TACTICS

In the journey of life, sometimes we find ourselves in difficult spots where we feel like we don't have power over what's happening. Dark psychological tactics can make us feel really small and like we can't change things. But there is a way to rise up and take back control— it's called empowerment. When you empower yourself, you give yourself the strength to step above those dark places and take the reins of your life back into your own hands.

Self-awareness is the first key to this secret door of empowerment. Think of self-awareness like a flashlight in a dark room. It helps you see where you are and what's around you. If you know more about who you are, what you care about, and what tricks people might use to try and sway you one way or the other, you're less likely to stumble in the darkness. For adults, self-awareness is this cool tool that helps you stand strong, even when things get rocky.

Education comes next. It's like adding a map to your flashlight. If you understand what dark psychology is and how it works, you're much more prepared to deal with it. Dark psychology is all about people using sneaky ways to get what they want, by playing on emotions, making you doubt yourself, or confusing you. If you know the signs, you can spot these tricks from a mile away. Reading books on the topic, going to events where smart people talk about their own experiences, or watching educational videos can all be part of learning more. It's like putting on a suit of armor that helps keep your mind safe. For adults, education is the difference between being fooled and being in charge of your own choices.

Self-care is the final, super important step. You could say it's like making sure your flashlight batteries are charged, and your map is well-read. It's how you take care of yourself, making sure you're in good shape to handle whatever comes your way. This could be simple stuff like getting enough sleep, eating foods that make your body happy, and finding time to just relax and enjoy life. Taking care of yourself also means learning ways to keep calm and focused, like breathing deeply or taking a nice walk. For an adult, self-care isn't a luxury—it's a must. Like keeping a car running bright light, and with it, you're way ahead of those trying to use the shadows to their advantage. Understanding dark psychology is like finding the magic spell for empowerment—it gives you the power back to live life on your terms, firmly in the driver's seat.

3
SHADOWS IN THE MIND: UNCOVERING THE DARK TRIAD

At the core of some of the trickiest human behaviors lies a group known as the dark triad. These are three traits that can be a bit scary when we see them in people. They are not like the heroes we admire. Instead, these traits make up a sort of 'unholy trinity' because they are a trio of not-so-nice personality features.

First, let's start with narcissism, which we've already discussed a bit. Imagine that one person who always wants to be in the spotlight, thinks they're better than everyone else, and doesn't really care how others feel. That's narcissism. Those with this trait love themselves a lot and want others to love them too. They think they're the most important and often don't feel sorry for others.

Next up is Machiavellianism. This one is named after a man from long ago who wrote about power and how to hold on to it, even if it meant playing dirty. It's a bit like being a puppet master. People with this trait are great at tricking others. They lie, they fake, and they don't care about what is right or wrong if it means they get what they want. These folks are like the sneaky characters who make secret plans and don't mind stepping on others to get to the top.

The third part of this dark trio is psychopathy. This one's tough because it's about people who often don't feel things the way most do. They don't understand others' hurt or fear. Psychopaths can do things that upset or hurt others without feeling guilty. They tend to be fearless in a way that isn't always good, daring to do things most of us would be too scared to try, and not in a cool, adventurous way, but in a risky and sometimes harmful way.

When we think of someone with these dark triad traits, it's like seeing a character in a movie who is the villain, not the hero. They seem hard to stop, they're cunning, and they're often steps ahead of everyone else. But unlike a movie, in real life, dealing with such people can be really tough.

Understanding these traits is important because they can influence how people act, especially those with a taste for power. All of us might have a tiny touch of these traits. Maybe we've wanted to be the best or to win at something, so bad we didn't play fair, or we didn't care enough about how someone else felt. But those with strong dark triad traits are different, they turn these feelings into actions that can be hurtful. By knowing more about these traits, we can be better prepared when we run into people who show them. We can protect ourselves and understand where their behavior comes from.

So, remember this trio – narcissism, Machiavellianism, and psychopathy – as the dark triad. They're the bad guys of personality traits. And knowing how to spot them can help us stay clear from trouble or handle it better when it comes our way.

NARCISSISM: THE SELF-ADMIRING PUPPETEER

In the realm of personality traits, there's a concept known to many as the "dark triad." This phrase might sound a bit mysterious or like something out of a storybook, but it's actually a term used by those who study how people think, feel, and behave. The dark triad refers to three not-so-nice traits: narcissism, Machiavellianism, and psychopathy. Today, we're specifically going to talk about one part of this triad: narcissism.

Narcissism, in the context of the dark triad, isn't just about taking one too many selfies or spending a bit too long in front of the mirror. It's about an extreme level of self-love, where someone believes they are more important than anyone else, and this belief is so strong that it shapes how they live their lives and treat other people. Imagine a balloon so full of air it's ready to burst – that's the narcissist's sense of their own importance. They see themselves as special, deserving of endless praise, and believe that their needs should always come first.

Think about a character like Don Draper from the TV show "Mad Men." He's a good example of a narcissist within the dark triad. On the surface, he's charming, successful, and seems to have it all. But as we watch, we see him using people to make sure he stays at the top, manipulating them to get what he wants and to keep up the shiny image of himself he presents to the world. While we may be drawn in by his charisma, we soon realize that there's not much room for anyone else's needs in Don Draper's world.

For people with dark triad narcissism, empathy isn't in their toolkit. Empathy is the ability to understand and share the feelings of another, to walk in their shoes. Without this, it's far too easy for narcissists to use others without feeling bad about it. If someone gets hurt along the way? that's not something they need to worry about. This missing empathy can come from a deep-rooted place where they genuinely cannot grasp or feel the emotions of the people around them. It's like they have a blind spot where everyone else's feelings should be.

This inability to recognize or understand others' emotions is a real problem because it allows them to exploit and take advantage of people without the brake pedal of guilt or regret to stop them. For example, a narcissistic boss might push an employee far beyond reasonable limits, not caring about the stress or exhaustion they're causing, all because it suits their goals. In the end, for individuals with narcissism in the dark triad, life is a one-person show, and everyone else is just scenery. Understanding this can help you identify these traits, protect yourself from potential harm, and approach relationships with a knowledgeable and cautious mindset.

MACHIAVELLIANISM: THE CUNNING MANIPULATOR

In the world of human behavior, there's a special term that sums up a way of acting that's all about looking out for number one: Machiavellianism. It's a big word, but here's what it means in simple terms: some people are very focused on winning for themselves, no matter what it costs to others. They are willing to twist the truth, act in sneaky ways, and forget about what's right or wrong if it means they will come out on top.

This idea comes from a man who lived a long time ago, Niccolò Machiavelli. He was an advisor to rulers, kind of like a coach for kings and queens, and he wrote a famous book called "The Prince." In this book, he told these leaders that it was okay to trick and lie if it helped them keep their power and control. Because of his book, when we see people acting this way, trying to gain more for themselves through cunning plans without caring if it's right, we call this Machiavellianism.

Now, you might be wondering, how does someone act Machiavellian? Imagine someone who is like a chess player, always thinking several moves ahead. This person isn't just doing things without thinking; they have a plan and are very careful about every step they take. The goal is to make sure they end up with what they want—be it a better job, more money, or just getting their way in general.

This kind of person sees others not as friends or partners, but more like tools or pawns—pieces they can move around and use to their advantage. They don't really play fair, because in their mind, life is like a game where the only thing that matters is winning.

Think about the TV show "House of Cards." The main character in that show, Frank Underwood, is a perfect example of a Machiavellian person. He's always scheming, plotting, and doing whatever it takes to climb higher and higher up the ladder, even if it means hurting others. He's got charm and can be friendly, but underneath, it's all about what he can get for himself. People like Frank are very careful with their choices, and their actions often surprise those around them when their true goals come to light.

When we talk about Machiavellianism, we're not just talking about a small trick here and there. It's about a whole way of being that treats life like an intense game where the stakes are high, and kindness or honesty can seem like weaknesses. People who act in a Machiavellian way might get ahead, but it can also mean making a lot of enemies and losing trust. It's a style that's all about personal gain and power, and as Niccolò Machiavelli's ideas continue to show, it's a path that has influenced people for centuries.

PSYCHOPATHY: THE EMPATHY-DEVOID PREDATOR

In exploring the subject of psychopathy, it's crucial to understand that this condition is not just something you see in movies or read about in crime stories; it's a real psychological phenomenon that has a significant impact on society. Psychopathy is characterized by a combination of antisocial behavior, a lack of empathy for others, and a set of bold traits that include being very confident, sometimes too much so. People with psychopathy can also have a strong sense of self-importance, and they tend to be very good at influencing others.

A person with psychopathy might do things that are risky or dangerous without stopping to think about what might happen as a result. For example, in the film "The Wolf of Wall Street," the character Jordan Belfort takes extreme risks with both his personal and professional life. He doesn't seem to care about the law or the possible damage he could do to people's lives, including his own. This same lack of concern for danger and consequences is often seen in real-life cases of psychopathy.

One of the most troubling aspects of this condition is the lack of remorse. People suffering from psychopathy usually don't feel sorry for the things they do, even if those actions hurt others. They don't share the feelings of another person, which is what we call empathy. For most of us, empathy is a natural part of how we interact with others—it allows us to understand and share the feelings of another person. But for someone with psychopathy, this part of human connection is missing. They see others not as individuals with feelings, but as tools to be used for their own goals.

Despite these challenging attributes, it can sometimes be hard to spot a psychopath. That's because they can also be very charming and likable. Their boldness isn't always seen as arrogance; it can come across as confidence or strength, which can be very appealing. They are often skilled at talking and can make themselves seem very good and trustworthy. It's this charm that makes it easier for them to manipulate others. They know how to play on people's emotions and can convincingly lie or twist the truth to get what they want.

It's important to note that psychopathy is a complex and nuanced condition and not everyone with these traits is a psychopath, nor are they inherently bad or dangerous people. This brief look into the mind of a person with psychopathy underscores the need for greater understanding and research in the realm of mental health, especially as it relates to how we as a society can manage and treat such challenging behaviors for the betterment of all.

INTERPLAY OF THE DARK TRIAD TRAITS

In a world that's as wide and deep as the ocean, understanding the human mind can sometimes be as tough as sailing through a storm. Think of personality traits as currents in the sea – often moving in their own directions, but sometimes they mix to create whirlpools. Three such powerful currents are narcissism, Machiavellianism, and psychopathy. When these traits come together, they form a personality that's as complex as it is harmful.

First off, let's look at narcissism. This is when a person has an endless need to be looked up to and loved by everyone. Imagine someone who looks in the mirror not just to comb their hair, but to remind themselves how great they believe they are. Now, this need for applause and "you're amazing" remarks can make a person do things that aren't exactly honest or kind. It may push them to trick others to get what they want. This sly behavior shows us how narcissism can waltz in time with Machiavellianism.

Machiavellianism is a fancy term that might remind you of a chess game where every move is carefully planned to win at all costs. People who are Machiavellian are masters of control and deception; they treat life like a game where they must outsmart everyone else. When someone is both narcissistic and Machiavellian, they can become a puppeteer who pulls strings without caring about who gets tangled up.

Let's add another layer to this: psychopathy. This trait is often seen as cold and heartless, like a winter night when the air bites at your skin. Psychopaths may not understand or care about how other people feel, which means they have no problem stepping over someone else to get what they want. Now, when you mix this lack of caring with the narcissist's hunger for attention, you have someone who not only wants to be the star of the show but also doesn't mind breaking a few hearts to get there.

When these three currents swirl together, you might find someone who is shockingly good at pulling the wool over people's eyes and getting away with it. Take Cersei Lannister from the TV show "Game of Thrones" – she's the perfect storm of these traits. She craves power and admiration, plays her family and foes like a fiddle, and shows barely a glimpse of true kindness. Cersei is a living example of how destructive this blend can be.

This toxic mix isn't just in stories; it's in the real world, too. It's the boss who steals your ideas and then smiles in your face, or the partner who says "I love you" while secretly twisting every word to keep you close. The mix of narcissism, Machiavellianism, and psychopathy can create someone who is very good at getting what they want – at everyone else's cost.

Understanding these traits isn't just about spotting villains in TV shows; it's about being able to navigate the trickier parts of the human sea without getting swept away. Just like putting on a life jacket before the waves get too high, knowing these signs can help keep us safe from those who might otherwise do us harm.

IMPACT OF THE DARK TRIAD ON RELATIONSHIPS AND SOCIETY

In our world, there are certain personality traits that can make life tough, not just for the people who have them, but also for those around them. These traits are often called the "dark triad": narcissism, Machiavellianism, and psychopathy. People with these traits can cause a lot of trouble, whether we're talking about families or at work.

Let's start with what these traits are all about. Narcissism means that a person thinks they are more important than anyone else, wants everyone to look at them, and thinks they deserve special treatment. Machiavellianism is when someone is really good at tricking others and doesn't care who they hurt to get what they want. Psychopathy is when a person doesn't feel bad about things that would make most of us feel really sorry, and they can be very charming to get their way.

Now, imagine your work life with someone around who shows these dark triad traits. It won't be easy. These folks might try to push others down to climb the ladder to success. They aren't afraid to bully coworkers by using mean words or making them feel small and unimportant. They might even spread lies or trick others to get ahead. It's not just about the teasing you might remember from school; it's serious grown-up stuff that can make people dread going to work.

It's not only at work, though. Think about friends or partners with these traits. Sadly, they often find it hard to care for others deeply. Since they don't genuinely feel for others, they can twist words and actions to get what they want. Somebody with high levels of these traits can end up hurting the ones they should love and support, all without feeling sorry about it.

Now, you're probably thinking, "Wait a minute! How can I tell if someone is like this—and what can I do about it?" Understanding these traits is the first big step. Knowing the signs can be like having a shield that helps you see these behaviors coming and take care of yourself.

If you're around someone who always wants to be the center of attention, who seems fake-charming, or is good at getting their way —even if it's not nice, they might have these traits. You can protect yourself by setting clear rules on what is okay and what's not in your relationship. And at work, being aware can help you steer clear of their tricks and stay focused on doing a good job with honesty.

Lastly, it's important to remember that having dark triad traits doesn't make someone a 'bad person'—it's not that simple. But it does mean that you have to be smart and careful in dealing with them, for your own well-being and for a healthier community around you.

4

THE FOG OF DECEPTION: UNMASKING THE ART OF GASLIGHTING

In this section, we're looking at something called gaslighting. Imagine someone quietly moving things around your house and then telling you nothing has changed. They insist you're just forgetting where things are. You might start doubting your own memory. Gaslighting is kind of like that, but with words and actions. It's when a person twists the truth to make you question what you know and feel.

The word "gaslighting" takes us back to a story from an old movie titled "Gaslight". In the film, a husband is very tricky. He plays with the lights in the house, making them dimmer and brighter. When his wife notices and asks about it, he tells her she's just seeing things, that the light hasn't changed at all. She begins to wonder if her mind is playing tricks on her. This is where the idea of making someone doubt what's real comes from.

Narcissists, or people who think they are more important than others and lack sympathy, love using gaslighting. Why do they do it? It's because they want to be in charge and look more powerful than everyone else. They use it like a tool to twist the truth so much that other people feel confused and unsure of themselves. When someone starts doubting their own thoughts and feelings, the narcissist can more easily control them.

But gaslighting isn't always loud and clear. It's often quiet and tricky to spot. If it were easy to see, it wouldn't work so well. That's the problem: gaslighting is sneaky. It can be little comments here and there like, "You're just too sensitive," or "I never said that." Over time, these comments can add up, making someone believe that there's something wrong with their memory or feelings.

For people who haven't heard of gaslighting before, it can take a long time to notice it's happening. Even when they do, they might not trust their own judgment. This is why talking about gaslighting is so important. It's like pointing out the tricks behind a magician's show. Once you know how the tricks work, they don't fool you anymore.

To sum it up, gaslighting is a secret form of trickery. People who love themselves more than anyone else might use it to trick others into questioning what's real and what's not. It's like deception wearing a disguise. Learning about it is like being given a special pair of glasses. With these glasses, you can see through the disguise and understand what's truly going on. In the next parts, we'll dive deeper into how this trick works, what it does to a person's thoughts, and how to spot it in your everyday life.

TOOLS OF A NARCISSIST: GASLIGHTING TECHNIQUES UNVEILED

In the world of relationships, understanding how people can twist the truth is key. Some folks, known as narcissists, can be tricky in the way they deal with others. They have a set of tools they use to confuse and control the people around them. This is often called gaslighting. Gaslighting makes a person question their own thoughts and memories.

One common tool in the narcissist's box is "denial." Imagine you know someone did or said something hurtful. You're certain of it. But then, they look at you and say it never happened. They deny it with such confidence that you start to question your own mind. Did I really hear that? Did it really happen? Even if you have an email or a message as proof, they'll argue it doesn't mean what you think it does. This can be very confusing, and that's the whole point. By denying their actions or words, the narcissist makes you unsure of what's true and what isn't.

Another tool is "diversion." This happens when you try to talk about something the narcissist did, but suddenly, they change the subject. They might turn the tables and accuse you of something else. For example, you might say, "I didn't like how you yelled at me," and they might reply, " you're defending yourself instead of discussing the original issue. This technique takes the focus away from their behavior and makes it hard to solve any problems.

Narcissists also use a method called "trivialization." This is when they make your feelings or worries seem small and silly. You might share that you're upset about something they said or did, and they'll respond with, "You're too sensitive" or "Can't you take a joke?" This can make you feel like you're overreacting and that perhaps your feelings aren't valid. And when that happens, you might stop bringing up issues, which lets the narcissist off the hook.

Lastly, there's the false hope technique. A narcissist will sometimes give you lots of kindness or affection. It's like the sun coming out after a storm. You might think, "Maybe they're really a good person after all. Maybe things will get better." But before you know it, the old patterns start again. This up-and-down of good and bad times keeps you hanging on, hoping they will change for good someday.

Understanding these tools is like having a map through a tricky forest. When you know the signs, you can navigate better and take care of your own well-being. It's tough to face these sorts of mind games, but knowing what's happening is the first step in handling the situation.

THE INVISIBLE WOUNDS: PSYCHOLOGICAL IMPACT OF GASLIGHTING

Gaslighting is a difficult word to think about. It means someone is playing tricks on your mind. They make you doubt what you know is true. This messes with how you feel inside and can change the way you see yourself and the world. Let's talk about how it really shakes someone up.

Imagine every time you remember something, someone tells you it didn't happen that way. Or when you feel something, they say you're wrong to feel like that. After a while, you start to question if you can trust your own mind. That's what we call "confusion" and "self-doubt." It's like trying to follow a map that keeps changing. You feel lost and start to wonder if you can trust your own memories and thoughts. This doubt makes you feel smaller inside, and you might be scared to trust yourself.

Now, think about having to be very careful every time you speak or act. It's like you're "walking on eggshells," tiptoeing around so you don't make a mistake. Living this way day in and day out is really tiring. It makes you feel on edge, never quite relaxed, always worried about doing something that will upset the other person. This is how living with constant fear twists inside you, turning into what grown-ups call "anxiety."

When this keeps going, a sadness can set in that feels too heavy to push away. This sadness is different from feeling sad about a bad day; it's a sadness that fills you up and makes everything seem gloomy. We call that "depression." People who are made to feel small and confused all the time can give up hope. They may stop seeing the bright side of life because they're weighed down by how hard it is just to feel okay.

In really bad cases, all this mind-twisting can hurt someone so much that it becomes a "trauma." This means it changes them in ways that don't go away when the gaslighting stops. They might start to have nightmares, feel scared all of a sudden, or have a racing heartbeat even when there's no danger. These are signs of something called post-traumatic stress disorder, or PTSD. It is like carrying a backpack full of rocks that makes it hard to walk, sleep, or find joy in everyday things.

The mind games of gaslighting can hurt a person very, very deeply. It can make them lose touch with themselves, fill their days with fear, and paint their world a color of sadness that's tough to wash out. This twisting of the truth is not just a mean trick; it's something that can change a person's life in big ways, making them feel alone and scared long after the gaslighting stops.

GASLIGHTING IN CONTEXT: RECOGNIZING THE SIGNS

Gaslighting is a sneaky kind of trick some people use to make you doubt your own thoughts and feelings. It can happen anywhere, but it's often found in places like our love lives and where we work. To keep ourselves safe and strong, we need to spot when it's happening. Let's take a closer look at how this plays out in different parts of our lives.

Let's say in a "romantic relationship", you have a partner who always makes you question your own mind. For example, imagine you remember a conversation where your partner promised to do the dishes after dinner. But when you bring it up, they act like the talk never happened. They might say things like, "You must be confused," or, "You never remember things right." You start feeling like you can't trust your own memory. That's a classic move in gaslighting. Or perhaps you're upset about something, and your partner tells you, "You're just too sensitive," or "You're overreacting," making you feel like your feelings aren't real or important.

Now picture yourself at "work". Perhaps you have a boss or a team-mate who's always putting you down or questioning your skills. They might take credit for your good ideas, or tell you that everyone else says you're not doing a good job. They make you feel like you're always the problem, even when you're not. When this happens, it can make you feel really small and question if you're good at what you do. That's also gaslighting – it's like they're trying to dim the light of your confidence bit by bit.

The first big step in dealing with gaslighting is knowing the signs. If you feel like someone's playing mind games with you, making you question your own world, or your feelings are always being pushed aside, take notice. It might not be just in your head. Trusting your gut and knowing that these are signs of someone trying to control you is important. Realizing this is happening is like turning on a light in a dark room. You see things clearly and can start finding the way out.

By knowing what gaslighting is and how people can use it against you, you're building a shield to protect yourself. The next chapter is going to go even deeper. We'll dive into other sneaky ways people, especially those who think only of themselves, like narcissists, might try to twist your reality. And we'll talk about how to stand strong against those tricks, too. Knowledge is like a key that unlocks doors, and you're already turning that key to keep yourself safe and sound.

5

MANIPULATION UNMASKED: COVERT TACTICS OF CONTROL

Within this chapter, we delve deep into the realm of manipulation, a cunning and often hidden strategy used by individuals with narcissistic personalities to sway others to their will. Knowing what manipulation looks like and how it operates is a vital piece of knowledge that can empower you to stand firm against such covert control tactics.

THE PUPPET MASTER: UNDERSTANDING MANIPULATION

At the heart of a narcissist's deceptive arsenal lies manipulation – a stealthy method of twisting your actions, feelings, and thoughts in directions that serve their needs and desires, often at your expense. Imagine a puppet master, pulling strings to make the puppet move, except in this scenario, the puppet is a person's will and the puppet master is the manipulator.

Narcissists, skilled in the art of bending others to their whims, use manipulation like an unseen force. You may not immediately see it, but you can feel the results when your behavior changes in ways you wouldn't normally expect of yourself. It's like being in a play where the narcissist is the director, but you never agreed to act in it.

For example, they might offer compliments or gifts, but these are not from the goodness of their heart. Instead, they act as hooks, subtle tricks to pull you closer and make you feel indebted. It's as if they are saying, "I've done something nice for you; now you owe me."

Manipulation can also take shape through more negative actions. A narcissist might twist your words or play the victim to make you feel guilty and yield to their desires. This form of emotional control is like a game of tug-of-war where you're constantly being pulled into the narcissist's emotional turmoil.

Another manipulative tactic is gaslighting. This sinister strategy involves making you doubt your own memories or perceptions, causing you to question your sanity. It's a way of eroding your confidence, with the narcissist suggesting that you're mistaken or have poor memory when you recall events, even when you're certain of what happened.

Recognizing these manipulative maneuvers is half the battle. The other half is knowing how to respond. Start by trusting your instincts; if something doesn't feel right, there's a good chance that it isn't. Set your boundaries firmly. Respond to unwarranted guilt with level-headed clarity. When gifts or favors come with strings attached, it's okay to say no thank you. If your memories or feelings are challenged, stand by them with confidence.

Understanding manipulation is like being given a shield. It provides a layer of protection against the invisible strings that a narcissist might try to attach to you. With knowledge as your ally, you are no longer an easy target for the puppet master's covert control.

When you spot the signs of manipulation, take a step back and examine the situation. Ask yourself what the narcissist might have to gain from their behavior and remind yourself that you have the power to control your own actions and emotions. With this awareness, you can counteract the puppet master's ploys and maintain control of your own life's narrative.

THE ART OF PERSUASION: COMMON MANIPULATION TACTICS

Narcissists have a toolbox full of tricks to make others bend to their will. One of their most powerful tools is persuasion, the art of getting someone to think or do something. Like a skilled painter choosing the right colors for a masterpiece, narcissists pick the right words and actions to control the minds and hearts of others.

Imagine sitting in a room where the lights keep changing. One minute it's bright, the next it's dark, and someone keeps telling you it's all in your head. This is what 'gaslighting' feels like. Narcissists make you doubt what you see, what you hear, and what you know to be true. They deny things they said, twist facts around, and make you question your sanity. When you believe you can't trust your own mind, the narcissist steps in to take the lead, deciding what's real and what's not for you.

Now picture the most amazing birthday party ever, with all the balloons, cakes, and presents you could wish for, thrown just to make you feel loved. This is a bit like 'love bombing.' At first, a narcissist will shower you with lots of attention, compliments, and gifts. They make you feel like the most important person in the world. But this isn't a party that lasts. It's all about winning you over quickly. Once they know you're hooked on that good feeling, they use it to their advantage, making you think you owe them something in return.

Let's say you're playing catch, but the ball goes through a window. Your friend, who threw the ball too hard, points a finger at you, saying it's your fault for not catching it. This is a small example of 'victim blaming.' Narcissists are experts at this game. They twist things around so that if they hurt you, they make it seem like it's because of something you did. They might say things like, "If you were more careful, I wouldn't get so angry." By shifting the blame to you, they avoid taking responsibility for their bad behavior and make you feel guilty instead.

Narcissists use these tactics smoothly, blending them into everyday life so it often goes unnoticed at first. But like pieces in a puzzle, once you know what to look for, you can see how they fit together. Understanding these tricks is like turning on a light in that room where the bulbs keep changing. It helps you see clearly, trust in your own thoughts, and stand up to the person trying to control you. Remember that you're allowed to trust your feelings and stand up for yourself. When you do that, you take the power out of the hands of the narcissist, and that's the first step towards taking back control of your life.

THE INVISIBLE CHAINS: EMOTIONAL MANIPULATION

Understanding emotional manipulation can feel like trying to see through a fog—it's confusing and unclear. But imagine that fog represents the tricky ways a person with bad intentions, let's call them a narcissist, tries to twist your feelings to their advantage.

First, let's take a look at three feelings the narcissist often targets: guilt, fear, and obligation.

Guilt is like a heavy backpack full of rocks that you're made to carry. A narcissist fills this backpack by making you feel responsible for things that aren't your fault. They might say things like, "If you really cared about me, you wouldn't spend time with your friends." This statement is unfair; it doesn't consider your feelings and needs.

Next, fear is like a dark room you can't find your way out of. Narcissists use words or actions that make you scared to disagree with them. They might tell you, "No one else will love you," to keep you close because they know that fear will make you not want to leave them, even if staying hurts you.

Lastly, obligation is an invisible rulebook that you didn't agree to. Narcissists expect you to follow these 'rules' because they believe you owe them something. They might remind you of a favor they did in the past and expect something in return now. It's as if they keep a score of every little thing to use against you later.

One of the sneakiest tricks in the narcissist's book is playing the victim. Playing the victim is like putting on a costume and acting in a play. They pretend to be hurt or targeted to make you feel sorry for them. This way, they take the light off the bad things they might have done and put it on their own fake pain.

For example, imagine you confront a narcissist about something unkind they did. Instead of saying sorry or admitting their fault, they twist the tale. They might say, "I did that because I've been feeling really down lately," or "I only did that because I've been under so much stress at work." Stories like these are designed to tug at your heart and make you feel bad for them.

Suppose you start to question their actions. In that case, they might even act as if they are the ones being treated unfairly, saying, "you always blame me," or "I try so hard, and you don't see it." This makes you the bad guy in the story, not them.

In this game of emotional chess, the narcissist seems always to stay two moves ahead. But once you know their strategies—how they use guilt, fear, and obligation, and how they twist situations to make themselves look like the victim—you can start to see the fog lift. You can begin to make decisions based on what's best for you, not just to keep them happy. And that's when you start to take back your power, piece by piece, until you're holding the whole backpack and can decide what to do with it: set it down and walk away.

THE WOLF IN SHEEP'S CLOTHING: IDENTIFYING SUBTLE MANIPULATION

In our world, there are many ways people can try to control or change our actions, often without us realizing what's happening. Manipulation is like a hidden force that can quietly twist situations to someone else's advantage, often leaving us confused, hurt, or even doubting our own feelings. Not all manipulation is loud and clear; some of it is so subtle that we might not even see it happening. These sneaky tactics can be just as harmful as the obvious ones.

One such hidden trick is known as the 'silent treatment'. Imagine you're in a relationship with someone who is very focused on themselves—what we often call a narcissist. When you do something they don't like, instead of talking it out, they might shut down all communication. They stop talking to you, don't respond to your messages, and act as if you don't even exist. This isn't just about needing space to cool off; it's a way to punish you. They know that being ignored can hurt, create confusion, and make you feel alone. It might even make you more likely to say 'sorry', even when you did nothing wrong, just to get back into their good graces. This tactic can be very damaging because it attacks our fundamental need for connection and leaves us feeling rejected and unworthy.

Another subtle manipulation method is called 'triangulation'. Picture this: the narcissist introduces another person into your inter- actions—maybe a friend, another partner, or a family member. Instead of talking directly to you, they might praise or spend more time with the other person. This can set off a competition of sorts, even if none was intended. You might end up feeling jealous or thinking you need to try harder to win the narcissist's attention and approval. Triangulation makes relationships feel like a game where there's a clear winner and loser. It can stir up tensions and insecurities, leading to a lose-lose situation for everyone but the manipulator.

These tactics can go unnoticed for a long time, causing the person on the receiving end to feel isolated and anxious. If you've ever experienced either the silent treatment or triangulation, you might understand how deeply it can affect your well-being. It's not as easy to spot as someone yelling or making a scene, but the silent messages sent by these actions can be just as loud.

As tough as it may be to deal with these subtle manipulations, it's important to remember that they say more about the person using them than about you. Tools like clear communication, setting boundaries, and knowing your worth can be your armor against such hidden tactics. Understanding these manipulation methods doesn't just help in defending against them; it empowers us to create healthier relationships and stand up for ourselves when needed.

WALKING ON EGGSHELLS: LIVING WITH A MANIPULATIVE NARCISSIST

Living with a manipulative narcissist can often feel as if you're moving across a floor scattered with eggshells, each step taken with utmost care, hoping not to cause a crunch. This type of environment generates a heavy air of caution, where you might find your steps measured, your words sifted, and your actions heavily weighed all in the effort to maintain a fragile peace. The strain of this dance can press deep into your everyday life, as you live alongside someone who shapes their world—and tries to shape yours—only to serve their needs.

The unpredictability paired with a narcissist's behavior can become a source of regular worry and fear. One moment might be smooth and peaceful, and with little warning, the mood can switch to stormy and tense. It's not unlike the fickle weather of a coastal town, where sunshine can be swiftly swallowed up by a brooding sky. You become like a weather vane, always alert, swiveling to catch the signs of a coming storm. This tension means that common activities like sharing a meal, watching a show, or even having a casual chat can turn into a nerve-racking event where you're bracing for an unexpected outburst or a cutting remark.

In the face of such behavior, you may find yourself becoming a sort of actor, performing in a play that has no script, no framework, only the whim of the narcissist to guide your lines and motions. Each day is an attempt to make the narcissist happy—or at least to keep them from becoming unhappy with you. You tell jokes to lift their spirits, compliment them to boost their ego, and often do things exactly as they like, all to sidestep the disapproval that can turn an average day upside down.

The constant effort to avoid conflict can feel like a full-time job with no breaks, no vacation days, and certainly no thanks. You gather their favorite food on your grocery trips, even if it means going out of your way. You pick out movie titles that you know they'll enjoy, setting aside your own preferences. And you nod along with opinions you don't share, silencing your true thoughts to keep the peace. This cycle can be exhausting, but it can also slowly become your version of normal—it's just how things are done to get through the day.

The strain of this invisible labor, the ceaseless efforts to please, might not be visible to others on the outside looking in. But to you, the one living it, the weight of each endeavor, each choice, feels as tangible as the very air you breathe. Balancing on this knife-edge demands not only your energy but also your sense of self, and sometimes, even your joy.

BREAKING FREE: STRATEGIES TO COUNTERACT MANIPULATION

Knowing what you're up against gives you strength. When someone tries to control you with sneaky methods, that's manipulation. Realizing these tricks puts you in a place to stop them. Like a game of chess, once you see the other person's moves, you can plan your next one. It's smart to spot these games early, so you don't get stuck in them.

Now, what can you do if you find yourself in this spot? Becoming assertive is a great way to start. Assertiveness doesn't mean being mean or pushy. It's all about being clear and honest about your thoughts and wishes without stepping on others' toes. It's like saying, "I respect myself, and I respect you, too."

But how does one become more assertive? It's like building a muscle; practice makes perfect. Try saying what you really think in small, low-pressure situations. For example, if your friend asks where you'd like to eat, suggest a place you'd enjoy instead of just going along with what they want. With time, this gets easier. When dealing with a person who's manipulative, being assertive helps you stay true to your own wants and needs.

Another big step is drawing clear boundaries, which means deciding where your limits are and sticking to them. It's like putting up a fence in your yard to let everyone know where your property starts and ends. In relationships, if you don't want someone calling you late at night, tell them. If they ignore your wishes, remind them of your boundary. If they keep ignoring it, you might need to stop answering those late calls. This shows you're serious about your boundaries.

Sometimes, though, you might need an extra hand, especially when it's tough to handle on your own. That's where professional help like counseling or therapy can be a game-changer. It's like having a coach in sports; they support you, teach you strategies, and help you stay on track. An expert can help you understand why you respond to manipulation the way you do and how to change it. They can give you tools to build your assertiveness muscles and guardrails to protect your boundaries.

Having those conversations with a counselor can also make you feel less alone. It's comforting to talk to someone who gets it and can guide you through the fog. They can teach you how to deal with a manipulative person without letting their games control you. This support can make a world of difference in finding your power and living the life you deserve—one where you call the shots, not someone else.

THE ROAD TO RECOVERY: HEALING FROM MANIPULATIVE ABUSE

Healing from manipulative abuse is much like embarking on a long walk through a forest you've never visited before. The path may not be clear, and sometimes, you might feel very alone. But remember this: with each step, you're moving forward, and with the right support and resources, you can emerge into the sunlight.

During your journey, practicing self-care is like packing the best hiking boots and a reliable compass. These things will support you and help guide your way. For many, self-care begins with mindfulness and meditation. These aren't fancy words for complex ideas; they're simple tools that everyone can use.

Mindfulness is just about noticing what's happening right now. It's like when you stop on your walk to look at the trees or listen to a stream nearby. During your day, take moments to just breathe and watch the world around you without trying to change anything. This can help you feel more calm and less tangled up in worries.

Meditation is like sitting down on a bench after walking for a long time. It's a time to rest and let your mind be still. You can find free videos on the internet that will guide you through short meditations, often as quick as five minutes. Taking this time can help manage stress and ease anxiety. It's not always easy at first, but like any new skill, it gets simpler with practice.

Another way to support yourself is to connect with others who understand what you've been through. Support groups, whether in-person or online, can be a safe place to share your feelings and experiences. Here, you find others who've walked paths like yours and who can nod and say, "I've been there." This can make you feel less alone and validate that what you're feeling is real and okay.

Lastly, one of the most powerful tools in your recovery backpack can be knowledge. Informative books are like maps and guides for your journey. One such book is "Psychopath Free" by Jackson MacKenzie. This book isn't a story about scary monsters but a guidebook that helps you recognize how manipulative people act and how their behavior can impact you.

Jackson MacKenzie's writing is straightforward. It doesn't confuse you with big words but speaks to you clearly, offering insight into why some people treat others badly, and how you can heal after such experiences. Through its pages, you'll gather wisdom and strategies to keep moving forward.

Recovery won't happen overnight. It's a journey with ups and downs. But by caring for yourself, connecting with others, and arming yourself with knowledge, you build strength. Step by step, day by day, you walk the path of healing, knowing that with each moving forward, you are getting closer to a place of peace and strength.

6

DRAWING THE LINE: BUILDING BOUNDARIES AGAINST NARCISSISTIC ABUSE

In the dance of human interaction, boundaries are the invisible protective shields that we put up around ourselves. They are the quiet yet firm lines that let people know where we draw the line between what we are okay with and what is not okay for us. For example, we set these boundaries when we say no to working late because we value our family time or when we choose not to share personal information because we want to keep some parts of our lives private.

Boundaries are not just physical; they encompass our feelings, thoughts, and needs. It's how we preserve our wellbeing and integrity amidst the pressures and demands of the world around us. When we lay out these limits for others, we're essentially defining what is acceptable and unacceptable behavior towards us.

With narcissists, setting boundaries becomes even more important. Narcissists often do not recognize or respect other people's limits. They may cross lines without thinking twice, expecting others to bend to their whims and needs. So, let's say you have a friend, and this friend often makes unkind comments about how you look. If this friend happens to have narcissistic tendencies, he might not even realize how hurtful his remarks are. Or worse, he might not care.

This is where you step in with your protective shield: your boundary. You gather your courage and tell your friend, "I won't tolerate disrespectful comments about my appearance." With this simple statement, you've drawn a line. You've declared to the narcissist—and to yourself—that you have self-respect, that you value yourself, and that you won't accept being treated poorly.

Admittedly, asserting this boundary might not be an easy task. You might worry about the reaction you'll get, or whether you'll be able to stand firm. But remember, it isn't just about the single instance of standing up for yourself; it's about creating a pattern of respect and reasonable expectations in the relationship.

Understanding this concept of boundaries and feeling comfortable with enforcing them is crucial when dealing with a narcissist. Without these invisible protective shields, you leave yourself open to being overwhelmed by the narcissist's wants and potentially harmful behavior. When your wellbeing is at stake, it's important to recognize your right to set these boundaries and to defend them as necessary.

Through practicing boundary-setting, you can create a space where your thoughts, feelings, and needs are acknowledged and respected. By doing so, you don't just protect yourself from narcissistic abuse; you honor your self-worth and lay the groundwork for healthier, more balanced relationships.

THE IMPORTANCE OF SETTING BOUNDARIES WITH NARCISSISTS

When we talk about boundaries, think of them like invisible walls. These walls keep us safe from people who might want to take more than we're willing to give. Some folks, like narcissists, are especially good at breaking down these walls. They often try to use our best qualities, like our kindness or care for others, against us. It's important we learn how to keep our invisible walls strong, so we can stay happy and healthy.

Let's say you're a very nice person. You love helping others. That's a wonderful thing! But sometimes, people might take advantage of that. Narcissists are experts at finding such good hearts and trying to use them for their own gain. They can make us feel like we have to give more and more of ourselves, even when it makes us feel bad.

A narcissist might be someone you work with, someone in your family, or even a friend. When you know someone like this, it's like they have a special button they push that makes you feel like you must do what they say. Maybe they make you think you owe them something or they make you feel guilty when you're actually not in the wrong.

Say you have a coworker who always asks you to do tasks that they should be doing. They might try to make you think it's your job, or that helping them will make you a better team player. But deep down, you know it's not right. This is where your invisible wall comes in.

Setting a boundary means you get to say "no" when something doesn't feel right to you. And you're allowed to do that! It's a way of protecting your own time and energy. You could say something like, "I'm happy to help when I can, but this time I can't do that task for you." That's a boundary. It tells the other person what you are and aren't willing to do.

These walls are super important because they keep your self-esteem and mental peace safe. Without them, a narcissist might make you feel small and tired, as they go on taking everything they can from you. When you set boundaries, it's like you're telling yourself and others that you respect yourself. You're saying that your feelings, time, and energy are important.

Setting boundaries doesn't mean you're being mean or selfish. it just means you're taking care of yourself. and that's something we all must do to stay strong and happy. once you start to set these boundaries, you'll notice that you feel better, and you won't get trapped in the unfair situations the narcissist tries to put you in. it takes practice, but setting boundaries is one of the best skills you can learn for a peaceful life.

HOW TO SET BOUNDARIES EFFECTIVELY

When dealing with someone who often thinks mostly of themselves —a person some might call a narcissist—setting limits is important. It's like putting up a fence around your personal garden so that not just anyone can trample your flowers. Boundaries help you keep that space safe and sound. To best protect your mental garden, you need to be clear and unwavering.

First, know what you expect from the other person and be very clear about it. Imagine if you were giving directions to a new place; you wouldn't just say "go that way," you would tell them the exact streets and turns to take. Likewise, be specific about your boundaries. For instance, you can tell a parent who often says hurtful things, "When you say these mean words to me, it hurts. If this happens again, I'm going to have to spend less time with you."

But it's not enough to just say what you don't like—you need to say what will happen if the line is crossed. That means talking about consequences. Think about when you were a kid and you were told not to jump on the bed. If you did, you knew you might get a time-out. As an adult, you decide the consequences. This isn't to punish the other person but to take care of you. If the hurtful words don't stop, you are allowed to say, "I'm going to hang up the phone or leave the room if you continue with this."

Assertiveness is the key to making these boundaries work. Being assertive isn't about being mean or rude; it's about speaking up for yourself in a strong, calm way. It means saying what you need without wobbling or backing down. Remember, you have the right to protect your feelings and your peace of mind—that's your garden, and you are the one in charge of it.

For example, let's say your father often pokes fun at your job. You can express this clearly: "Dad, when you make jokes about my work, it feels like you don't respect me. I need you to stop. If you can't, we're going to have fewer conversations." It's like putting up a sign in your garden that says, "Do not step on the flowers." And just like that sign, if someone keeps stepping on the flowers anyway, you have the right to stop them from coming in.

In short, confronting a person with these traits isn't easy. It takes firmness and courage. But remember, you're the keeper of your garden. By being clear, specific, and assertive with your boundaries, you help ensure that your space stays peaceful, just the way you want it.

OVERCOMING CHALLENGES IN SETTING BOUNDARIES

Setting boundaries with people who have a strong focus on themselves – narcissists – can be a tough task. When someone is used to having all the attention and making things go their way, the idea that someone might set up rules that limit them doesn't make them happy. They may see boundaries as walls stopping them from getting what they want or from controlling situations and people around them. Knowing the rough spots that may come up on this journey can be a helpful guide to dealing with them.

Let's say you've told a partner who always wants things their way, "I need to have time for my hobbies and friends without you getting upset." That seems fair, right? this might seem like you're denying them the constant attention they crave. The way they respond might be harsh – they could get angry, try to make you feel sad or guilty, or completely ignore what you've said.

It's critical to stand your ground when your boundaries are tested. Picture this as drawing a firm line in the sand. The wind might blow, and they might try to erase it with their foot, but you keep drawing that line over and over. This takes strength and won't be easy. They'll notice you're serious, and that's what you want.

For example, if your narcissistic partner tries to make you feel guilty for spending time on your interests instead of with them, it can be tricky not to give in. They might say things like "You don't love me if you'd rather do this than be with me." Or they could twist things around so you start wondering if you're being selfish. This is a classic move called a guilt trip. They're trying to fly you straight to "Sorry Land" where you give up your needs for theirs.

Recognizing these sneaky plays is like having a secret map that shows you where the traps are hidden. When you hear the guilt-tripping beginning, it's a sign to hold on tight to what you've decided. It's your right to have your own space, time for what you enjoy, and peace of mind.

In dealing with someone who only thinks of themselves, keeping to your boundaries is like setting up a fence around your garden. It tells them where they can and cannot go. They might be annoyed that they can't trample all over your beautiful flowers anymore, but this fence keeps your garden – your life – safe and sound. It's not to be mean, it's to take care of what's valuable to you. Remember, every time you stand by your rules, you show yourself respect, and that's something everyone deserves.

MAINTAINING BOUNDARIES: A CONTINUOUS PRACTICE

Maintaining boundaries is like caring for a garden. It takes time, attention, and patience to keep it healthy and thriving. Just as a gardener must consistently care for each plant, water it, and protect it from pests, you must tend to your personal boundaries regularly to ensure they stay strong.

Consistency is the tool you must use day in and day out. It's the daily watering of your garden. When setting limits with others, doing so on a steady basis is key. Just as a plant might wilt if watered irregularly, your boundaries may weaken if they are not consistently upheld. If you're always changing the rules, it might confuse others, much like how a plant can get stressed and wither if its care is inconsistent. Others may begin to think that your boundaries are not serious and can be changed or ignored whenever they want. It's as though you would leave a gate open for rabbits to hop in and nibble away at your garden.

To continue this important work, it can be very helpful to have support – like calling in a friend to help you clear away weeds or tend the garden when you're not able. Trusted friends, close family members, or even a mental health professional can act as these helpful gardeners in your life. They can encourage you when you're feeling worn out and remind you of why your boundaries are important. They can also give you advice on what has worked for them or offer a listening ear when you need to vent your frustrations.

Take, for example, a family member who seems to always step over your lines. This person might take up too much of your time, always ask for favors without giving anything in return, or make you feel uncomfortable with their words or actions. If you have a relative like this, it's like dealing with a stubborn weed in your garden that keeps popping up, no matter how many times you pull it out.

To deal with this, you would need to be like a seasoned gardener – patient, firm, and persistent. Each time this person tries to step past your set boundaries, you would need to clearly and firmly remind them of your limits. It's not always easy, and it might feel like you have to repeat yourself too many times, but eventually, they will begin to understand that you mean what you say. The message will be clear: these are the edges of your garden, and they need to be respected. Bit by bit, your garden — your space and peace of mind — will flourish under this careful watch.

The job is never completely done. just as a garden is always growing and changing, so too will the process of maintaining your boundaries. it's a journey that requires resilience, but with steady work and the support of your friends, family, or a professional, your garden will thrive.

HEALING THROUGH BOUNDARIES: REGAINING CONTROL AND RESPECT

Establishing and maintaining boundaries is a crucial step in the journey to recovery from narcissistic abuse. When a person has endured a relationship with a narcissist, they often experience feelings of being out of control. Narcissists have a way of making their needs the center of everything, often ignoring or trampling the needs and feelings of others. In order to heal from the hurt and regain a sense of self, setting firm boundaries is essential.

Boundaries act like invisible lines that help protect your emotional space. They are the rules and limits you set for yourself in relationships, defining what you find acceptable and unacceptable from others. Think of them as a personal property line that tells others how close they can get, both physically and emotionally. Setting these boundaries can help you regain control over your life—a control that's often taken away in a relationship with a narcissistic individual.

In the process of healing, self-respect blooms when boundaries are established and maintained. It's a statement to yourself and others that you value your wellbeing and will not allow it to be compromised. It's acknowledging that your feelings, thoughts, and needs are important, and you have the right to protect yourself from being hurt further.

Self-care goes hand in hand with self-respect when it comes to healing. After a narcissistic relationship, it's vital to prioritize taking care of your mental, emotional, and physical health. Setting boundaries is a form of self-care because it allows you to take space from harmful interactions and situations that can further deplete your energy and peace of mind.

Let's imagine you're moving on from a narcissistic partner. A clear and direct boundary might be choosing to limit conversations with them only to necessary communication, such as discussions about children or shared responsibilities. Or, it might be healthier to cut off communication entirely if the situation allows. It's not about being mean or rude; it's about taking the steps you need to protect yourself.

In practice, establishing boundaries with a narcissist may not be easy. They might push back against your newfound limits or even pretend not to acknowledge them. However, staying firm in your decisions is key. Consistency tells the narcissist—and more importantly, yourself—that you are serious about your healing journey.

You have the power and the right to decide who has access to your life and on what terms. it's not about punishing the other person; it's about taking care of you. you are worthy of having your needs met, and setting boundaries is a powerful step toward making that happen.

7
THE ART OF NON-ENGAGEMENT: MASTERING THE GREY ROCK METHOD

In this essential part of our book, we're going to dive deep into the Grey Rock Method. This is a tool you can use to protect yourself from people who try to mess with your mind or control you – we call these people narcissists. Imagine a narcissist as a person who loves seeing a big reaction. What the Grey Rock Method does is teaches you how to not give them the reaction they want.

Let's break down the Grey Rock Method. You might have seen a grey rock at a park or on a walk. It's plain, not bright or shiny, and most of the time, you just walk by it without noticing. That's what you aim for with this method – becoming like that rock: quiet, simple, and forgettable. When you talk to a narcissist using the Grey Rock Method, you keep your words and reactions so plain that they lose interest in bothering you.

The Grey Rock Method was thought up by Skye Sherman. She said it's like you make yourself as dull and unremarkable as a grey rock. That's the picture we want to paint here. It's a way of talking and acting that doesn't give off anything interesting, fun, or worth talking about to a narcissist. They usually like it when things are exciting or when they can make someone else upset or happy – basically, when they can control how someone else feels.

But when you go grey rock, that's when their tricks stop working. You respond to them with simple 'yes', 'no', or 'maybe' answers. You don't tell stories or share your feelings. Your face doesn't show anger, joy, or sadness. It's like you become a human version of, "I don't know you, and I'm just going to keep it moving."

Going grey rock makes the narcissist find someone else to try and upset, because they're not getting any fun from you. This method doesn't feed their hunger for drama or the spotlight. Remember, a narcissist is kind of like a person who loves to stir the pot or see things get all twisted up. If you don't give them any of that – if you stay calm and boring like a rock – they'll go looking for someone else who will.

Using this method isn't always easy. It takes practice to hold back and not react when someone is pushing your buttons. But keep this in mind: every time you don't give in to the drama, you're taking a step to keep your peace, your power, and your control. You're choosing not to play their game. And by doing that, you're winning.

WHEN AND WHY TO USE THE GREY ROCK METHOD

The Grey Rock Method might sound strange at first like some old magic trick, but it's actually a smart way to handle tough situations with certain difficult people. Imagine a grey rock—nothing special, right? It's easy to walk by a grey rock and not even give it a second look. Now picture you could be like that rock when dealing with someone who, let's say, isn't very nice or makes you feel bad—like a person who always needs to be the center of attention. We call these people narcissists because they think about themselves a lot and often try to feed off other people's reactions.

However, this method is not your number one tool for every single bump in the road. It shines in specific problems where you still have to deal with a narcissist regularly. Perhaps you share children with this person, which means you'll need to talk and see each other for your kids' sake. Or maybe you work at the same place, and it's not like you can just pick up your desk and move to another building, right? In these situations, running away isn't your best choice or maybe not a choice at all.

This is where the Grey Rock Method can really help. Narcissists love to be in the spotlight and play with other people's feelings to get there. They're like emotional vampires—they'll try to get a rise out of you, looking for a reaction, any reaction. When you act like a 'grey rock', meaning you become as dull and uninteresting as possible, you don't give them the drama they're looking for. No more than you'd give that unnoticed rock on the sidewalk.

You might give short answers like "Hmm," "I see," or "Okay." Or maybe you nod and not say too much. You keep your face calm and don't let any of your feelings show. This might seem simple, but it can be harder than it sounds. The trick is to stay calm and not let their words or actions change your cool.

Sarah Newman, an expert with fancy degrees, wrote about this in a big article on a website called PsychCentral. She said that when you can't stay away from a narcissist completely, the Grey Rock Method might just be your secret weapon. By not giving them the energy and reactions they want, you're protecting yourself. It's like you're invisible to their games.

The goal isn't to be rude or mean. it's about keeping your peace and your power. you talk when you need to but keep it like the weather—simple, everyday stuff. let the narcissist look elsewhere for their drama. meanwhile, you stay cool, collected, and most of all, safe—just like that unremarkable but steady grey rock.

PRACTICAL STEPS TO IMPLEMENT THE GREY ROCK METHOD

Implementing the Grey Rock Method can be a useful strategy when you need to interact with someone who thrives on drama, such as a person with narcissistic tendencies. It requires you to take on the unremarkable nature of a grey rock, becoming as dull and unengaging as possible, so the person loses interest in trying to provoke a reaction from you. This approach can minimize the emotional energy you spend dealing with such personalities and keep your peace of mind intact.

To apply this method effectively, you need to develop a level of emotional detachment. This means that even if the person tries to push your buttons, you maintain control over your reactions. It's like you're building an invisible shield around your emotions, keeping them safe from the drama and games.

When you need to have a conversation with the person, keep it strictly factual. You avoid sharing anything personal that they could use to get a rise out of you. Instead, talk about neutral, mundane topics that don't invite further discussion. For example, you could discuss the weather, mentioning it's sunny or looks like it might rain later. Such conversations are usually brief and are not emotionally engaging, which is precisely the aim of the Grey Rock Method.

Moreover, it's vital to exhibit no emotional reaction to the narcissist's attempts to engage or provoke you. They might try to say something to get under your skin or to bait you into an argument, but with the Grey Rock Method, your goal is to not let them see any change in your demeanor. Imagine your expression and tone of voice as unchanging as a rock's surface—consistent and undisturbed, no matter what's happening around it.

Psychologist Sherrie Campbell notes the value in this emotional steadiness. In an article for Entrepreneur, she emphasizes that "the less reactive you are to provocations, the more you can use your better judgment to handle the situation." It's sound advice because when you're not caught up in responding to every provocation, you're in a better headspace to think about how best to deal with the person and protect your well-being.

In essence, the Grey Rock Method is about conserving your emotional energy. It's not about being rude or dismissive; rather, it's a tactic to deflect unwanted attention and negative energy. By keeping your interactions simple, you discourage the person from engaging in the kind of emotional drama they feed on. This creates a safer and more controlled environment for you and prevents the emotional toll that can come from dealing with someone who has narcissistic behaviors.

THE CHALLENGES OF THE GREY ROCK METHOD

Silence speaks volumes—it's an old saying that holds a well of truth, especially when dealing with someone who craves attention like a flower craves sunlight. That's where the Grey Rock Method comes in, a technique as simple yet as powerful as a quiet stream of water shaping the toughest rocks over time. However, wielding this method is not without its own set of hurdles.

Imagine, for a moment, you're at a family gathering. There's food on the table, laughter echoing off the walls, but there's that one person —the one who always has to turn the spotlight onto themselves. They're a whirlpool of charisma and energy, sucking you into their drama, spinning tales where they're always the hero or the victim. That's the person you're using the Grey Rock Method on. You keep your words and your reactions plain, like a pebble, nothing for the drama to catch on to. But even pebbles can get heavy.

Here's the twist: keeping your feelings hidden away, schooled into a mask of indifference, it's tough. It can weigh on you because, sometimes, the person you're being a grey rock for is someone you used to laugh with, share secrets with. Holding back can feel like locking a piece of yourself in a box. Long term, this is emotionally exhausting. You're in a constant battle not to let your real feelings show, not to react. And this can leave you feeling lonely, misunderstood, or even numb to your own emotions.

Now, let's talk about balance. Imagine a seesaw, with your emotional engagement on one side, and the Grey Rock Method on the other. Tip too far into the Grey Rock, and you might find yourself becoming less responsive not just to the narcissist but to others as well. You start to draw back, building walls because it starts to feel safer that way, except now, friends and family—who don't deserve that rock treatment—feel pushed away. Your dog might still get tail-wags a'plenty and joyful energy from you, but people might just get a nod or a bland smile.

Dr. Karyl McBride, wise in the ways of family dynamics, recommends a release valve. Writing in Psychology Today, she advises finding those "safe others" in your life, like a best friend who's always there or a cousin who's like a sibling. These are the people you can show your real face to, who can hold your sorrows and your joys gently in their hands while you navigate the minefield of your more challenging relationships. They're like the soft grass you can tumble onto when you're tired of being a rock.

So, the Grey Rock Method, while a tool of resilience, can't be all you are. You've got to keep that balance, find those moments for your true emotions to shine safely, to keep yourself from turning into the very thing you're using to protect yourself—a rock.

STAYING RESILIENT: SELF-CARE DURING THE GREY ROCK PROCESS

Maintaining your mental health is just as important as taking care of your body. Think of it like giving your mind a daily dose of vitamins or going for a brisk walk to keep your heart healthy. When using the Grey Rock Method—which means staying calm and not reacting in a big way to someone who's difficult—it's essential to also take steps to keep your mental health strong.

Imagine your mind is a garden. Just as a garden needs regular watering and sunlight, your mind needs care too. Stick to a routine that includes activities that make you feel good. This could be as simple as reading a book, taking a long bath, or walking in nature. It's like putting on a suit of armor that protects your feelings each day.

Don't forget to fill your life with laughter and joy. Maybe that means watching funny movies or playing games that make you smile. When life feels heavy, these moments of lightness can be a breath of fresh air for your soul.

Talking to people you trust can make a huge difference, too. Friends and family can offer kind words and remind you that you're not alone. Even when facing tough times, a good chat can be like finding an unexpected treasure in your day. Imagine you have a special team —the people who stand by you, no matter what. Turn to them when you need a cheerleader or a listening ear.

Another powerful tool is seeking guidance from a mental health professional. Picture them as a guide who helps you navigate through a dense forest. They can provide tools and a safe place to talk about your feelings, and they're trained to help you cope with stress and worries. It's their job to support you on your journey.

Lastly, consider connecting with people who truly understand what you're going through—like joining a support group. Just as a circle of friends catch each other when they fall, a support group serves as a network of understanding and care. The National Domestic Violence Hotline recommends such groups because they provide a secure place to express yourself and learn from others facing similar challenges. You might even pick up new ways to handle situations that you hadn't thought of before.

In all of these steps, you're giving your mental health the same attention as a gardener gives to their precious plants. Joining a support group, talking it out with friends, or finding a little joy in your daily routine are all ways of nurturing your well-being. Like tending to a garden, it's important to pay attention to your emotional landscape every day. This ensures that while you're using the Grey Rock Method, your inner world stays vibrant and strong.

8

SILENCING THE ECHOES: DEALING WITH THE NARCISSIST'S FLYING MONKEYS

In life, just like in the story of 'The Wizard of Oz', there are people who might not realize they are being used. You know, like how the Wicked Witch sent out her winged helpers to do her bad tasks? we call these helpers 'flying monkeys'. These are usually folks who, without even knowing it, help a person who only cares about themselves, often called a narcissist.

Now, let's talk about these 'flying monkeys' and their role. These enablers, they're not the main troublemakers, but they can still cause a lot of hurt. Why? Because the narcissist, the person who's always thinking they're the best and ignores others' feelings, tricks them into helping. It's like when someone pulls the strings on a puppet. The puppet might not know it's being controlled, but it's still doing what the puppeteer wants.

These 'flying monkeys', they can come from anywhere. They might be your buddies who you grab a bite with, your relatives who you spend holidays with, or even folks you work with at your job. But here's the catch: they've been fooled into thinking that the narcissist is right, and you're wrong. They start doing things that help the narcissist and give you a hard time, and trust me, that's not fun at all.

So, imagine you're having an argument with a narcissist and all of a sudden, you're not just facing them, but also a bunch of other people who have taken their side. It feels unfair, right? That's because it is. These 'flying monkeys' might not even get why they're doing what they're doing; they just think they're helping out a friend or family member, but in reality, they're making things tough for you.

But here's the good news: once you know about these enablers and their tactics, you're a step closer to dealing with them. We're going to learn how to spot when someone's being a 'flying monkey'. Then we'll talk through some clever ways to handle them and make sure they don't throw your life off track.

It's not about being mean or getting back at anyone. it's about understanding what's going on and taking care of yourself. by spotting these 'flying monkeys', you can avoid a lot of headaches. you'll be able to see when someone's trying to pull the strings and you'll be ready to snip those strings before they get all tangled up in your life.

THE PUPPETEER'S STRINGS: HOW NARCISSISTS MANIPULATE THEIR FLYING MONKEYS

In the tangled web spun by a narcissist, there are those who become unknowing pawns in the game – often called flying monkeys. Like the characters in a classic tale whisked away to do the bidding of the wicked witch, these individuals are manipulated to do the narcissist's bidding, serving their agenda and keeping the narcissist's image shiny and clean.

At the core of this manipulation is a toolbox of emotional tricks. The narcissist is skilled at tapping into deep feelings—guilt, fear, a sense of duty, or even the sweet honey of flattery. They know just what strings to pull to get their flying monkeys to dance to their tune.

Picture a family dinner where one seat is empty. The narcissistic parent tells the gathered siblings that their absent brother didn't come "because he believes he's better than us." The parent shakes their head, trying to look sad, but their eyes don't have true sadness in them. Yet, this act is enough to stir a mix of guilt and anger in the other children. The words, unsaid but understood, hover in the air – "You're not disloyal like him, are you?" And soon, the flying monkeys take flight, defending the parent and turning against the sibling who has been cast as the outsider.

In the workplace, the dynamics are strikingly similar. A narcissistic boss may call a meeting and lament the decline in team spirit, all the while laying the blame at the feet of one absent co-worker. "We must all pull together," the boss might say, suggesting in the same breath that the co-worker is pulling in the wrong direction. Authority amplifies the boss's words, and colleagues are nudged one step closer to turning on their own team member.

The methods of turning others against you can be subtle yet powerful. Rumors, which are often disguised half-truths, become the narcissist's smoke and mirrors. They never lie outright, but the truths they tell are coated in deceit. They build a narrative where they are the victim who needs protection, and you are the villain from whom others must be guarded. It's a clever trick – because if someone else tells the tale, the narcissist remains at a distance, their hands seemingly clean.

Over time, this can have a devastating impact. Relationships falter, reputations suffer, and the narcissist watches, their control over the narrative tight. It's a sad reality for those caught in the crossfire, but understanding this manipulation is the first step in countering it. Being aware of these tactics can be like drawing back the curtain, revealing that the grand wizard is just a person – a person pulling levers and desperately hoping no one notices the truth behind the disguise.

CUTTING THE STRINGS: STRATEGIES FOR DEALING WITH FLYING MONKEYS

Dealing with flying monkeys can be really hard. These are not the winged creatures from stories, but people used by a narcissist to keep their control over you. Flying monkeys might be friends or family who don't understand they are being used. They do what the narcissist asks them to, often hurting you without meaning to.

It's important to see the flying monkeys for who they truly are – tools in the narcissist's game. Their words or actions might sting, but remember, they're just repeating what the narcissist told them. They might not even see the truth behind the things they do or say. Because of this, do your best not to take it to heart. It's not really about you; it's about the narcissist trying to hold on to power.

Setting clear boundaries with these people is key. Think of boundaries like invisible lines that show what is okay and what is not. You do not have to listen to flying monkeys when they try to twist your thoughts or make you doubt yourself. And you definitely don't owe them any explanations about your life or choices.

Let's say a friend begins asking odd questions about your personal matters. Maybe they're doing this because the narcissist asked them to. You can handle this by being polite but very clear. Say something like, "I appreciate our friendship, but I'm not comfortable talking about these things." This tells them the subject is off-limits. It's like putting up a "No Trespassing" sign on parts of your life.

Also, it's good to keep in mind that you cannot change how flying monkeys will act. The truth is, they might keep doing what the narcissist wants. But, and this is where your power lies, you can choose how you will react to them. When you respond with strength and calm, you are taking back control. Instead of getting upset, give yourself a quiet nod for handling it well. This is not about winning a fight; it's about keeping your peace of mind.

In all these situations, being kind to yourself is so important. Remember that flying monkeys often do not see the whole picture and are caught in the narcissist's tricks too. You can only take care of how you react and keep your well-being first. Stand firm in your truth, knowing that you are not part of their game. You have your own path, and that's where your focus should be.

HEALING FROM THE ATTACKS: OVERCOMING THE DAMAGE CAUSED BY FLYING MONKEYS

Dealing with the damage caused by the so-called "flying monkeys" – people who have been influenced by a narcissistic individual to cause trouble for you – can leave you feeling hurt and exhausted. But I assure you, by adopting the right approach, you can begin to mend the emotional harm and find peace once again.

One fundamental step in your journey to healing is to pull away from the flying monkeys. This means that when they try to confront you, resist the urge to argue with them or defend your actions. Doing that is like giving extra wood to a fire—it only makes it burn brighter. Instead, if you calmly step away, you're denying the fire that wood and the flames will slowly die down. Also, remember that these people are likely not acting fully on their own. They are doing what the narcissist wants them to do. Your best move is to not play this game at all.

Now, stepping back from the chaos doesn't mean you're alone in this fight. There are people out there who will understand what you're going through. One powerful source of support can be a professional counselor or therapist. These are folks who have studied for years to help people just like you. They can lend an ear, give wise advice, and offer a hand to hold (figuratively speaking) as you move forward.

Moreover, there are groups composed of people who have been in your shoes, coping with the tricks of narcissists. You might be surprised by how many there are! Places like Reddit and Quora are home to online communities where you can share your story and hear others'. Talking to people who truly get your experience can be like finding an anchor in a storm.

Another essential part of getting better is caring for yourself. Think of self-care as building up a shield against future hurt. Simple activities like sitting quietly and watching your breath (meditation), moving your body through different poses (yoga), or writing down your feelings and thoughts in a book (journaling) are powerful ways to handle stress and work through your emotions.

Lastly, I want to stress that there's absolutely nothing wrong with needing help along this path. It's a strong move, not a weak one, to reach out when you need a hand. Bringing people and activities into your life that bring light and strength is not just smart, it's necessary.

So let's embrace both our independence and our need for community. It's not about one or the other—it's about having the wisdom to know when to step back and when to hold out your hand. Just as we wouldn't think twice about calling a friend when our car breaks down on a lonely road, we shouldn't hesitate to seek support when we're dealing with the damage of flying monkeys. No one should have to face this situation by themselves.

9
CHAINS OF THE HEART: UNRAVELING TRAUMA BONDING

THE INVISIBLE CHAINS: DEFINING TRAUMA BONDING

Imagine a tie between two people, where one hurts the other, but the hurt person still feels a strong pull towards the one causing the pain. This kind of tie is what we call trauma bonding. It's like an invisible chain that's hard to break, and it happens when someone faces regular mistreatment or emotional harm from another person but still feels a deep connection to them.

Patrick Carnes first talked about trauma bonding in his book back in the late '90s. He explained that this powerful bond is not something kind or good. Instead, it's like a trick, making people stay in relationships that hurt them. Think about it like a loop: something bad happens, later something good or sweet follows, and this back and forth creates a confusing mix of good and bad. The heart goes on a roller coaster, and that can make someone think, "Maybe it's not all bad."

But there's a catch. This back and forth isn't normal in a healthy relationship. When someone is loving one minute and mean the next, it twists the idea of love and caring, making it hard to see the situation clearly. Why does this matter? Because understanding this can be the first step in getting free from that invisible chain.

Therapist Terri Cole talked about how trauma bonding looks a lot like Stockholm Syndrome. That's when people who have been taken and held by someone end up liking or even defending the very same person who captured them. It sounds odd, right? But it happens more than we think. When affection and hurt get mixed up, it turns into a very sticky, tangled bond.

So, why talk about trauma bonding in this chapter? Because knowing about it is key in recognizing it in ourselves or others who might be stuck in a harmful relationship. Sometimes, someone might feel trapped with a person who is all about themselves—a narcissist—because of this strong emotional chain. Narcissists can make someone feel special, then worthless, then special again in a cycle that keeps on spinning.

Realizing there is such a thing as trauma bonding helps us understand that the feeling of being unable to leave isn't because the relationship is good. It's because the pattern of hurt and comfort has created a deep, confusing bond. Breaking free starts with seeing the invisible chains for what they are—not ties of love, but of trauma. Understanding this can be the start of choosing to walk away and heal.

THE NARCISSIST'S TUG OF WAR: EMOTIONAL HIGHS AND LOWS

Life with a narcissist is like being on a roller coaster that you never agreed to ride. It's full of ups and downs and can leave you feeling dizzy and confused. People often wonder why it's so hard to walk away from such a relationship. The answer lies partly in the way a narcissist's behavior can trap you in a cycle that alternates between kindness and cruelty.

In the first phase, the narcissist floods you with gestures that seem like love. This phase is known as "love bombing." At this point, the narcissist showers their target with compliments, gifts, and undivided attention. You feel special, perhaps even like you've met the perfect friend or partner. This intense level of attention is designed to get you hooked. But this is not a true or healthy form of love; it's a set-up.

Unfortunately, this warmth doesn't last. Once the narcissist feels secure in the bond they've formed, their attitude shifts dramatically. This is when the devaluation starts. Suddenly, the person who couldn't praise you enough begins to find fault with everything you do. They may criticize your looks, your intelligence, or your abilities. They may even become mean or abusive. This sudden shift can be jarring and hurtful, and you may find yourself working harder to get back the affection you once received so freely.

Dr. Rhonda Freeman, an expert on brain patterns and emotions, explains that this switch creates an emotional attachment that is incredibly hard to break. When you're subjected to this kind of push and pull, your mind and heart start to link these intense experiences. The kindness feels even sweeter after you've been treated poorly, and the cruelty hurts more after being loved. It's not unlike a gambler who keeps playing for the next big win: when you occasionally get that hit of affection again, it's powerful, and it keeps you coming back for more, hoping the bad times will end for good.

To illustrate, imagine your partner greets you with a warm hug and tells you how much they missed you – your heart soars. Then, out of nowhere, they make a cruel joke about your new haircut or scoff at your work accomplishments, and you crash back to the ground. You're left reeling, feeling uncertain, and anxious, which is precisely what anchors you to them. You start to long for the good moments because they're so dazzling and intense, creating a cycle of abuse and affection.

It's no wonder that you might find yourself stuck, unable to leave even when you know on some level that the relationship is harmful. The emotional roller coaster has created a trauma bond – a connection rooted in the cycle of hurt and comfort. Breaking this bond requires immense strength and often, support from others. Understanding the cycle is the first step in recognizing it's not merely a rough patch in the relationship but a deliberate pattern of control.

SHACKLED BY SHAME AND FEAR: THE POWER OF TRAUMA BONDING

When someone goes through a very hard and hurtful relationship, they sometimes develop a thing called trauma bonding. Imagine a strong, invisible thread that ties a person to someone who hurts them, both in their body and feelings. It's a kind of link that makes leaving this person seem as tough as climbing the tallest mountain without any help. This connection isn't a sign of true love, even though it might trick a person into thinking it is.

Trauma bonding can make people who are hurt by their partner feel really stuck. They might know deep down that the situation is bad for them, but they're caught like a bug in a web. This web is made not from spider silk, but from a mix of fear, loyalty, and a hope for better days. This is what keeps them returning to the person hurting them, hoping for a tiny piece of care, even when most times all they get is pain.

Dr. Lisa Firestone, a smart person who understands a lot about the mind, explains that people stuck in trauma bonds often think it's their own fault they are being mistreated. They might say to themselves, "If only I were better, this wouldn't happen." It's like wearing a backpack filled with rocks of guilt. They carry it everywhere, and it makes it much harder to walk away.

This happens a lot with people who live together but hurt each other – we call it domestic abuse. It's incredibly sad because you could hear stories of people living with their abuser for not just months but years. These people are unable to cut the trauma bond, even though they might want to.

Why is it so hard to leave? It's not because they're weak. Not at all. It's because the bond messes with their feelings and thoughts. Imagine you have a little bird that lands on your hand every day. The bird pecks you, and it hurts, but you want to believe it still loves you. Sometimes the bird even sings a pretty song. So, you hold on to the good moments and forget about the pecks. Now, think of the bird as the abuser and the hand as the victim's heart.

The heart wants to hold on to the good, even if it's tiny and comes with lots of hurt. The hurtful person might say sorry, or be kind for a short time, and make promises of changing. And like the bird's song, these rare happy moments can make the bad times seem less bad. So the heart keeps hoping, and the mind keeps making excuses.

Breaking that trauma bond is a huge step, and it's tougher than most things in life. But it's the first step towards a brighter and safer day. It means putting down the backpack of guilt and letting go of the harmful bond that connects them to the one who causes pain. It's a journey that begins with understanding that the hurt isn't their fault and they deserve to be treated kindly.

BREAKING FREE: OVERCOMING TRAUMA BONDING

Overcoming a trauma bond is like walking through a thick, dark forest. The path is hard to see, and it's easy to lose your way, but once you find that path and walk it step by step, you get closer to a place of peace and wellness. Here, we talk about what Dr. Linda Hatch, an expert on healing from deep hurts created by love, shares with us about starting the journey to get better.

First, we must understand the situation. A "trauma bond" is a strong, unhealthy link that forms between a person hurt by someone, and the person who hurt them. It's like being tied to someone who has hurt you, but you can't seem to break free. This bond can make a person keep choosing a relationship that is not safe or good for them.

Dr. Linda Hatch knows a lot about this kind of pain and the road to feeling better. She tells us that to begin healing, we must be honest about the bond we have with the person who hurt us. This is hard. It means facing our fear and pain, and admitting that someone we care for has caused us deep harm.

After we see the bond for what it is, Dr. Hatch advises we look for help from people who understand our pain. This could be a therapist or people in support groups. Support groups are like circles of friends who have walked on paths similar to ours. They've felt the same fears and faced the same darkness. When we sit with them, we learn we're not alone. We share stories, and as we do, we find pieces of our strength we forgot we had.

Moreover, Dr. Hatch says it is key that we take good care of ourselves. When we're wounded, we need to be kind and gentle with ourselves, like we would be with a best friend. Self-care is how we do this. We might try being still and calm, which is sometimes called "mindfulness," or we might take deep breaths and clear our mind, which is part of "meditation." When our heart hurts, things like this can calm the noise in our mind and give our hearts a break.

Remember that this path isn't one we must walk alone, nor will it be quick or easy. But every small step we take is a step toward freedom from the pain. By facing the truth, finding a circle of support, and treating yourself with tender care, you are building a new road—one that leads you out of the dark forest into a place where you can see the skies clearing and feel hope shining on your face again.

10

BREAKING FREE: UNTANGLING THE KNOTTED TIES OF TRAUMA BONDING

Recognizing the Trauma Bond

When you are in a relationship with someone who is constantly nice to you one moment and then mean the next, you might find yourself stuck in something called a trauma bond. It is a strong hold, a sort of invisible chain, that can play with your feelings and make you think that you need that person, even when they hurt you. It's a serious thing that doesn't only tie you to the person but also messes with your heart and mind.

The trauma bond is a sneaky trap. It starts when someone does or says bad things to you, which can make you feel sad or scared. But then, they turn around and do something very kind. This roller coaster of bad and good times leaves you confused. You feel grateful for the good moments and might even think that the bad times weren't so terrible because, look, they're being nice again!

The problem is, you begin to believe that the kind moments are more important than the hurtful ones. You find reasons to stay, to forgive, and to put up with the pain, all while the trauma bond grows stronger. That's because your feelings are being toyed with. When someone is kind to you right after being mean, it can almost feel like a reward, and that messes with your head.

The scariness of leaving this kind of see-saw relationship comes from the intensity of the bond. If you think about leaving, you might feel scared or like you can't live without that person. And that fear could keep you stuck there, in a place where you're not treated the way you deserve to be treated.

In a study done in 2015 by scientists in the University of Illinois, it was found out that people who have these trauma bonds feel a very strong emotional connection that is so powerful it can make leaving the tough relationship even harder. The study showed that when you go through this cycle of bad and good treatment, it can get even more difficult to remember your worth and to see the relationship clearly. It's like being tied to someone who can lift you up with one hand while pushing you down with the other.

Understanding the trauma bond is important because it's the first step in breaking free. Just like when you're playing tug-of-war, once you see the rope in your hands, you realize you can let go. Knowing that what you're feeling is because of a trauma bond means you can start to undo that knot and move towards healing your heart. It's about learning that your well-being matters more than the roller coaster of kindness and hurt, and that you have the power to say "no more" and walk away into a calmer, happier life.

OVERCOMING COGNITIVE DISSONANCE

Cognitive dissonance is like sitting in a boat that's rocking back and forth because of two very different waves. On one side, you have your thoughts about someone you know who might not treat you well. You might feel like you care for them, and sometimes they can be really nice to you. This makes you want to stay close to them, like a warm, sunny spot on a cold day. On the other side, you have the wave that comes crashing in when they hurt you with their actions or words. When this happens, your feelings get all mixed up because you know it's not right.

This rocking boat can make you feel stuck, like your foot's caught in thick mud. You want to leave, but something pulls you back. This trap is something we call a trauma bond. It's a sneaky link that ties you to someone who's not good for you, and it's tough to break.

Now, imagine you have a personal rule or belief, like "Treat others as you would like to be treated." You believe in kindness and respect. But the person you're stuck to keeps being mean or selfish, and that doesn't match with your values at all. You might try to brush it off, thinking, "Oh, they had a bad day," but deep down, you feel that something's wrong.

Experts like Dr. Stephanie Sarkis tell us that seeing this mismatch is key. It's like realizing you're wearing a red sock and a blue sock when you thought they matched. Once you see the difference, you can't unsee it. Recognizing this clash is the first step to untangling yourself from the messy ropes of the trauma bond.

We all want to make sense of things, to have a story that flows nicely without big gaps or snags. But staying with a narcissistic person—it's like trying to read a book with pages ripped out. Dr. Sarkis encourages us to look at those ripped pages and ask, "Do these missing pieces align with who I am and what I believe in? Is this the complete story I want to live?"

When the actions of the narcissistic person keep clashing with your beliefs, it's time to listen to that jarring note in the melody. It's tough. It's like admitting your favorite sweater has a hole in it. But acknowledging the problem means you can start to fix it—or find a new sweater.

By recognizing this discord and understanding that you deserve a story that's whole and true to you, you can begin to loosen the grip of cognitive dissonance. It won't be easy, but imagine the relief when that boat stops rocking, and you're on solid ground, walking in a direction that feels right to you. This is your journey to finding peace and getting back to a place where your thoughts and feelings are in harmony, like a gentle tune that soothes the soul.

EMOTIONAL DETACHMENT: CREATING DISTANCE

Breaking free from a trauma bond with a narcissist is tough. It's like untangling yourself from a web that's sticky and confusing. But it's a critical step to healing and finding peace. One very strong tool in your toolkit for this is emotional detachment. Let me walk you through what it is and how you can make it a part of your life.

Emotional detachment isn't about not caring or shutting down your feelings. It's about taking a step back so that your emotions don't control you, especially when dealing with a narcissist whose influence has been harmful to your well-being. Emotional detachment is about finding a space where you can observe your feelings without letting them dictate your actions.

Imagine your feelings are like wild horses. Without a skilled rider, they can run in any direction they choose. Emotional detachment is like becoming that skilled rider. You're learning to guide your emotions rather than letting them run away with you.

Mindfulness is a great way to start practicing emotional detachment. It's about living in the present moment and noticing what's going on around you and inside you. When you're mindful, you recognize what you feel, but you don't get swept away by those feelings. You might notice, for example, "I am feeling sad" or "I am feeling angry," without letting those emotions determine your next action.

Meditation goes hand-in-hand with mindfulness. It's like giving your brain a break. For a few minutes every day, you sit quietly and focus on something simple, like your breath or a word you repeat in your mind. If thoughts come, and they will, you gently push them away without getting upset at yourself. Meditation creates a calm space within you, and this calm stays with you, helping you stay detached in emotionally charged situations.

Practicing emotional detachment, as explained by Perpetua Neo, a psychotherapist, is not about running away or ignoring your feelings. Instead, it's about managing them in smarter ways. Neo describes this as being in charge of your feelings so you can respond rather than react to situations. This means, instead of instantly reacting to something the narcissist does or says—which could start a storm of emotions—you take a moment. You breathe. You recognize your feelings. And then, deliberately, you decide how you'll respond.

This kind of response gives you power because it comes from a place of choice, not habit or hurt. Emotional detachment helps break the cycle where the narcissist's behavior triggers an automatic emotional reaction from you.

Healing is a journey, and it takes time. but each day as you practice emotional detachment through mindfulness and meditation, you'll find you're a step closer to freedom. little by little, those wild horses of emotion can be tamed, and you'll have the reins firmly in your hands.

BUILDING A SUPPORT NETWORK: YOU'RE NOT ALONE

Recovering from a difficult experience, especially one that involves another person who may not have treated you family members or new acquaintances who have faced similar challenges—people who understand what you're going through and can offer the kind of help you need.

A solid support network doesn't just cheer you on. It's like a safety net, catching you when you feel like you might fall. These people, or groups, provide emotional support to help you through the hard times. Sometimes, just knowing you are not alone in your feelings and experiences can be comforting. If you are feeling sad or frustrated, a support network can offer kind words and a listening ear. They can remind you of your strengths and the progress you've already made, which can be a great boost when you're feeling down.

Besides the emotional part, a good support network can give practical advice. Maybe they've been in your shoes before and can share what helped them recover. They can assist in finding resources like books, helpful articles, or professionals like therapists who specialize in helping people who have been hurt by others.

In today's world, the internet can be a powerful place to find people who get what you're going through. Take Reddit's r/Narcissistic-Abuse forum, for example. It is an online space filled with people from all over the world who have gone through or are currently navigating the impact of being close to someone harmful to their well-being. If you're awake in the middle of the night feeling alone with your thoughts, someone across the globe might be there to talk to you. They might share their story and show you how they're working to feel better. This can give you hope and show you that recovery is possible.

If you prefer connecting with people in person, check out your local community centers or places that offer therapy groups. You may find workshops or groups curated for people who have had similar experiences to yours. Going to these can be scary at first, but finding the courage to step into a space where others are waiting to lend you a hand can make a big difference in your recovery.

Don't forget to reach out to trusted friends and family, too. They might not fully understand what you went through, but if they care about you, they'll be there to support you in any way they can. Even if it's just a friend to sit with you, sharing a coffee and a laugh, that kind of support matters too.

With a supportive network, both online and in the real world, you're not walking the path to recovery alone. Every message, every meetup, and every kind word is a step forward, and with each step, you get stronger and more capable of overcoming the challenges you face.

SEEKING PROFESSIONAL HELP: THERAPISTS AND COUNSELORS

When someone experiences a trauma bond, their connection with another person is not built on mutual kindness and respect. Instead, it's like being stuck in a loop where they feel powerless and yet deeply tied to someone who hurts them. This can happen in different kinds of relationships, like with family or even a partner.

Therapists and counselors play a crucial role in aiding individuals who are struggling to break free from trauma bonds. They are like skilled guides who can help you find your way out of a confusing and often painful maze. These professionals have a toolbox full of methods to help their clients understand what a trauma bond is, how it affects them, and the ways to move beyond it.

Getting professional help may seem like a big step, but it's often a necessary one to heal and find a happier life path. A big part of the work involves learning about trauma bonds. It's like getting a map that helps you see where you are and where you need to go. With the help of a therapist or counselor, you start to notice the patterns that keep you tied to the hurtful relationship.

There are specific organizations, like the International Society for the Study of Trauma and Dissociation (ISSTD), that have experts trained in helping people recover from deep emotional wounds. These folks understand the tricky nature of trauma bonds and they know how to support you on your journey to break free. They're like teachers who specialize in a subject, giving you the focused help you need.

One of the tools these therapists often use is called cognitive-behavioral therapy, commonly known as CBT. Think of CBT as a process that helps you clean out and reorganize a closet full of thoughts and behaviors that no longer serve you well. It helps you question and change the harmful ideas that the trauma bond has planted in your mind. For example, you might believe that you deserve to be treated badly or that you can't live without the person who hurts you. CBT helps you challenge these thoughts and replace them with healthier, more accurate beliefs.

It's like switching the lens on a camera to bring a clear picture into focus. With the therapist's help, you practice new ways of thinking and acting that support your well-being. It takes time and sometimes it's uncomfortable, like learning to ride a bike after only ever walking. But with patience and practice, the new habits can take hold, making it easier to steer away from the trauma bond and towards a brighter, healthier relationship with yourself and others.

In sum, therapists and counselors are invaluable in dealing with trauma bonds. With their specialized knowledge and tools like CBT, they can light the path to a better understanding of oneself and the development of stronger, more positive connections.

SELF-CARE AND RECOVERY: HEALING FROM WITHIN

When someone has been hurt by a person who thinks only of themselves—a narcissist—it's like walking through a storm without an umbrella. Recovering from such an experience can feel like drying off and warming up after being cold and wet. Self-care is the warm blanket and hot tea that can help the heart and mind find comfort again.

Self-care is about looking after yourself in a kind and loving way, just like you might care for a delicate flower in a garden. It involves actions and thoughts that can help you feel better and healthier— not only on the outside but also deep inside where your emotions live. Taking care of yourself can help you get back the strength that the stormy relationship with a narcissist might have taken away.

One self-care practice that is especially helpful is writing in a journal. Imagine having a special book that listens to all your thoughts without judgment or interruption. That's what a journal can be. When you write down your feelings, you give yourself a chance to understand them. Seeing your thoughts on paper can also help you notice patterns and learn more about yourself. Journaling is a place to be completely honest, which can be a step to healing.

Mindfulness exercises are also a gentle tool for those who have felt the sharp edge of narcissistic abuse. These exercises help by teaching you to live in the present moment, to breathe deeply, and to be aware of your surroundings. Mindfulness means paying attention to now, not the painful yesterdays or the uncertain tomorrows. It's like giving your busy mind a break and saying, "For right now, let's just be still and quiet."

Adding physical activity to your daily routine is another key part of self-care. Do you remember how free you felt as a child when running around or dancing just for fun? Moving your body can bring back some of that joy. Whether it's a simple walk, yoga, or dancing to your favorite song in the living room, physical activity gives you a chance to let out stress and welcome in fresh, positive energy.

Dr. Ramani Durvasula, a wise teacher on the journey to heal from narcissistic abuse, speaks strongly about the power of self-care. She knows how tough the path can be and reminds us that just as you might wrap a wound with a bandage to heal, self-care wraps your spirit in protection and love. Dr. Ramani urges people to make self-care a regular part of their lives, not just something you turn to in tough times.

The road to recovering your emotional health and well-being after being with a narcissist is not a race. it's a personal journey, and it's important to take it one step at a time. like a garden after the rain, with patience, love, and care, you can bloom again, brighter and stronger than before. self-care is the sunshine and water that help you on your way.

RESILIENCE AND EMPOWERMENT: MOVING FORWARD

You've been through a storm, one that has twisted and turned your world upside down. But here you are, standing firm. Know this: that stand is your power, your bravery in its purest form. It's you, showing off a strength that you might not have recognized before. It's what we call resilience. And overcoming a challenge so big—like dealing with someone who has hurt you with their self-centered actions, what you know as narcissistic abuse— that knowledge of your own resilience. Think back to the days, the moments, when you felt down and out, yet you got back up. You moved ahead. Those weren't just bad times; they were steps on a path that was about to make you stronger. It doesn't take a cape or superpowers. It's just you, and that amazing ability to bounce back, that's what we celebrate here. That toughness is your own personal tool, like a trusty hammer in a toolbox. It helps you build and shape the life you want, from today onward.

Then there's this journey—yes, it's a tough one. It's also something more. It's your chance to really, truly learn about who you are. Underneath all the noise, past the hurt, there's a person there that deserves to be known, by you most of all. This journey, as you peel back the layers, can be so exciting, like opening a gift that keeps getting better the more you unwrap it. That's your self-discovery, that's your growth. It's as though you've been given a map to the most amazing treasure, and guess what? That treasure is you.

Dr. Megan MacCutcheon, a smart person who knows lots about how our thoughts and feelings work, reminds us that making it through hard, painful times like surviving abuse from someone who only thinks of themselves can actually help us grow strong like a tall, solid tree. It's not just getting through the storm, it's using the storm to find our inner strength, our true selves.

This part of the book, this chapter, is like a friend reaching out a hand. I'm here to help with advice that you can really use, to help you step away from the pain, to heal those deep hurts, and to start building a fresh, new life for yourself. Yes, it might be tough. The road may be long. But with each step, remember that it's your mighty resilience, your newfound empowerment, carrying you forward. You have all that you need within you to not just rebuild, but to build something even more beautiful, a life where you are in control, smiling with the knowledge of just how strong you truly are.

UNLOCK THE POWER OF EMPATHY
ILLUMINATE A PATH WITH YOUR REVIEW

"Helping one person might not change the whole world, but it could change the world for one person."

— ANONYMOUS

Did you know that people who extend a helping hand without expecting anything in return tend to experience more joy and satisfaction in life? If there's a chance to spread such happiness, I believe it's worth every effort.

Here's a thought I'd like to share with you...

Would you consider shining a light for someone wandering in the dark, even if your paths might never cross?

Imagine someone out there feeling as lost and confused as Emma, stuck in the shadows of a relationship that dims their spirit. They're searching for a way out, a signpost to guide them through the maze of manipulation and gaslighting, yet they don't know where to find it.

Our purpose is to bring understanding and healing to those entangled in toxic relationships. Every action we take is rooted in this cause. But to truly make an impact, we need to reach... everyone.

This is where your kindness can make a world of difference. People often choose books based on their covers and, crucially, on the experiences shared by others through reviews. So, on behalf of someone out there who desperately needs this book but hasn't discovered it yet, I kindly ask for your assistance:

Please leave a review for this book.

This simple act requires no monetary investment and only a moment of your time, but it could be the key that unlocks a new beginning for someone else. Your review has the potential to:

- Light the way for another soul trapped in the darkness of narcissistic abuse.
- Empower someone to recognize and escape the cycle of manipulation.
- Offer hope to those questioning their reality and seeking validation.
- Help an individual understand the complex web of dark psychology they're entangled in.
- Inspire a journey towards self-discovery and freedom from codependency.

To share your light and truly make a difference, all it takes is a moment to...

leave a review.

If the idea of guiding someone out of their struggle warms your heart, then you're exactly the kind of person I hoped to connect with. Welcome to the circle of empathy - you're one of the light-bringers.

I'm eager to support you on your path to understanding, resilience, and liberation, more swiftly and effectively than you could imagine. The guidance and insights ahead promise to be enlightening.

Thank you sincerely for considering this heartfelt request. Together, let's continue to illuminate paths.

Your devoted guide, Natalie M. Brooks

PS - Remember, sharing knowledge is a powerful act of kindness. If you believe this book could serve as a beacon for someone else, don't hesitate to pass it along. It's a beautiful way to extend your light to others.

11

NAVIGATING THE MAZE: YOUR LEGAL AND PROFESSIONAL RIGHTS AND RESOURCES

When dealing with someone who may be a narcissist, it can feel like you're trapped in a tricky puzzle. But there's hope because you can learn about your legal rights, which is like finding a map that can help guide you out of that puzzle.

Let's start with a situation that's really tough: when someone faces narcissistic abuse at home. It's important to know that if you're in this spot, you're not alone and there are laws to help protect you. If you or your kids are not safe, you can ask for a restraining order or protective order. These orders are like a strong shield; they tell the person who's hurting you that they must stay away or there will be serious consequences.

Now let's talk about work. Sometimes, a person might face a narcissist at their job. This can be really hard, too. If someone is being really mean to you at work, and it makes you feel scared or uncomfortable all the time, that's not okay. You have the right to speak up. You could start by talking to Human Resources. They're there to make sure everyone feels safe at work. If talking doesn't fix things, you might have to think about taking legal action, which means asking for help from the law.

Whether at home or work, one smart thing to do is keep a record of what's happening. Imagine you're a detective collecting clues. Write down everything about the bad behavior: when it happened, where you were, and what the narcissist said or did to you. Keep these notes safe. This is super important because if you decide to ask for help from the law, these notes are like puzzle pieces that show the full picture of what's been happening to you.

And guess what? If there were people around who saw what happened, they could help tell your story, too. Their words can add more pieces to your puzzle, making it clearer for everyone to see the truth.

So, remember this key takeaway: knowing your legal rights is like turning on a light in a dark room. It shows you the way out and makes you feel strong and sure about what to do next. Whether you're dealing with a difficult situation at home or a hard time at work, understanding the law gives you choices. And with these choices, you can start to stand up for yourself and take steps toward a happier and safer life.

PROFESSIONAL RESOURCES: ALLIES IN YOUR JOURNEY

Meeting with a person who studies the mind, like a therapist or a counselor, can be a big help when dealing with a tricky character like someone with narcissism. Imagine having a guide who knows the ups and downs of the path ahead. This guide could show you how to navigate the journey and help you move forward.

Therapists who know a lot about how to help people who have been hurt by someone with narcissism are special. They can give you a set of tools to help you feel stronger and teach you how to protect your emotions. They can show you how to build a fence around your heart and mind, so the words and actions of the narcissist can't hurt you as much.

When you have someone in your family or a partner who acts in this selfish way, it can feel like you're in a boat with a tiny hole in it. The water keeps getting in, no matter how fast you try to get rid of it. Therapy for couples or the whole family could be like a patch for the boat. It can stop the water from getting in, so you can start fixing the boat. But remember, the person who helps you in therapy needs to really understand how narcissism works. Otherwise, it's like using a patch that doesn't stick to the boat.

Sometimes, dealing with a person who always puts their needs first can lead to tough legal issues. Legal experts are like captains steering you through rough sea waters. They know the maps and the stars and can guide you to a safe harbor. They can help you understand complicated rules and laws, making sure you know your rights.

If you're in a marriage that's breaking because one person is too self-centered and you have kids together, you might need to talk to a special lawyer who knows all about families. They can help you sort things out, making sure that your kids' needs come first and that they have a stable home.

And if your boss or someone you work with is showing these selfish traits and making your work life miserable, an employment lawyer might be who you need. They can listen to your story, tell you if the law can help, and plan the best way to make things better for you at work.

Using the right experts can be like having a strong team supporting you in a tough game. They have the skills to help you understand the rules, make smart decisions, and keep moving forward to a happier and healthier life.

SUPPORT GROUPS: YOU'RE NOT ALONE

Support groups represent something powerful for those who've faced the hurtful behaviors of a narcissist. They're like a warm, safe room where you're finally heard. This piece of your healing journey helps rekindle hope, understanding, and strength by connecting with others who've been where you stand. Let's talk about how support groups, both online and offline, can help people bouncing back from narcissistic abuse.

When you take part in a support group, you find a circle of friends who truly "get it." They've faced the harsh words, the mind games, and the loneliness that come from such a relationship. And by listening to their stories, it's like a light turns on, showing you that you're not the only one who's gone through these hard times. It's not about reliving the bad moments; it's about knowing others have climbed the same mountain and found their way to better days. Here, in these groups, when you talk about your own path, it's like planting your flag on the mountaintop and saying, "I'm still here, and I'm moving forward."

In today's world, finding these groups can be as easy as a click or tap on a screen. Online communities like the subreddit named r/NarcissisticAbuse have grown into spaces where voices echo with similar tales and kind words. Folks share their journeys, offer a shoulder to lean on, and reach out with tips that have worked for them. These online rooms are open night and day, letting anyone slip in and read words of encouragement or lay down a bit of their own story when the time feels right.

However, sometimes you might need help right this moment, and that's when you can turn to something like the National Domestic Violence Hotline. It's a line where someone is always waiting to pick up the phone. The caring folks on the other end are trained to help in these very moments. They listen, they understand, and they can point you to places close to you that can offer the help you need. Most importantly, everything you say to them is just between you and them—confidential.

These hotlines do more than just listen; they give advice and real steps you can take to feel safer and stronger. They're like a lighthouse, standing tall in a stormy sea, guiding boats to harbor. Whether it's bright day or darkest night, these people are there, a dependable presence ready to lead you towards calm waters.

Walking out of the shadow of narcissistic abuse takes time, and it's okay to lean on others. support groups are there to remind you of your worth, help you reclaim your story, and assure you that each step, no matter how small, is one more towards a sunny horizon.

STAYING INFORMED: KNOWLEDGE IS POWER

In life's tough moments, knowing what you can do and where you can get help is like holding a bright lantern in a dark room. When you're dealing with someone who thinks highly of themselves and cares little for others' feelings—a narcissist—this knowledge becomes even more vital. These individuals can cause real troubles in your life, and it's important to know your rights and the help that's out there for you.

One invaluable source is the National Domestic Violence Hotline website. You may wonder, "Does this relate to me?" If a narcissist's behavior is hurting you, it might. This website offers not just a nugget, but a whole mine of information. You'll find phone numbers you can call to speak with someone who will listen and care, and give you advice. The website also talks about the types of harm that aren't just physical—they can be mental tricks and games, too. And those can hurt a lot.

Now, let's talk about books. Just like a good friend, the right book can give you courage and knowledge. There's one called "The Narc

Decoder: Understanding the Language of the Narcissist" by Tina Swithin. Reading this, it's like you're getting special glasses that help you see through all the confusing things a narcissist says. It shows you ways to stay strong when they talk and talk, trying to make you feel small.

Knowledge is power, as they say. It's important to learn about narcissism itself. When you understand this thing is a real problem, not just a bad way of being, it can change your world. You'll see it's not your fault. There are even books to guide you, like "Disarming the Narcissist" by Wendy T. Behary. This book doesn't just talk about the hard stuff. It shows you how to talk back with kindness and how to reach out to the good part of the narcissist, if it's there.

It's a bit like understanding a complicated game. Once you know the rules and the tricks, you can play it better. By learning and using the right words, sometimes, you can even stop some of the pain the narcissist tries to throw at you. Even if the other person doesn't change, you'll feel different. You'll feel stronger, and you'll know you're not alone.

While books and websites can be super handy, sometimes you need more. it's okay to ask for help from those who know these games and reaching out for help when needed, you won't just cope with a narcissist—you'll take steps to reclaim your life and happiness.

MOVING FORWARD: IT GETS BETTER

When you find yourself in a tough spot with a person who has a narcissistic personality, it can feel like you're stuck in a never-ending battle. This person might always want to be the center of attention or may never seem to care about your feelings. But hold on tight because, with time and effort, things will look up.

Firstly, it's vital to have people who you can lean on—friends, family, or even professionals who understand what you're going through.

They can be your rock, the ones you share your thoughts with when times get hard. Furthermore, there are many groups and communities out there filled with individuals who have walked a similar path as you. You're not walking this road all alone.

Now, let's talk about navigating the twists and turns you might face if legal or work matters come into play. If you're dealing with a narcissist, you might find yourself needing a lawyer or advice for work-related issues. The key is to find experts who have experience with these kinds of situations. They can guide you through the confusing stuff and help protect your rights.

While you're going through this process, remember that you are a priority. It's like when you're on an airplane and they tell you to put on your own mask before helping others. Keep your body healthy by eating good foods and getting enough sleep. Rest is like recharging your body's batteries.

Moreover, taking care of your mind is just as critical. Simple things can make a big difference. You could try taking walks, listening to calming music, or even learning to say "no" when you need to. It's not being mean; it's being mindful of your own needs.

Journaling can be another helpful tool. Write down your thoughts and feelings as a way to let them out. This can help clear your mind. Think of your journal as a safe place where your thoughts can rest.

And please, don't be too hard on yourself. Dealing with a narcissist can sometimes make you feel like you're not good enough or that it's all your fault. It's not. Be kind to yourself. Remember, it's not about being perfect; it's about doing the best you can.

Lastly, consider seeking professional help if you're finding it too hard to cope. There are counselors and therapists skilled in helping people who are dealing with difficult relationships. They can give you tools and strategies to manage your emotions and help build you back up.

Things do get better. it might not happen overnight, but with the right support and resources, you will come out stronger on the other side. take it one day at a time, and trust that you're moving toward a place of peace and healing. you've got this.

12

BREAKING THE CHAINS: HEALING AND MOVING ON AFTER NARCISSISTIC ABUSE

In the journey of picking up the pieces after a storm of narcissistic abuse, the first step must be to see the need to move forward. This is no small feat. Acknowledging that the connection you had with another person was toxic is not easy. It might be a friendship, a love, or the bond with someone in your family. But the truth is, to heal, you must first see the relationship for what it was, and understand how it affected you.

Narcissistic abuse often involves a pattern that can break your spirit. You may have been made to feel small, unworthy, or constantly at fault. You may have faced manipulation so subtle that you questioned your own reality. Now is the moment to put the pieces together and see the whole picture. Don't blame yourself; it's not a sign of your weakness. Narcissists are skilled at control and often leave chaos in their wake.

Realize this: you cannot force a narcissist to change. More importantly, you need to believe in your heart that you deserve better. It's not just okay but absolutely necessary to put yourself first sometimes. Your feelings are important, and your well-being is priceless. Choosing your own health and peace is not selfish—it's self-respect.

As you look ahead, it might feel like you're in a deep hole of pain and sadness. These feelings are your soul's way of saying that being mistreated is not okay. Betrayal cuts deep, and it's natural to be hurt by someone you opened your heart to. It's also normal to grieve not only the end of your relationship but also the loss of the person you wanted to believe in. You might have held an image of who the narcissist could be—but that was a mirage, a false promise that left you stranded.

Moving forward isn't about pretending none of it ever happened. You don't need to forgive or forget the hurt caused by a narcissist to heal. To move on is to liberate yourself from the emotional chains that bind you to those painful memories. It's about saying "no more" to being defined by how someone else treated you.

The road to reclaiming your life is about building a new story, one where you choose the narrative and turn the pages at your own pace. Healing is letting the past be a lesson, not an anchor. And in this new chapter, it's the light of your regained strength that illuminates the way. Welcome to your recovery, where each step forward is an act of courage, a personal triumph, and a reclaiming of the life you were always meant to live.

CUTTING OFF CONTACT: BUILDING PHYSICAL AND EMOTIONAL BOUNDARIES

When you're dealing with a narcissist, it can feel like you're stuck in a storm of tricky mind games and hurt feelings. Just remember, it's okay to find a way out of that storm. Cutting off contact with the person could be your safe harbor, a way to stop further hurt and tricky behavior from happening.

Imagine you have a phone that keeps getting messages that make you feel bad or uneasy. One way to keep your peace is by blocking that person's number. You can do the same with social media, where they might try to reach out to you or follow what you're doing. By blocking them, you create a little bubble where their words can no longer reach you.

Now, let's say you live in the same house or your homes are close by. It's like living next to a noisy street that's always disrupting your calm. In this case, it could mean finding a new place to live or changing your routine so you don't cross paths with them. It's like moving to a quiet neighborhood where you can relax and breathe easier.

But keeping away is not just about physical distance. It's also about the invisible fences we put around our feelings. Think of it as wearing a raincoat in a downpour — it keeps you dry no matter how hard it rains. You don't let the narcissist's hurtful words touch your heart. And it's important to remember, whatever they do or say, it's not your fault. There's no good reason for someone to treat another person badly.

Of course, making the choice to step away can be really hard. You might feel a weight of guilt on your shoulders or fear like a dark cloud over your head. The person you're distancing yourself from might try to make you feel wrong for wanting to leave. They might say things to make you feel guilty or even scare you into staying.

That's when talking to people you trust can be a big help. Friends and family can be there for you just like a sturdy umbrella in a storm. They can remind you that you deserve to be treated well. Sometimes, it helps to talk to a counselor who is trained to help people going through hard times. They're like the lighthouse guiding ships away from rocky shores.

By choosing to block out a narcissist and protect your feelings, you're taking steps toward a happier, healthier life. It's like choosing sunshine after so many days of rain. And while it can be challenging, with good support and strong boundaries, you can navigate away from the hurt and toward a brighter, quieter horizon.

SELF-CARE PRACTICES: NURTURING YOUR MENTAL AND PHYSICAL WELL-BEING

Taking good care of yourself is like putting on a life jacket when you're about to brave wild seas. It's a strong step in the right direction on your path to feeling whole again after dealing with a harmful person, who may have left you feeling lost or small. Think about the simple things you do every day, like what you eat, how long you sleep, and how you move your body. These basics are the building blocks of your comeback.

Imagine your body as a garden that needs the right food to grow. Just like watering plants, eating good foods can make you strong. If you eat a lot of sugary or fatty foods, you might feel slow or tired. But if you eat lots of fruits, veggies, and other healthy bits, your energy can bloom like sunflowers in the sun. And don't forget rest – good sleep is like the quiet night that helps the garden cool down and get ready for the next day. Aim to sleep enough so that you wake up feeling fresh.

Moving your body is also key. This doesn't mean you have to run marathons or lift heavy weights. It can be as calm as doing yoga, which stretches your muscles and brings peace to your mind, or taking a walk, which lets you breathe in fresh air and watch the world go by. These activities can be like a soft melody that brings harmony to your day.

Now, let's talk about the inside of your mind. Just like a house needs cleaning, your thoughts and feelings do too. Mindfulness, which means paying attention to the present, can be your broom and mop. Maybe try sitting quietly and letting your thoughts pass like clouds, or writing in a journal to help sort out the jumble of feelings inside you.

Sometimes, though, you might need a friend who knows a lot about healing from hurtful relationships. A therapist is like a guide who has walked the path many times and knows where the tricky parts are. They've seen the effects of someone else's mean ways and can give you special advice. And nowadays, help can come right to your phone or computer through websites like BetterHelp or Talkspace. It's never been easier to find someone to talk to.

Finally, remember the things that make your heart sing. Everyone has something they love to do. It might be reading a book and getting swept away in a story, painting a picture with colors that express your feelings, or walking among trees and listening to birds. Doing things like these can bring back the sparkle in your eyes and remind you of who you are, a person full of life, far away from the shadow of the narcissist. Rediscover the activities that make you, you – and let them lift you up, like the sun breaking through the clouds after a storm.

BUILDING A SUPPORT NETWORK: YOU ARE NOT ALONE

Rebuilding your life after facing tough times can feel like starting from scratch. It's like planting a new garden after a storm has turned everything upside down. The first seeds you'll want to sow are the ones of connection with friends and family. They are the people who can offer you a kind of comfort nothing else can, like a warm blanket on a chilly night. This kind of support feels like a gentle pat on the back, telling you that you're doing just fine.

However, it's important to pick who you share your story with as if you were picking out the ripest, juiciest apples from a tree. Look for those friends and family who truly listen, those who understand and support you. When you speak with them, it should feel like your words are safe, tucked away in a cozy spot where they won't be picked apart or looked down on. These people see your strength and remind you that it wasn't your fault.

In the same way, there are some apples on the tree that aren't so nice - ones that are sour and make your face squish up. These might be people who, when you tell them your story, say things that aren't fair or kind. They might even make it sound like you could have prevented the hurt. It's best to step away from these folks. Let them be, like the apples you leave behind on the tree; they're not the ones that will help you heal.

Finding a group of people who have walked a path like yours can feel like coming home. A support group is like sitting around a campfire, where everyone shares their own tales and listens to yours. You'll see reflected in their eyes your own feelings - and that's a powerful thing, realizing you're not in this alone. You could start somewhere simple like the subreddit r/NarcissisticAbuse or the Survivors of Narcissistic Abuse Facebook group. These are places peppered with stories that might sound much like your own, and they're right at your fingertips.

In these groups, speaking your truth can echo back hope from others. Hearing their stories is a reminder that the storm you've been through is one that others have survived. It gives you a map to find your way out. Their courage can wrap around you like vines, supporting and lifting you towards the sunlight.

Lastly, remember - asking for help is a sign of bravery, not weakness. Sometimes, we think we need to stand alone to show we're strong, but even the mightiest of trees have deep roots that reach out for water and support. It's okay to say, "I need a friend" or "Can someone help me?" Adjusting to a life after tough times isn't a road anyone should walk with just their own shadow for company. Lean on others, and let them walk beside you. This road to healing, just like a garden, grows richer with the care of many hands.

EMBRACING THE FUTURE: LIFE AFTER NARCISSISTIC ABUSE

When we begin the journey to mend our hearts and minds after experiencing narcissistic abuse, it's essential to understand that this path is far from straight. Healing from such deep wounds requires time, and it's more than okay to have days that feel tougher than others. It's a gentle reminder to be kind to yourself. Just as a wound on the skin doesn't heal overnight, the scars left on your inner self from manipulation and abuse need moments to breathe, to build new, healthy tissue, and sometimes, that process can feel uncomfortable or downright painful.

Walking the path of recovery, you will undoubtedly encounter moments where it feels like the world is pressing down on you, where memories come flooding back, and days when you question your progress. These lows do not erase the steps forward you have taken. They are a natural rhythm in the music of healing. Acceptance of these ups and downs is pivotal. You are not a machine set to 'recovery mode;' you are a human being, beautifully complex and capable of a vast spectrum of feelings.

Amidst this, don't forget to honor every little triumph. Healing is not only about overcoming the big hurdles; it's also about the collection of tiny victories along the way. Celebrate the moment when you recognized a trigger and sidestepped it with grace. Applaud yourself for the day when you chose self-care over self-criticism. No success is too minor because in the grand tapestry of your recovery, every stitch counts.

This journey may also open the door to profound personal growth. With each step forward, you learn more about the shadowy mechanism of narcissistic control and discover ways to shield your spirit from future harm. Knowledge, in this case, becomes your armor. Simultaneously, this passage delivers you to the shores of self-discovery. As you travel, stripping away layers of pain and deceit, you unveil the raw strength and passion that was always within you. Perhaps you rediscover an old hobby that sparks joy or find confidence in a new skill that brings purpose to your days. This is the silver lining—this blossoming of your truest self.

At the heart of all this is the steadfast belief that there is life after narcissistic abuse—a life where respect, love, and happiness are not just distant dreams but tangible realities. Yes, the road may be uneven, the skies could be gray at times, but the power within you to rebuild a future of positivity and peace is immense. Always carry with you the knowledge that every effort you make is a stepping stone toward a world created on your terms, filled with the love and respect you rightly deserve.

13

SELF-CARE SANCTUARY: NOURISHING YOUR MIND AND BODY

Self-care is like a strong foundation for a house. When you've been through tough times with someone who didn't treat you right, like in narcissistic abuse, it's like your house has been shaken. Now it's time to rebuild, and self-care is the tool you use.

Let's explore what self-care really means. It's not just about treating yourself to a bubble bath or a chocolate treat, though those things can be nice. Self-care is deeper. It's about taking care of all parts of you—your thoughts, your feelings, your body, and even your spirit. Think of it like feeding your whole self the good stuff it needs to grow and get better.

Imagine you're a plant. After a storm, you might be a bit droopy and sad. Self-care is like the sunlight, the water, and the soil that help you stand tall again. The World Health Organization, a big group that knows a lot about health, says self-care has many parts. It's got to do with staying healthy, stopping sickness before it starts, and taking good care of yourself if you do catch a cold or something worse. It also means looking after others who need you, like kids or older folks, and getting back on your feet if you've been knocked down.

For someone who's been hurt by a person who thinks only of themselves, like a narcissist, self-care is especially important. You might have forgotten how to listen to what you need because you've been too busy worrying about them. Now, it's time to tune into your own station.

Self-care can look like many things. For your mind, it might be picking up a book and getting lost in a story, or learning something new that excites you. What about your heart? That's where emotional self-care comes in. You could write down your thoughts and feelings or talk to someone who helps you make sense of them.

Your body needs attention, too. Moving around, eating foods that make you feel good, and getting plenty of rest are like giving your body a big hug. And your spirit—that quiet, sometimes whispering part of you—might like some quiet time, maybe sitting outside and just being, or finding a special practice that fills you with calm and wonder.

Doctors and scientists agree that taking good care of yourself is a big deal. It can make you feel less stressed, happier, and healthier. The University of Kentucky found that folks who practice self-care bounce back better from hard times. And the American Psychological Association, a big group of experts on how people think and behave, reminds us that self-care is key for getting through tough stuff, like the kind of hurt caused by narcissistic abuse.

So let's remember, self-care is your friend. A friend that helps you heal and get strong again. It's the steps you take every day to take care of you. And when you do that, slowly but surely, you start to feel like yourself again.

BUILDING YOUR SELF-CARE PLAN: PRACTICAL STRATEGIES AND ACTIVITIES

A self-care plan is a special way of looking after yourself that's made just for you. It's like having a map that shows you how to feel better in your mind and heart. This kind of care is all about doing things that are good for you and that you like to do. It's like putting together a recipe for a happy, healthy you.

When creating this plan, think about what works for your life. Choose things that you like and can do often. This could be something you do every day, once a week, or even once a month. What's most important is keeping it regular. It's like watering a plant; do it often enough, but it doesn't have to be a lot each time.

Here are some good things you might add to your self-care plan:

Move your body: Getting your body active is a great way to lift your mood, shake off stress, and help you sleep better at night. You could take a walk in the morning, try some fun stretches, or even dance to your favorite tunes. Pick something that makes you smile and try to do it as often as you can.

Eat yummy, healthy food: Eating well is like giving your body the fuel it needs to run smoothly. Aim to eat more things that grow from the earth like fruits and veggies, and foods that make your body strong like fish, chicken, and grains. These foods help you feel more awake and ready for the day.

Get enough sleep: Having enough sleep every night is very important. It makes you feel good and helps you think clearly. Try to go to bed at the same time each night and make your bedroom a peaceful place. You could read a little or listen to calm music before bedtime.

Be still and quiet: Taking time to be quiet and still helps your mind slow down. This could mean sitting still for a bit, taking slow breaths, or thinking about things that make you happy. Doing this helps you deal with stress better and gets you to know yourself more.

If you've been hurt by someone who always put themselves first, like a narcissist, it might be hard to start taking care of yourself. But it's okay to go slow. Try little things first and be kind to yourself. Self-care helps you heal.

Studies, like one from the University of Minnesota, show that beginning with little changes in your life can help you stick with them longer. So remember, looking after yourself isn't selfish. It's really important for helping you feel better. This is especially true when you're trying to heal from a tough time.

OVERCOMING OBSTACLES TO SELF-CARE: PRACTICAL TIPS AND SOLUTIONS

Self-care is like giving your body and mind a helping hand to feel better, even when life is busy or hard. It is very important when getting better from hurt caused by someone who only thought of themselves, like in narcissistic abuse. But making it part of your day isn't always easy. Let's look at what might stop you from taking care of yourself and how you can move past these challenges.

The first hurdle is finding the time. You might think you need hours to do self-care right. But the truth is, little drops can fill a big bucket over time. If your days are packed with jobs, family, or other big things, you can still sneak in moments for yourself. It can be as quick as taking deep breaths for five minutes, going for a short walk while you have your lunch break, or enjoying a few pages of a story before you sleep. These small acts can give you a boost without needing a lot of time.

Another roadblock is the feeling of guilt. After dealing with someone who always put their needs first, you might feel wrong when you start to think about yourself. You might worry that taking care of yourself means you're not caring for others. But this is not true. Looking after yourself isn't just okay; it's very important. It helps you heal and be strong, so you can be there for others too. Think of it like when you are on an airplane, and they tell you to put on your oxygen mask before helping others. Self-care is your oxygen mask.

Then there's the matter of what you have to work with. Maybe you believe you need a lot of money or fancy things to take care of yourself. But self-care doesn't need to cost a lot. It can be as simple and free as making a meal that makes you feel good, walking in a park and watching the trees and animals, or calling a good friend to chat. These things can relax you and make your day brighter.

Taking care of yourself means making a space where you feel safe and can heal. It's about getting back the time, being kind to your body, and feeling good that was taken by someone who didn't treat you well. The National Alliance on Mental Illness says that when you take care of yourself, you can handle stress better, enjoy life more, and keep yourself healthier for a long time. Remember, looking after yourself is a big step to feeling better and living a happier life.

14

MINDFUL MOMENTS: HARNESSING INNER PEACE AMID CHAOS

Healing from the hurt of being with a person who only thinks of themselves is a tough road. It can leave deep marks on the heart and mind. One strong tool we've got in fixing those hurts is something called mindfulness.

Now, what is mindfulness? It's a kind of skill that lets us be totally here and now. We pay close attention to this very moment, nice and easy, without our minds running off to think about yesterday or worrying about tomorrow. Imagine you're sitting at a park. Mindfulness is taking in every bit of that scene: the fresh green grass, the way the breeze feels, the kids playing at a distance. We just soak it all in without judging if it's 'good' or 'bad.'

A smart person named Jon Kabat-Zinn, who knows a lot about mindfulness, says it's like this: it's "paying attention in a particular way: on purpose, in the present moment, and nonjudgmentally." That means we look at what's happening right now, on purpose, without saying it's good or bad. Just noticing and accepting.

For those who've been hurt by a person who tries to control every-thing and thinks they're the best – what we call a narcissist – mind-fulness is like an anchor. When memories of bad things try to pull you back, or fears of the future try to scare you, this anchor holds you safe in the here and now. You don't get tossed about by the waves of past hurts or future worries.

Scientists have put mindfulness to the test and guess what? They found out that it does some good stuff for us. It can help us feel calm and less stressed. For instance, a report from 2013 in "Perspectives on Psychological Science," a big, important magazine for people who study the mind and behaviour, shared that mindfulness meditation helps people feel less stress and worry.

When you've been through a lot with a narcissist, your mind gets really used to feeling stressed and on edge. You might find yourself always ready for the next bad thing to happen. Mindfulness helps to change that. It teaches your mind to rest in the now, to take a break from fighting battles that are either long gone or haven't even started.

So, how do you do mindfulness? You can start simple. Find yourself a quiet spot. Sit down, let your hands rest, and begin to notice your breath. You breathe in, you breathe out – just pay attention to that. When thoughts about yesterday or later Tonight pop up, you just gently bring your attention back to your breathing. That's the start of being mindful. It's like a muscle, the more you practice, the stronger it gets, and the better you get at staying in the present.

When the storms inside get wild because of the hurt a narcissist caused you, remember that a calm and peaceful spot exists in the now, and mindfulness can help you get there.

INTEGRATING MINDFULNESS INTO DAILY LIFE: SIMPLE TECHNIQUES

In the swirl and rush of our days, it's easy to feel lost or unsettled. But there are simple ways to find calm and stay rooted, like with mindfulness. Mindfulness is being fully there in the moment, noticing everything around you and inside you without judgment. This can help manage stress and keep you steady even when things are wild.

One easy way to start is by using the "5-4-3-2-1" grounding technique. It's like a game for your senses that you can do anywhere. First, name five things you can see. Maybe it's the bright red of a stop sign, the soft curls of a dog in the park, or the dance of leaves in the wind. Next, notice and name four things you can touch. It might be the cool smoothness of your phone screen, the warmth of the sun on your arm, or the feeling of your feet on the ground. Then, close your eyes and name three things you can hear. You might hear the chatter of people nearby, the hum of cars on the street, or the distant song of a bird. After that, name two things you can smell. Maybe it's the fresh grass or the sharp tang of coffee from a nearby cafe. Finally, name one thing you can taste, even if you're not eating—perhaps the minty taste of toothpaste from brushing your teeth or the linger of orange juice from breakfast.

Another practice is mindful breathing. This is when you pay close attention to your breath. Sit comfortably, take a slow breath in, and feel the air fill your lungs. Hold it for a brief moment, and then let it out gently. Notice the sensation of air moving in and out of your nose or mouth, the rise and fall of your chest or belly. Whenever you feel jumbled up inside, come back to this feeling. Just a few minutes can make a difference.

Mindful eating is also a great way to weave mindfulness into daily life. So often, we eat while we're doing other things and don't really taste our food. But try this: take a small bite of something, maybe a piece of fruit. Chew slowly. Notice the texture, the taste—it's sweetness or tartness, the way it feels in your mouth. With each bite, take your time. It's not only a way to enjoy your food more, but it also helps you listen to when your body says it's full.

Mindfulness doesn't have to be complicated or take a lot of time. Simple practices like these can fit into any schedule and can be anchors that bring you back to the here and now, making space for peace amid the hustle of life.

THE POWER OF MEDITATION: CULTIVATING INNER PEACE

Let's begin by looking closer at meditation. Picture it like exercise, but instead of moving your body, you're exercising your mind. The main goal? To help you find peace and stability within yourself.

Now, imagine if each thought in our mind was a loud noise in a crowded room. Meditation helps turn down the volume, so we can hear our own voice clearer. One way to meditate is by using mindfulness. This means paying attention to what is happening right now, in the present moment, without getting lost in thoughts about the past or future.

Another way to meditate is by focusing on something specific, like your breath, a sound, or even an object. By doing this, it's like you're training your brain to stay on one path, instead of wandering off into many different directions. Like when you're exercising, staying on track can be hard at first, but with practice, it gets easier.

Meditation is like a tool that can help fix some of the hurt and stress life throws our way. Think about stress; it's like carrying a heavy backpack all day. Now, what if meditation could help you take that backpack off for a bit? Research, like the study from "JAMA Internal Medicine," tells us that it can. It's also been found to improve how we understand our feelings and it can make us feel better about ourselves and our lives.

Why is this important if someone has experienced harm from another person, especially someone who thought only about themselves? This kind of hurt can leave you feeling stressed and anxious. Meditation can be a quiet space for your heart and mind to heal. It's like giving them a kind and gentle hug.

If you've never tried meditation, or the idea seems a bit strange, there are helpers out there in the form of apps. Headspace and Calm, for example, are like friends who can guide you along the way. They use simple words and instructions to walk with you into the world of meditation. You don't need any special equipment, just you and maybe your phone or computer.

And remember, like learning any new skill, it takes time. You won't turn into a meditation expert overnight, and that's perfectly okay. The key is to be patient with yourself and keep going, even if it's just for a few minutes each day.

OVERCOMING OBSTACLES TO MINDFULNESS AND MEDITATION

When you've been hurt by someone who only thinks about themselves—a narcissist—finding peace can feel like a tough journey. Being mindful and meditating are like super tools that can help fix your heart and mind. But it's not always easy to pick up these tools and get to work. As you try to heal, you might bump into a few roadblocks on the way.

One big roadblock is not having enough time. You might think, "I'm so busy! How can I add one more thing to my day?" But good news: finding a calm moment doesn't have to take long. A smart group of scientists showed in 2014 that even if you just sit quietly and breathe for a couple of minutes—like 2 or 3—you can chase away some stress and find a little bit of calm. Think about it, that's less time than it takes to make a cup of tea!

Each tiny moment you give yourself to just be can help build a stronger you. Even on a busy day, you can take a short walk, breathe deep while waiting for the bus, or just be still before you start your car.

But let's talk about another bump you might hit. Some people think that to meditate right, you need to make your mind as blank as a fresh piece of paper. But that's not true. Our minds are always buzzing like a busy bee with thoughts, and that's okay. Meditation isn't about fighting those thoughts; it's more like sitting by a river and watching leaves float by. You see them, but you don't have to grab them. You let them drift without making a big fuss.

Starting out, it's normal to feel like you're not getting it or to get antsy sitting there. Maybe you're thinking, "Why isn't anything happening? Shouldn't I feel different by now?" But remember, it's like planting a seed. You can't rush a flower to bloom, and the same goes for mindfulness and meditation. It grows a bit each day.

When you first start, make it simple. Do it just a little. Maybe today you sit for two minutes, and next week you try three. It's all about taking baby steps. Before you know it, those minutes will add up, and you'll start seeing changes, like feeling a bit lighter inside.

So, even though there might be obstacles, please don't give up. Remember, every little bit counts, and it's okay to start small. Keep at it, and slowly but surely, you'll find your way toward healing from the hurt a narcissist has left behind.

MINDFULNESS AND SELF-CARE: PRIORITIZING YOUR WELL-BEING

In this important part of your healing journey, self-care should stand high on your list of things to do. The term "self-care" often brings to mind images of taking long baths, eating healthy foods, or getting enough sleep. But there's a part of self-care that's just as key, though sometimes less talked about. This part is about looking after your mind and your heart. It's about being kind to yourself by learning how to be in the moment—this is where mindfulness and meditation come in.

Mindfulness is about being totally present. It means paying attention to what you're doing, how you're feeling, and what's happening around you right now—not in the past, not in the future, but at this moment. When you've gone through tough times, especially if someone with a very strong and tough personality has hurt you, your mind may keep running back to those tough times or worrying about the future. Mindfulness can help you put those thoughts to the side and focus on what you're feeling right now.

Starting to practice mindfulness can be as simple as taking a few moments to notice how you're sitting or standing. Feel the ground or chair support you, notice the air around you, listen to the sounds that usually slip past you. By doing this, you give your mind a rest from the heavy thoughts it's been carrying.

In comes meditation, which is like a workout for your mindfulness muscles. It's taking time to sit quietly and just be. There are lots of ways to meditate, but a simple one is to sit in a quiet spot, close your eyes, and pay attention to your breathing. When you breathe in, be aware of the air filling your lungs, and when you breathe out, imagine you're letting go of all the stress and tightness. If your mind starts to wander to other thoughts (and it will), that's okay—just gently bring your focus back to your breath.

By making mindfulness and meditation part of your daily routine, you start building a habit of tuning in to your feelings and needs. This can make a huge difference. You learn to notice when you're getting tired or upset and can then decide to slow down or ask for some help. It helps you spot what your heart needs and if you're being too hard on yourself.

Remembering to take care of yourself isn't selfish. It's actually really important. Picture yourself as a garden. Without water and sunlight, the garden can't bloom. You're the same. By giving yourself the kindness of mindfulness and meditation, you're watering your spirit and letting light in. Those small moments of peace make you stronger, more able to deal with life, and put you on a path where healing can begin.

15
UNLEASHING THE HEALING POWER OF WORDS: EMBRACING JOURNALING FOR RECOVERY

Journaling is like opening a door to a safe room where you can let out all your feelings without anyone telling you you're wrong. It's a personal space, just for you, where you can write down your thoughts and feelings. When something bad happens—like being hurt by someone who only cares about themselves, which we call narcissistic abuse—journaling can help a lot.

Imagine your mind is like a garden. Just like a garden can have weeds, your mind can have tough memories or feelings. Journaling helps you pull out these "weeds" so the beautiful parts of your garden can grow better. When you have been treated badly, writing it down can make the heavy feelings easier to carry. It's like having a friend who listens and doesn't judge you.

How does journaling do this? Here are a few ways:

1. **A place for your feelings:** When someone messes with your feelings, making you question what's real—this is something called gaslighting—it can confuse you. Writing helps put those twisted feelings into words, making them clearer to see.

2. **Understand the patterns:** If you keep a journal, after some time, you can look back at what you wrote and notice if the same bad things keep happening. This can help you see it's not your fault, and it's really the other person who is being mean.

3. **Heal your heart and mind:** Just like cleaning up a scratch on your knee helps it heal, writing about what hurts your heart helps it heal too. It might not be easy, but it's a big step in feeling better.

Now, you might wonder, "What should I write about?" Here are some ideas to help you start:

- Write down what happened today that made you feel bad, and then write about what could make it better.

- Think about what you would say to someone else who's been hurt the same way you have. Write that down.

- Ask yourself what you really want to be different in your life. Describe this dream day in your journal.

The key to journaling helping you is doing it often. make it part of your day, like brushing your teeth. it doesn't have to be for a long time, just enough to get your thoughts out. pick a certain time, maybe in the morning or before bed, and stick to it.

Don't worry about mistakes or making it perfect; it's just for you. The pages of your journal don't mind if you're angry, sad, or even happy — they just hold your story for you. Keep taking small steps, and one day, you'll look back and see just how far you've come.

JOURNALING PROMPTS: GUIDING YOUR PATH TO SELF-DISCOVERY AND HEALING

As you turn the pages of this book, consider it as a close friend who encourages you to speak your heart out. Writing in a journal is like having a conversation with yourself. It's a safe space where you can explore your feelings and thoughts, especially after going through tough times with a person who may not have been kind or fair to you.

Starting with the prompt, "How am I feeling today and why?" can open the door to understanding your emotions. Picture it as if you're sitting down for coffee with a friend and they ask, "How's your day going?" Take your time to think and then jot down your feelings. Are you feeling sad, happy, mixed, or blank? Thinking about why you feel that way will help you see what things in your life are making you feel good or not so good.

Next, ask yourself, "What is one thing I can do for myself today?" This is like giving yourself a small gift. Maybe it's taking a walk in the sunshine, or perhaps you would enjoy reading a chapter from your favorite book. Whatever it is, make sure it's something that brings you a little bit of joy.

When reflecting on your experiences with the difficult person in your life, use the prompt, "What patterns am I noticing in my relationship with the narcissist?" This is like playing detective with your past. By writing down patterns, you may start to see how things happened over and over again. It's a step towards understanding what you've been through.

Another reflective question to consider is, "What strengths have I discovered in myself through this experience?" This is like looking for treasures within you. You may find that you're stronger or more patient than you realized. Writing these strengths down is like collecting gems to remember how capable you are.

It's also important to think about the road ahead. With the prompt, "What would I like my life to look like a year from now?" imagine you're an artist painting your future. What colors and images would you put on your canvas? Let your imagination guide you, and write about the life you wish for yourself.

Then, think about "What steps can I take today towards my healing?" This is like plotting a path on a map for a trip. Consider small, doable steps that can lead you towards feeling better. Write these down to remind yourself of the direction you want to go.

Finally, consider, "What qualities do I want in my relationships?" and "What boundaries will I set in my future interactions?" This is like building a house where you decide what materials to use so it's safe and strong. Write down the qualities you want from others and how you'll make sure to keep your relationships healthy.

These journal prompts are just starting points. They can be the keys to unlock what's in your heart and help you to heal and grow stronger. Remember, each word you write in your journal is a step forward on your path to a happier life.

THE ART OF CONSISTENT JOURNALING: BUILDING AND MAINTAINING YOUR PRACTICE

When you pick up your journal, it's like opening a door just for you, where your thoughts can breathe and stretch out. To get all the good you can from writing in this book, it helps to do it a lot—like how if you want to get strong, you might do push-ups every day. Imagine doing a kind of workout for your heart and mind—that's what journaling can be when you make it part of your regular life.

You might choose to write every day or every week. By doing it on a schedule, it will become something you count on, just like eating lunch or brushing your teeth. What's awesome about this is that when you look back at what you've written, you can see how you've changed, spot things that happen again and again, and notice how you've gotten stronger over time.

Wouldn't it be great if after going through tough times, like dealing with someone who was not good to you, you had a secret strength-training tool? That's what journaling can be. Creating a comforting rhythm with your writing helps heal the hurt and adds structure to days that might sometimes feel messy.

But, let's be real, keeping this up isn't always easy. On days when the couch and a good show call your name, it can be tough to pull out your pen and paper. To make it easier, think about setting up a space that makes you smile—a cozy corner with a comfy chair, a plant or two, and maybe some soft music. This is your special spot where you can snuggle into the words and let them flow.

You can also hook your writing time to something you already do. Maybe in the morning, when the world is quiet and your coffee is steaming. Or at night, slipping words onto paper as your eyes grow heavy. It's like inviting journaling to join you at these familiar times, and before you know it, reaching for your journal will feel as natural as reaching for the light switch.

Remember too, there's no perfect way to do this. Your journal is not a test, and there are no grades. It's okay if some days your writing is just a few scribbles and others it's pages deep. This is your space, your story, your journey. Take the pressure off. When you realize your journal is your friend, one that's happy to hear whatever you've got to say, you'll keep coming back.

Having this little book can be a soft place to land on hard days and a treasure box for your brightest moments. With each word you write, you're building a bridge to a stronger, more peaceful you. Keep walking on it, one page at a time.

OVERCOMING JOURNALING CHALLENGES: NAVIGATING EMOTIONAL BLOCKS AND RESISTANCE

When writing about the hard things in life or the big feelings that shake us up, you might find it isn't easy. Sometimes, trying to put those thoughts on paper can make us stop in our tracks. It's like hitting a wall inside our minds that makes us want to run the other way. But it's important to remember that it's normal to feel this way. Everyone who tries to heal through writing will face this at some time.

As you sit down with your journal, ready to let your emotions flow onto the page, be kind to yourself. Imagine you're talking to a good friend. You wouldn't rush them or be tough on them. So, treat yourself with the same kindness. Healing isn't a race; it's more like a walk through your own story at your own pace.

Let's say you've got a big, scary emotion or a memory that feels huge and heavy. If thinking about it makes you feel like you can't breathe, it's okay to put your pen down. You don't have to write about it now. It's not going anywhere. Instead, you might choose to write about something smaller that day. Maybe talk about what you had for lunch or the bird you saw on your walk. There are no rules that say you must write about the hard stuff first.

If you're ready to try tackling those big feelings, here's a way to make it a bit easier. Think about breaking it up into pieces. Instead of trying to write the whole story, just write a little bit. Even one sentence is a good start. Write a little, then take a break. This makes it less scary and more doable.

Before you even start writing, you can do something to make yourself feel calm and safe. This could be taking three deep breaths, listening to a song you love, or even hugging a pillow. Find a calm exercise that works for you, and do it before you write to create a safe space for your thoughts.

Lastly, remember it's okay to ask for help. Talking with someone you trust can make a world of difference. It could be a friend, a family member, or maybe a therapist who understands how journaling can help you heal. Sharing what you're going through can lift some of the weight off your shoulders. Then, you're not alone with those big feelings. They're there to listen and support you as you write your way to feeling better.

No matter what you face inside your journal, be patient. It's your story, your healing journey, and you're doing just fine.

BEYOND WORDS: EXPLORING ART AND VISUAL JOURNALING

Journaling is often thought of as writing down words—your day's stories or your heart's whispers. But journaling doesn't have to be just about words. Art or visual journaling is another wonderful way to say what's on your mind or in your soul. This kind of journaling is about using pictures, colors, shapes, and forms to share your feelings and thoughts, especially those that might not come out easily in words.

Imagine trying to say how you feel when words just aren't enough, or when what's inside you is so big or mixed up that you can't find the right words. That's when art journaling can shine. It gives you the freedom to let your hand move and your mind wander, without worrying about making sentences or spelling things right. By drawing or painting, you can show your emotions or what you've been through in a way that is personal and just for you.

Some people think they're not good at art, but art journaling isn't about being good. It's about letting what's inside you out in a different way. When you tap into making art, you wake up a different side of your brain. This creative side can take you on new paths, showing you new ways to see yourself and how to heal.

Let's talk about how you could do this. One day, you might feel sad or happy, confused or clear, and instead of finding words, you pick up colors that speak for those emotions. You start to draw or paint how you feel. Another day, you could cut pictures from magazines or print them, and arrange them into a collage. These pictures might show different parts of your life, like footsteps on a long road, showing where you've been and where you're going. Sometimes, symbols or metaphors—a key, a bridge, a storm cloud—appear on your pages, telling a story about your experiences or feelings.

It doesn't matter how it turns out. what matters is that it's true for you. in art journaling, every color smeared on a page, every line, and every symbol is a part of your story. no judging, no rules. if it's real for you, then it's perfect. the goal is to express yourself.

Art journaling is a door open for you whenever words aren't enough, or when you just want to see your life in colors and shapes. It's a way to heal, to understand yourself a bit more, and to say without words, "This is me, and this is my journey."

16

THE TIES THAT BIND: NAVIGATING AND HEALING FROM A NARCISSISTIC RELATIONSHIP

In this detailed section of the chapter, we're going to look closely at someone's journey through a tough relationship with a narcissistic partner. When we talk about narcissism, we mean a way some people are that makes them think they are the most important person in the world and that their feelings are the only ones that matter.

When this person first met their partner, it was like a dream come true. Their partner was so lively and seemed to light up the room. They told exciting stories and made big promises that made the future look bright.

But as time went on, the dream started to feel like a trick. The partner, who had first seemed like the star of a happy movie, was starting to show signs that were worrying. You see, the partner loved to talk – but only about themselves. Every conversation, no matter how it started, ended up being about their thoughts, their wants, and their stories. It was like they were the sun, and everyone else, including our friend in this story, was just a planet spinning around them.

It wasn't just that they talked about themselves a lot, either. They acted as if they were the smartest and most talented person around. They could do no wrong in their own eyes and they wanted everyone else to agree. They would tell tales of things they did that seemed too good to be true. And often, they were. The partner liked to make their life sound like a grand adventure, with them as the hero, even if it meant stretching the truth.

The most painful part for our friend, though, was how cold their partner could be. When they had a rough day or were feeling down, the partner didn't seem to care. If our friend was happy about something, the partner would find a reason why it wasn't such a big deal or would switch the topic to their own successes. There was no comfort, no shared joy – just a one-sided relationship where only one person's feelings mattered.

This left our friend feeling lonely and confused. They started to question their value and wonder if their feelings were worth anything. It's tough to stand strong when someone you care about only sees you as a background character in their show.

But our friend's story doesn't end here. As we move on, we will see how they began to see these patterns for what they were – red flags of a narcissistic behavior. And once they spotted them, they could start on their path to healing, which we'll explore further in the next sections of this chapter.

GASLIGHTING AND MANIPULATION: THE NARCISSIST'S TOOLS OF CONTROL

As the relationship moved forward, things began to change in ways that were hard to see at first. The partner, who once seemed so kind and understanding, started playing mind games. These games are tricks a person might use to get someone else to do what they want.

It's like they were following a hidden plan, a way to make sure they were always the one in charge.

One of their tricks was to mess with the truth. Sometimes when something happened, and it was clear as day, the partner would say it didn't happen at all, or it happened in a whole other way. This made their partner feel confused. "Did I remember that right?" they would wonder. It was like trying to grab onto water; the more they tried to hold onto what really happened, the more it seemed to slip through their fingers.

Then there were the small, hurtful comments. Whenever the partner shared their thoughts, the other would laugh or say they were being silly. "You're just too sensitive," they'd say when their partner spoke up about feeling hurt. Over time, this made their partner quiet down. They stopped sharing as much because every time they did, it felt like those words went into a black hole, never to be seen or heard.

Guilt turned into an invisible chain that kept their partner close. If there was something the partner wanted to do that didn't match what the other wanted, suddenly there'd be talks about how much they had given up for the relationship, or how ungrateful their partner was being. "After all I've done for you, how could you be so selfish?" they'd ask. So the partner, not wishing to be seen as bad or ungrateful, would drop what they wanted and fall in line.

Blame was another card played often. Let's say there was a mistake, or something happened that wasn't great. Instead of talking it out, or sharing the blame, it became a game of 'hot potato.' The partner always ended up holding it, being told it was their fault, even when it wasn't. This made them feel like they were always walking on eggshells, careful with every step, every word.

This blend of turning the truth upside down, making someone feel small, using guilt as chains, and always being blamed can make a person really tired. It can make them start to believe that maybe they're not so smart, or that their feelings aren't right to have. It's a way to make someone hand over their power piece by piece, without even knowing they're doing it. The partner ended up feeling like they were in a fog, trying to find their way back to who they were before it all started.

THE IMPACT: EMOTIONAL TURMOIL AND CONFUSION

As days turned into weeks and weeks into months, the changes in their emotional well-being were impossible to ignore. It was like an invisible weight had started to press down on their shoulders, growing heavier with each day. Dealing with a partner whose words twisted reality was like living in a warped mirror maze, where every reflection cast doubt on what they saw, thought, and even felt. This relentless mental game had a name: gaslighting. It's when someone makes you question your own memory and sanity, and that's exactly what was happening to them.

The individual began to doubt their judgment on even the smallest things. When they tried to recall an event or a conversation, their partner would insist it had never happened or had occurred in a completely different way. Such constant questioning made them feel like they couldn't trust their mind. It was like trying to walk on eggshells that were scattered on an unstable floor. One wrong step and they might upset their partner, so they tread carefully, but the eggshells of doubt never stopped cracking under their feet.

This confusion led to anxiety - a feeling of unease that buzzed in their chest like a trapped bee. At times, it bloomed into full-blown worry storms that raged within them, making it hard to focus on anything else. Their partner's harsh words, like gusts of wind, would wipe away any warmth from complements or encouragement they had once heard. Depression, a sadness that felt like an ocean wave crashing over them and pulling them under, also began to set in.

They found themselves less energetic, less hopeful, and struggling to find joy in things they once loved.

Their self-view started to change too. Every negative comment from their partner, every small criticism, stuck to them like burrs on a sweater. These belittlements stuck and pulled at their self-esteem, until they viewed themselves with the same critical eyes. They felt small, incapable, and unworthy – none of which were true, but that's what constant put-downs can do to a person's heart.

Their relationships with other important people – friends and family – started to weaken. Their partner had built walls of doubt around them, convincing them that others wouldn't understand, or worse, that they would judge them for not handling their relationship better. They were cut off from those who could offer a different, kinder reality, which left them feeling alone in a cold, empty space.

The toll on their mental health spilled over into every part of their life. At work, their concentration faltered, and the spark that once fueled their passions dimmed. Nights once used for rest became battlegrounds for restless thoughts. The happiness that used to brighten their days faded like a sunset, leaving behind a long, difficult night filled with shadows. This wasn't just personal turmoil; it was affecting every thread in the fabric of their life, unraveling it bit by bit.

SEEKING HELP: THERAPY AND SUPPORT

At a certain point, our hero recognized that they were stuck in a harmful loop that just kept repeating. Every time they thought things were going to get better, the same old pains and problems would show up like unwelcome guests. That's when they understood that something needed to change. After thinking hard and gathering their courage, they decided it was time to get some professional help. This was a big, brave step on the road to feeling good again.

The journey to healing began with their first therapy session. It was through a service called "BetterHelp", which is a place on the internet that connects people with real therapists without having to leave home. This was perfect because it meant scheduling and attending sessions could squeeze into life's busy timetable much easier. In these sessions, they started to untangle the confusing feelings and experiences they'd been carrying around.

The therapy helped them learn about something called 'narcissistic behavior.' This is when someone thinks they are the most important person, and they try to control and hurt others to keep feeling that way. Understanding this was like a lightbulb moment. Our friend could finally see that the problems weren't their fault and that what they had been going through had a name. The therapist shared that such behavior could really mess with someone's head and heart, and that's exactly what had been happening.

But therapy was just one slice of the pie. Wanting to connect with others who understood what it's like, they joined a support group in their community. This group was filled with folks who had been through the same storms. They met once a week in a cozy room at the community center, where they shared stories, passed around support like a precious gift, and learned how to cope in healthier ways. It was a relief to talk with others who really 'got it' — people who nodded and said, "I've been there too."

In between therapy and support group meetings, our hero devoured information from websites like "Psychology Today." This site had articles that were easy to understand and covered all sorts of topics about mental health. Reading these pieces, they armed themselves with knowledge about narcissistic behavior and found smart ways to put the broken pieces back together. There were tips on how to stand up for themselves, how to build boundaries as strong as a fortress, and how to sprinkle seeds of self-care that would grow into a garden of inner peace.

With each step, each appointment, each article, and each shared story in their support group, the individual felt a little more in control of their life. The toxic cycle that had once seemed like an endless merry-go-round was slowing down. It wasn't easy, and it sure wasn't quick, but they were on the path of healing, with fresh hope blooming like morning sun on the horizon.

BREAKING FREE: ENDING THE RELATIONSHIP AND HEALING

The last step in this tough journey was to say goodbye to a hurtful relationship for good. This wasn't a choice made lightly. After all, it's hard to let go of someone you once cared for, even if they weren't good for you. But for the sake of their own heart and mind, it was time to leave and heal.

With the backing of their therapist and friends who knew about these kinds of tough times, they created a plan to leave safely. It was key to make a smart exit strategy because emotions could run high, and they wanted to avoid any trouble. They set a date, organized a place to stay, and had a close buddy ready to help out. They even practiced what to say for when the tough moment arrived.

After they left, the next big step was to keep no ties with their ex. To do this right, they needed to cut off all ways of chatting or bumping into each other online or through texts. This meant blocking phone numbers, emails, and any profiles on social media. The point was, no more talking, no more messages — total silence between them. This way, their ex couldn't twist their words or make them second-guess their choice to move on.

Next up was caring for themselves, a very important part. They poured their feelings into a journal instead of bottling them up inside. They sat quietly, taking deep breaths, and let their thoughts pass by like clouds in the sky — that's meditation. Little by little, they became more aware of the present moment instead of being caught up in the past. That's being mindful. These new habits didn't erase the pain but helped them to manage it better.

A big help on the road to feeling stronger was a workshop they joined, called "Surviving Narcissistic Abuse." This was held by a group that knew a lot about mental health in their area. At this workshop, they met other people who had been through similar heartaches. They learned how to spot a person who wasn't being kind or honest. They picked up ways to protect their feelings and put up boundaries so that they wouldn't be hurt again. The workshop gave out papers and contacts for more help, which made everyone leave feeling more hopeful.

This chapter of their life wasn't a simple one. It took courage and a lot of small steps to find peace after being with someone who didn't treat them well. But bit by bit, with smart choices, good advice, and taking care of their own needs, they began to heal. The end of this relationship wasn't just an ending — it was the start of being kind to themselves and moving forward, stronger than before.

LIFE AFTER NARCISSISM: REBUILDING SELF-ESTEEM AND MOVING FORWARD

Breakups can be tough, especially when the person you were with wasn't kind to your heart. But life after saying goodbye to a partner who brought you down can lead to a path of self-discovery and newfound strength. This chapter takes a close look at someone who found the courage to move on from a harmful relationship with a person filled with too much love for themselves – a narcissist.

When a relationship ends, sometimes your confidence goes with it. But this person, let's call her Ana, took important steps to rebuild her sense of self-worth and create a happy life for herself. Ana kept meeting with her therapist and friends in her support group. These meetings were like a soft place for her to fall. Each time she shared her feelings and heard guidance from others, she felt less alone and more ready to take on the next day.

Ana also found strength in words – powerful little thoughts she would tell herself. Words like, "I am worthy," "I am loved," and "I can do this." When she repeated them every day, it was like planting seeds of confidence that started to grow little by little. Ana gave herself the care she deserved, too. She made time for bubble baths, reading books, and going for walks – anything that let her breathe easier and enjoy her own company.

With time, Ana started reaching back to her friends and family. She had pushed many of them away while she was in her troubled relationship. Some conversations were awkward at first, like trying to dance when you've forgotten the steps. But as she kept trying, the rhythm of her old connections came back, and her circle of support grew stronger.

The story didn't stop with just feeling better; Ana turned towards new roads she had never walked before. She picked up a paintbrush and let colors tell stories she couldn't say out loud. She learned how to make food that not only tasted good but made her feel good too. And as these new pieces of her life started to fit together, she realized she had a story to share – one that could light the way for others in the shadows of their own tough relationships.

Ana started a blog, writing down the tough stuff, the successes, and the everyday steps in between. In sharing her journey, she found purpose and connection with others who were also trying to find their way back to themselves after being lost in someone else's shadow.

This chapter isn't just about ending things with a narcissist. It's a tale of coming back to life after feeling invisible. It shows that with time, care, and the courage to reach out, anyone can heal from the wounds of a toxic love. Ana's story is a shining example that when your world feels upside down, there's hope for setting it right again, one step at a time.

17
NAVIGATING THE JUNGLE: HANDLING NARCISSISM IN THE WORKPLACE

When you're at work, you might cross paths with a coworker or boss who seems to really love themselves - a lot. We call this kind of person a narcissist. But in a job setting, spotting a narcissist isn't always easy because some of their traits might look like just being super ambitious or having a strong personality. Even so, there are clues that you can watch out for that reveal a person might be more than just really confident.

First off, it's helpful to understand that in the workplace, narcissists often go after what they want without thinking about how it will affect others. They tend to have big plans and goals, which isn't bad on its own, but the problem is they can be willing to push others down to lift themselves up. So if you see someone who's always talking about how amazing they are and not thinking about the team, you might be dealing with a narcissist.

One of the big warnings is when someone seems to be playing games to make themselves look good at the expense of others. They might spread rumors, take credit for other people's work, or even tell lies to make themselves shine. All of these actions can create a lot of stress and unhappiness at work, especially if you're the one being stepped on.

An example that really shows what a narcissist can do in a professional setting is the story of Elizabeth Holmes. She was the boss of a company called Theranos. She became famous for promising that her tech could do amazing things that nobody else could do. But it turned out, she wasn't being honest. She told stories to make the tech seem better than it was, and she managed to convince a lot of very smart people, including her own employees, that her lies were true. Holmes's actions were a really big deal because they didn't just affect her company; they even tricked people outside the company who invested a lot of money.

So, if you're working with someone who always wants the spotlight, doesn't care about the team, and is okay with being sneaky to win, you might just be working with a narcissist. Recognizing these signs is the first step to figuring out how to work with them without letting them make your job miserable. You'll want to protect your own work and make sure that you don't get caught up in their games. By understanding what makes a narcissist tick, you can keep your cool and focus on doing a good job, which is what really matters in the end.

EFFECTIVE COMMUNICATION STRATEGIES

In any workplace, being able to talk straight and strong is important, especially when you're dealing with someone who might be full of themselves. We often call this type of person a narcissist. They can be tricky to work with because they love attention and often think they're always right. So, how do you deal with a coworker or boss like this? Let's dive in.

Firstly, let's talk about setting boundaries. It's like drawing an invisible line that tells others what you're okay with and what you're not.

These boundaries tell the other person how they can treat you and what's not going to fly. For example, if a coworker tries to give you more work that's not yours because they don't feel like doing it, you might say, "I can see that you need help, but I have my own work to complete. Perhaps we can find another solution together?" This is a respectful way of saying no and keeping things fair.

Standing your ground like this isn't easy, but it's necessary to make sure you're not pushed around. When you do it right, you show that you respect yourself, and often, the other person will start to respect you too. If they're reasonable, they'll understand and back off. If they're not, you've still shown them you can't be manipulated easily.

Next comes the art of using "I" statements. Imagine if you tell someone, "You're always taking credit for my work!" That's going to make them defensive. It's attacking and puts them on edge – not what you want. Instead, using "I" statements makes the conversation about your feelings rather than their actions. You're not pointing fingers; you're just explaining your side.

Here's an example that can make a big difference in how your message is received: "I feel left out when I don't get credit for my contributions." It's softer. It's more about sharing how you feel than blaming the other person. Surprisingly, it often helps them listen better because they don't feel like they're being accused of something.

To put it into practice, let's say your boss didn't include you in a meeting where your project was being discussed. Instead of saying, "You never include me in meetings," you could approach them later and say, "I realized I was not part of today's meeting. I feel that being there could help me contribute more effectively to the project."

This approach is not just about being nice. It's smart communication. It's showing that you know how to express your thoughts without causing a fight. And in a workplace, that's a powerful skill.

With a little bit of practice, anyone can make these strategies a part of their everyday conversations. That's how you keep your cool and your self-respect, no matter who you're dealing with at work.

SELF-PROTECTION TECHNIQUES

In the daily dance of work life, keeping your mind healthy is as important as any task on your to-do list. This is especially true when you find yourself working with someone who thinks they are the center of the universe—a narcissistic individual. Their need for constant praise and attention can drain your energy and can make you feel small. Here's how you can protect your peace in such a thorny situation.

Let's start with a simple yet powerful rule: Keep your personal stories and information just for you or people you trust deeply. Why? A narcissistic coworker might take the bits and pieces of your life that you share and twist them in ways that can hurt you. They might use what you say to make themselves look better or to put you down. Imagine you tell them about a mistake you made last year; they might bring it up when you least expect it, maybe even in a big meeting, just to make you look bad. Keep your cards close to your chest, and you'll have fewer problems.

Next, seek allies in your workplace. These are the colleagues who understand teamwork, who you feel good around, and who see you for who you are. If you're lucky, you might also have a mentor—someone with experience who can guide you and help you understand that the problem isn't you; it's the challenging person you're dealing with. They'll offer a shoulder and good advice. When a situation with the narcissist gets confusing or hurts, these are the people who can help you see clearly and remind you that you're okay.

Remember that your job isn't your whole world. It's crucial to find a balance—like a seesaw, with work on one end and the rest of your life on the other. Make sure it doesn't tip over by fitting in things you love to do. Maybe that's stretching into different shapes with yoga that make your body feel good, sitting quietly and letting your thoughts pass like clouds with meditation, or diving into a book that opens your mind to new ways of thinking. "The Power of Now" by Eckhart Tolle is a great book to start with; it's about living in this moment, not the past or future, which can be a calm place to be.

Taking care of your mental health isn't just good for you, it's smart. It helps you stay strong and ready for each day's work challenges, even with a narcissistic coworker trying to stir up trouble. Protect your stories, find your people, and keep that work-life seesaw balanced. Your mind will thank you for it, and you'll be able to outlast any storm with your peace intact.

NAVIGATING OFFICE POLITICS

Title: Staying Afloat in the Office Sea: Navigating the Waves of Office Politics

In the busy world of office life, understanding how people work together—and sometimes against each other—can make a big difference in your career. Office politics are like undercurrents in the sea; they're not always easy to see, but they can certainly sweep you off your feet if you're not careful. And when there's a person with a narcissistic approach in the mix, those waters become even trickier to navigate.

Imagine a coworker who always wants to be the center of attention, often takes credit for others' hard work, or quickly puts the blame on someone else when things go south. That's often the narcissist at work. To handle these rough seas without finding yourself thrown overboard, you need strategies to sail smoothly.

First, think of staying neutral like staying afloat. Just as a lifeguard tries to stay calm and collected during a rescue, you want to avoid getting pulled into arguments or conflicts. When you remain impartial, the narcissist finds it hard to use you as a piece in their chess game. By not picking sides, you keep your power and stay in control of your position at work.

Second, maintaining a professional attitude is like having a sturdy ship to weather the storms. When you're at work, act like you're the captain of your ship. Speak kindly, don't spread rumors, and steer clear of talking badly about your colleagues. If you avoid gossip, the narcissist has less chance to twist your words or involve you in their schemes.

Staying neutral means if two people are in a disagreement, try not to take sides. Even if you think one person is right, it's usually better to keep that to yourself. Instead, focus on your work and do your best every day. This way, you don't give the narcissist a chance to create drama with you in the middle.

Lastly, don't forget that there are lots of resources out there that can be your navigational guides. LinkedIn, a big network for professionals, has many articles and tools to help you understand and handle office politics. Taking some time to read and learn from these can offer you more tips and tricks to keep the narcissist at bay and keep your career sailing smoothly.

Your job is more than just doing tasks—it's also about being smart in how you handle relationships. by staying neutral, keeping a professional demeanor, and learning from experts, you put yourself in the best position to succeed at work and avoid the narcissist's traps. you might not be able to change how the narcissist behaves, but you can definitely control your own course and keep your journey through office politics as smooth sailing as possible.

SEEKING HELP AND ESCALATING ISSUES

Working in a place where someone's self-centered behavior impacts your day can be tough. We've all come across someone who seems to think the world revolves around them. When this attitude doesn't get better and starts to make your work life difficult, it's time to take more serious steps. Here's how you can wisely deal with these challenges while staying professional.

Firstly, don't just watch and hope things will change. Start keeping a record. Every time this narcissistic behavior shows up, note it down. Write the date, the time, and where it happened. If it was during a meeting, jot that down. If it occurred in the lunch area, note that, too. And if people were around who saw what happened, they can back up your story, so list them as well.

You're not doing this to be sneaky. you're protecting your work life and maybe even helping others who feel the same way but are too scared to speak up. imagine this record as evidence. you're building a case to show what's going on isn't right. write down everything: the big things and the small things. did they take credit for your work? write it down. did they shut down your ideas without a good reason? that goes on the list, too.

Once you have enough evidence, it's time for the next step: go to someone higher up who can help. Before you talk to them, check your company's rules. Every workplace has its own steps on how to handle these kinds of problems. Some places ask you to talk to your boss first. Others might have a special team you need to go to, like the human resources department. By following these rules, you show that you're serious and you respect the process. Plus, it makes sure you don't accidentally get in trouble for not doing things the right way.

When you sit down with your boss or HR, bring your records. Show them the clear pattern of this person's behavior. Your company should see that it's not just a one-time problem but something that keeps happening. Stay calm and stick to the facts. This isn't about getting someone in trouble for no reason; it's about making the work environment better for everyone.

Lastly, there's a website called Glassdoor where people can share their work stories, both good and bad. You can look at Glassdoor for advice or to read about other people's experiences with tricky work situations. You'll see you're not alone in dealing with difficult people at work. Lots of others have been in your shoes, and their stories can help you figure out what to do next. But remember, every workplace is different, so while their stories can give you ideas, your company's rules should always guide your actions.

HEALING AFTER LEAVING A TOXIC JOB

Once you decide to step away from a toxic work environment, it's like setting down a heavy bag you've been carrying for too long. Your shoulders may feel lighter, but your hands might fumble, missing the weight they've grown used to holding. It can be liberating to walk away, yet challenges wait on the path to healing and moving forward. It's a journey that asks for both courage and patience.

As you find yourself outside those office walls, it's essential to recognize that it's okay to grieve the loss of your job. Much like any significant change, leaving your position, even one that hurt more than it helped, is a big deal. Grief isn't just for good things lost; it's also for the bad ones that were part of our daily lives. You may grieve for the routine you had, the colleagues who were also friends, or even the identity you tied to that job title. Acknowledge these feelings; they are signposts of transition, markers that show you're moving through a process that'll take you to a better place.

In your healing journey, you might benefit from professional guidance. A therapist can help you explore the tangle of emotions that quitting a job can stir up. From feelings of relief to threads of doubt and worry about the future, a therapist provides a safe, supportive space to unpack these emotions. They are there to listen, to understand, and to assist you in finding strategies for coping and growing beyond this experience.

On the other hand, a career coach can serve as your guide to what comes next. Together, you can examine your skills, strengths, and interests to map out a career path that aligns better with your values and goals. They can help you polish your resume, practice for interviews, and build the confidence you need to dive into new opportunities. Career coaching isn't about finding just any job—it's about finding the right one, a place where you can thrive instead of just survive.

Additionally, the internet is a treasure chest of resources for those who've left toxic work environments behind. One such gem is The Muse, a website specifically designed to support job seekers and individuals recovering from negative work experiences. It offers articles about self-care, tips for job hunting, and stories from people who've been where you are now. This website can be a companion in your journey, offering advice, encouragement, and tools to help you move toward a brighter professional future.

Leaving a toxic work environment can indeed be a daunting task initially. But it's also the first brave step towards rediscovering your worth and creating a career that's not just a job, but a joy. With time, support, and resources like The Muse, you can heal from the past and build a future where work is a source of fulfillment, not frustration. Remember, the road ahead is yours to shape—step by step, and day by day, towards a place where you are appreciated and can grow.

REBUILDING CONFIDENCE AND TRUST

Working in a place where your boss or coworkers make you feel small can be tough. It's like carrying a heavy weight every day, making it hard to feel good about yourself. If you've been in a situation like this, it can feel like the color has faded from everything you do. You might doubt your skills or wonder if you're good at anything at all. This is often what happens when someone's been hurt by a person who only thinks of themselves – a narcissist.

First, know that it's not your fault. People who behave this way can make anyone doubt themselves. But now that you're out of that negative space, it's time to remind yourself of who you are and what you can do. Think of it like fixing a bike with a busted wheel – it's not the bike's fault it's broken. With the right tools and a little time, it'll be good as new.

One tool to patch up your confidence is to practice saying positive things about yourself. This might sound simple, but it's mighty powerful. Stand in front of a mirror each morning and say nice things to yourself, like "I'm smart," "I'm kind," or "I'm great at my job." It might feel strange at first, like patting yourself on the back for tying your shoes. But just like muscle grows with exercise, your self-esteem will get stronger with this practice.

Having people who believe in you helps too. Reach out to your friends, family, or someone you see as a guide – like a mentor. Talking with these people can be like having a good meal after being hungry for a long time. Share your story and let them remind you of your worth. Their words can act like a warm light in a chilly room, pushing away the shadows of doubt.

Sometimes, we need a fresh voice to ring through the noise of our worries. TED Talks are like windows into new ways of thinking. One talk, called "The Power of Vulnerability" by Brené Brown, is like finding a guidebook when you're lost in the woods. She talks about being brave enough to show who you are, bumps and bruises and all. This can give you a step to lift yourself up on. Her words encourage you to embrace your story – even the rough patches – because that's where your true strength lies. With insights like these, you can start filling your toolbox with ideas and strategies that rebuild your confidence.

Rebuilding trust in yourself after a rough experience at work is a journey, one step at a time. like healing a scrape on your knee, your confidence needs a bit of care and time. use these tools: self-affirmation, support from loved ones, and uplifting talks like brené brown's. with these, you'll not only mend the cracks but also become even stronger than before.

18

MENDING THE BROKEN BONDS: HEALING FROM NARCISSISTIC PARENTAL ABUSE

In the shadows of family life, a particular kind of harm can go unnoticed. It's the injury that comes from a parent who thinks only of themselves, a narcissistic parent. Too often, people think that just because someone is a parent, they always do what's best for their kids. But that's not always true.

A narcissist parent sees their children not as separate people but more like things they own. They can twist the way their kids see the world, making them doubt their own minds and feelings. Picture a child who is told that the sky is red when they know it's blue. They might start to wonder if their own eyes are tricking them. That's what it's like for these kids, only it's about their whole lives, not just the color of the sky.

Carrying this weight around every day, a child can start to break down inside. As they grow, they might be more likely to feel nervous or down all the time. They could even suffer from something called C-PTSD, which is like a wound in their mind that just doesn't heal.

Narcissistic parents often treat their children as if they're just part of their own image. If the child does harsh words like cold wind might blow their way. This makes the child think they're only as good as what they can do, not just for being themselves.

A narcissistic parent might even turn siblings into rivals. They might give love to one child and not the other, to make them compete for attention. This is a sneaky way to keep control, like a king who keeps his knights fighting each other so they don't notice what he's up to.

Such a tough home life doesn't just hurt the kids; it splits them up when they need each other the most. Without the help of brothers or sisters, a child may feel utterly alone and without help. It's like being in a small boat in the middle of the ocean without a paddle.

From all this, it's clear that the hurt from a narcissistic parent is deep and tangled. But knowing about it is the first step to getting better. Once the truth is in the light, healing can start. It's a journey, but with the right help and understanding, those hidden wounds can start to close, and life can get brighter.

THE ROAD TO RECOVERY: HEALING FROM NARCISSISTIC PARENTAL ABUSE

When a person has gone through some very bad and unfair treatment by a parent, it's a very big step to say out loud what has happened. To say, "Yes, my mom or dad hurt me, and it wasn't right," is hard. People often think families should always be close and never hurt each other. But sometimes, that's not the way it is.

Realizing the truth about the hurt can feel like a heavy weight has been lifted. It's like finally telling your story and having people nod, saying, "We see you. We understand." That can feel very good because it means you are not alone, and what you feel inside is real and matters.

Talking to someone who knows a lot about this kind of hurt can help a lot. They are called therapists, and they have special ways of helping people feel better. They can teach you how to handle the memories and bad feelings that come from being treated badly by a parent who should have been kind.

The experts in feeling better after bad things have happened use special kinds of talking and thinking exercises to help. They've found out that these exercises work well. One big study by some very smart people who study the mind said so in 2017.

If you still talk to the parent who hurt you, you need to draw a line in the sand. You decide what you're okay with and what you're not. Maybe you choose to only see them sometimes, or you don't talk about certain things with them. This is very important for you to start to feel better. A study done by some smart people who write about feelings and being treated badly showed in 2016 that drawing this line really does help people feel more at peace.

Taking care of yourself in a way that makes you feel good is also key. Doing things like stretching and running, or breathing while sitting quietly, can make the scared and sad feelings take a back seat. Some doctors from a big school that studies how to stay healthy said that moving your body can help your heart and brain feel happier in 2018.

It's also really nice to find people who get it, who have been there, too. There are places on the internet where you can talk to people who have had a mom or dad hurt them as well. You can find these groups in the online world or through local places that help with feelings. Here, you can share your story and listen to others, and it makes you feel like you belong to a group that truly gets it.

In short, saying it like it is, accepting it, getting some help, making rules with the parent who hurt you, doing things that feel good, and meeting people like you can all help a heart start to heal after a mom or dad has been unkind.

SHAPING YOUR FUTURE: MOVING BEYOND NARCISSISTIC PARENTAL ABUSE

Moving past the hurt caused by a parent who only thinks of themselves can be tough. Your heart and mind might feel like they're stuck in a not-so-nice place. Your parent might have told you things that make you believe you're not enough. That's a heavy weight to carry. But there's a path forward, a way to drop that weight and find the real you—that strong, amazing person you're meant to be.

First things first, you have to notice those dark thoughts—the ones that say you're not good, smart, or loving enough—and then stand up to them. It's like telling a mean bully, "Hey, you're wrong about me!" Easier said than done, sure, but every time you do it, you're one step closer to feeling better about who you are.

One way to find the awesome person you are inside is through doing things that let your soul sing. Maybe it's painting a picture with colors that show your feelings, or writing stories that have been tucked away in your heart. Making something that comes from you is a powerful way to see how special you are. Plus, it feels pretty great to create something that's all yours.

Another step is to shape a world where you're surrounded by people who cheer you on. You need friends who listen, who care, and who give you space to be you. They're the kind of folks who say, "I get it," and mean it, especially when times are tough. In fact, smart folks in the business of studying happiness found out that having these kinds of positive chats and hangouts can actually make your heart feel lighter and your days brighter, especially if you've been through rough patches.

Learning is another super tool. It's like giving your brain a gym workout. Reading books by doctors who've helped others like you or watching talks by experts can shine a light on what you went through. Now, that might sound a bit school-like, but remember, understanding is power. It helps you say, "Aha! So that's what was happening." It's like someone turned on the light in a dark room.

But you can't just look back; you've got to look forward too. Setting your sights on what's ahead—maybe it's a dream job, starting your own family, or digging into a hobby—is like drawing a map to a sunnier place. Each small step you take is a step away from those tough times. And before you know it, you're not just moving on; you're building a brand-new story, one where you're the brave hero at the center, writing your own happy ending.

19
NAVIGATING THE HEALING PATH: SEEKING PROFESSIONAL HELP

Recovering from the deep scars left by someone with narcissistic traits can be a winding and tough road. Finding a good direction on this journey is where therapists and counselors become your guides. They are not just regular people; they are educated and skilled people who spend their days learning the best ways to help folks like you.

Imagine you've got a shattered leg. You wouldn't just wait and hope it gets better, right? You'd probably go to a doctor, someone who knows exactly what to do. That's what therapists and counselors do for your heart and mind after narcissistic abuse. They have strategies and understanding to help patch up the hurt on the inside.

It's not always easy to see the effects of narcissistic abuse, but it wraps around your thoughts and feelings, sometimes in ways that are hard to untangle by yourself. The American Psychological Association pointed out in 2007 that cognitive-behavioral therapy (CBT) is one of the remedies. This sort of therapy can be like a map, showing where the thorns of narcissistic abuse are and how to carefully remove them.

Some folks are worried that asking for help might make them seem weak. But it's actually a mighty and brave step. It means you're ready to face the challenges head-on and that you're taking control to change things for the better. Think of it as picking up a tool to build a sturdier you.

Even though lots of people could use a helping hand when it comes to their mental well-being, there's this wrong idea that it's some sign of failure. But, truly, it's no different from dealing with a cold or a twisted ankle. The National Alliance on Mental Illness says that so many people experience mental health troubles, but less than half get the help they need. This is where knocking down those false beliefs about therapy really matters.

When you walk into a therapist or counselor's office, you're stepping into a space as safe as a fortress. Here, no one is going to judge you for feeling hurt or confused, and nothing you say leaves that room. You can let out all the stuff you've been carrying, the parts that feel too heavy, and find real understanding.

The therapist sits with you, truly hears you, and sees your struggle. They can't change the past, but they can hand you the tools for a brighter tomorrow. And remember, opening up to a therapist or counselor doesn't mean your feelings aren't real or valid. It's the exact opposite. It's saying, "My well-being is worth fighting for," and that's about the bravest thing anyone can do.

FINDING THE RIGHT THERAPIST

Selecting the right therapist is a big step in your path to feeling better. If you've faced hardship because of someone who thinks only of themselves and hurts others, it's even more essential to find a therapist who really gets it. Like finding the perfect pair of shoes, you need a therapist who fits you just right. The impact this match can make on your healing is powerful.

Consider therapists like experts in different subjects. Some might be wizards with work stress, while others might know all about how to handle scary thoughts. Because you're dealing with hurt from someone with a narcissistic behavior, you want a therapist who's seen this before and knows just how to help.

Finding this person may sound tough, but there's help out there. Websites like Psychology Today let you search for therapists. You can type in what you're dealing with, like "narcissistic abuse," and see who pops up. The American Psychological Association has a similar tool. These sites are like maps, guiding you to the help you need.

When you reach out to a therapist, remember it's kind of like you're hiring them for a job. That first talk you have, think of it like an interview. Ask questions to make sure they understand your situation and know how to support you. It's okay to talk to a few therapists to see who feels right.

Now, if fitting therapy into your busy life sounds hard, online therapy could be your answer. With options like BetterHelp or Talkspace, you can get support over video, phone, or even text message. These online spaces often have lots of therapists to choose from. That means you've got a better chance of finding someone who knows how to help with the specific pain you're going through.

Besides one-on-one therapy, joining a group can be super helpful. In these groups, people who have been through stuff just like you come together. They share what happened, talk about what works, and give each other support. Think of it like a team, all working together towards feeling better.

To find these groups, you can look online. Organizations like the International Society for the Study of Trauma and Dissociation (ISSTD) can point you to the right place. Or you might find communities on social media, like the Survivors of Narcissistic Abuse group on Facebook. These can be spaces where you feel understood and supported in a way that's different from solo therapy.

Reaching out for help is a big, brave step. and finding the right person to help you can make your journey to feeling better a whole lot smoother. it's about connecting with someone who gets you, supports you, and walks the path with you, at a pace that feels right.

OVERCOMING COMMON OBJECTIONS TO SEEKING PROFESSIONAL HELP

Title: Taking the Step for a Healthier Mind: Overcoming Hesitations About Therapy

As you read this, you might find yourself nodding in understanding or shaking your head in disagreement. That's okay. It's very normal to feel unsure about reaching out for professional help when it comes to our mental well-being. You may have all sorts of thoughts and worries about this step. Let's calmly talk them through together.

One common worry is about the cost. "Therapy is too expensive," is a thought that holds many back from getting the help they may deeply need. But here's something you might not know: a lot of therapists really want to help people, no matter how much money they have. So, they adjust their charges based on what you can afford. This is called a 'sliding scale.' What this means is, if you don't have a lot of money, you pay less. It's as simple as asking about it, and you could find yourself able to afford the support you need.

Also, the world of therapy has grown. Now, there are online therapy websites where chatting with a professional can be less costly than in-person visits. Plus, don't forget to check your health insurance, as many plans are starting to include mental health, making the cost of therapy more manageable.

Then there's the "I'm too busy" thought. The feeling of our days being packed from dawn till dusk is a reality most of us live with. And putting something else on that to-do list? It feels impossible. However, this is where online therapy platforms shine again. These platforms often have more of a come-as-you-can approach. This means you can find a time for therapy that fits into your busy life, like early morning before work or late at night after the kids sleep. Your mental health matters, and giving it time is an investment in yourself that pays off in every part of your life.

Lastly, the concern about what others will think. "What if someone finds out I'm going to therapy?" Here's something worth repeating: there is no shame in wanting to be the best you can be. Seeking help isn't a sign of weakness; it is a sign of strength and taking care of yourself. Remember, many people turn to therapy. They just don't all talk about it. By reaching out, you're joining a quiet army of folks who are committed to living more healthy, peaceful lives. They are people just like you, who one day just decided that they deserved better and bravely took a step toward change.

You're not alone, and it's okay to ask for help. Taking care of your mind is just as important as taking care of your body. Remember, everyone needs a hand sometimes, and reaching out might just be the change that lights up your life.

THE ROLE OF MEDICATION IN THE HEALING PROCESS

When someone has been through the tough times that come with narcissistic abuse, it can leave marks on their heart and mind. They might feel really anxious or deeply sad. It's like carrying around a heavy backpack filled with rocks, every step feels harder. So, it's okay to need a bit of extra help sometimes. Medicine isn't a magic fix for the hurt caused by narcissistic abuse, but think of it like a walking stick that can help you keep moving on a hard hike.

Before thinking about medicine, it's super smart to talk with a doctor or someone who knows a lot about health. This person is like a guide. You wouldn't explore a dark cave without someone who knows the way, right? So, you shouldn't start taking medicine without talking to a healthcare professional, either. They know what could be helpful and will listen to how you're feeling. They'll also make sure the medicine won't mess with any other meds or health issues you've got. Chatting with them is the first step on the path to feeling lighter.

Medicine for your brain and emotions does its best work when it's part of a team. Imagine a soccer game where there is just one player trying to score a goal without any help; it's pretty tough. Therapy or counseling is another key player in this team. These are the people you can talk to about everything that's weighing on you. They help you understand your feelings, where they come from, and how to handle them. Medicine can make you feel stable, but therapy does the digging to get those rocks out of your backpack for good.

When you do start medicine, remember it's really important to take it just like your healthcare professional tells you. If they say take it with food, eat a little something. If they say take it in the morning, make it a part of your get-ready routine. And if something feels off or you notice changes in how you feel or act, let them know right away. They're there to make the journey easier, not scarier.

No one should feel alone or lost after dealing with narcissistic abuse. Medicine can be a helpful friend on your journey, but it's the mixture of meds, talking, and understanding that really leads to healing. It's a big step to reach for that walking stick and open up to a guide, but it's brave and wise. It's part of taking back control and finding your way back to sunshine and solid ground.

CULTIVATING A SUPPORTIVE NETWORK

When life gets tough, especially after experiencing the challenges of being with someone who has narcissistic tendencies, it's not just okay to ask for help, it's smart. Remember, we are social beings by nature, and having good people around us can make a big difference. In addition to professional help like therapists or counselors, there's great value in building a circle of support with friends, family, or people who've walked a path like yours.

Friends and family can be your cheerleaders. They know you, care for you, and can offer a shoulder to cry on or an ear to listen. When you're feeling overwhelmed or just need to talk about your day, they can be there to lift your spirits and remind you that you're loved and valued. These are the people who can make you laugh when it feels like you'll never smile again. They provide that safe space where you can be yourself, without judgment.

Beyond your personal circle, there's a whole world of folks out there who know exactly what you're going through. They're in online forums and social media groups where they share their own stories, tips, and heartfelt support. One useful place to find such a community is the subreddit r/NarcissisticAbuse. Here, thousands of people, all dealing with the impact of narcissistic abuse, come together to talk, share, and help one another. Reading their posts, you may find stories that sound like pages from your own life. It can be a relief to discover you're not alone.

Another online haven is the Survivors of Narcissistic Abuse Facebook group. It's a place where you can make new friends who won't get tired of listening because they truly understand. They've felt similar fears, asked the same questions, and fought the same inner battles. These platforms not only offer comfort and companionship, but they also give practical advice. From learning healthy ways to respond to a narcissist to strategies for rebuilding your self-esteem, these communities can be a treasure trove of guidance.

It's okay to lean on these people. You're not weak for wanting support; you're human. And you don't have to do this alone. Walking this path with others can make the journey less scary. So take a deep breath and reach out. Send that message, make that post, or call that friend. Your support network is a lifeline – an extended family you choose – and they can add strength to your wings as you learn to fly again after the storm.

It's not just about getting through the dark times, but also about finding moments of joy and companionship along the way. together, you can make it to the other side of this experience, not just surviving, but thriving.

20

A WORLD OF WISDOM: FURTHER READING AND LEARNING RESOURCES ON NARCISSISM

In this important part of our book, we are going to share with you a list of other books and resources that you can look into to learn even more about tough topics like narcissism, dark psychology, gaslighting, and manipulation. We understand that having one book or one perspective is not enough when you want to really understand a subject. This is similar to wanting to know all sides of a story or looking at a sculpture from all angles. To help with the hurt and confusion these issues may cause, we want to guide you to more information.

First let's talk about "The Covert Passive-Aggressive Narcissist" written by Debbie Mirza. This book dives deep into the sneaky and often hidden ways someone can control and play mind games without being loud or aggressive. Usually, when we think of a narcissist, we imagine a very self-centered person who loves being the center of attention. However, this book talks about a different, quieter kind of narcissist who might be hard to spot. Reading it can make you more aware of the signs of such behavior and give you the tools to deal with people who act in these ways.

Another book, "Rethinking Narcissism" by Dr. Craig Malkin, turns the table on how we traditionally view narcissism. Dr. Malkin suggests that narcissism isn't always bad and that a bit of self-love can be healthy. However, too much self-love can damage relationships and hurt others. This book is helpful for understanding the balance between being self-assured and being self-absorbed, as well as how to notice the difference in others.

For those who have grown up with parents that made everything about themselves, "Children of the Self-Absorbed" by Nina Brown can be a lifeline. It's common for adults who had narcissistic parents to face a lot of emotional struggles because of their childhood. Nina Brown's book helps readers understand how their past can affect their present, and how to heal and move forward.

It's important to note that these books are written for normal people —just like you and me—and not only for doctors or experts. The language is simple so that you can learn and figure things out without getting lost in difficult words or scientific talk. We think that when you choose to read these books, they can act as friends on your journey to understand a complex topic that affects many people's lives.

These resources are just the beginning. They open doors to new ways of thinking and understanding yourself and the people around you. As you explore these books, remember that learning is like putting together a puzzle; every piece of information helps make the whole picture clearer. Dive in, keep an open mind, and equip yourself with the knowledge you need to navigate these challenging interactions and relationships in your life.

PODCASTS: LISTENING TO SURVIVORS AND EXPERTS

Audio resources like podcasts have become a handy tool for many. In our busy lives, taking time to sit and read isn't always possible.

That's where the power of podcasts shines through. You can listen while you're doing other things – exercising, cleaning, or driving. They're like having a personal talk show in your pocket, ready whenever you are. The beauty of podcasts is that they feel like a friend talking to you, offering advice and sharing stories that can make you nod your head in agreement and feel less alone in your experiences.

"The Narcissist in Your Life" podcast, hosted by Linda Martinez-Lewi, is one such audio resource that brings comfort and understanding to those dealing with narcissists. Linda's voice comes through the speakers with warmth and clarity, like a guide leading you through a difficult journey. Each episode dives deep into the world of narcissism, explaining how a narcissist thinks and behaves. It's educational but simple to follow. Linda uses examples that feel like real life because, for many listeners, they are. It's like sitting down for coffee with an expert who can explain why that person in your life makes you feel unseen or unimportant.

Christine Hammond's "Understanding Today's Narcissist" is another gem in the podcast world. Christine has a knack for breaking down complex ideas about the narcissist's mind into pieces that are easy to digest. While you fold laundry or wait in line at the grocery store, you can uncover the reasons behind a narcissist's actions and learn ways to cope with them. Christine's podcast is like a short class that gives you "aha moments," as if a lightbulb goes off in your head when you suddenly understand something that confused you before.

Finally, "Narcissist Apocalypse" gives a microphone to those who have survived narcissistic relationships. It offers something special: a community. Each story shared is unique, yet you might find pieces of your own story woven in. Hearing a voice shake or a breath taken with courage reminds you that these are real people, just like you. This connection is what makes podcasts so special. There's comfort in shared experiences and knowing that you are not the only one to have lived through challenging times with a narcissist. When people share on this podcast, you feel a part of a larger group of survivors, each supporting the other through their audio testimony.

These podcasts not only educate but also heal. They are free, they are accessible, and they bring people together. In a world where dealing with a narcissist can make you feel very alone, podcasts offer an invisible handshake, a silent nod, saying, "I understand, and you are not alone in this."

ONLINE LEARNING PLATFORMS: COURSES AND WEBINARS

In a world where information is as close as a tap on a screen, structured courses and webinars stand as powerful tools for those seeking to understand complex topics comprehensively. Let's dive into the benefits of such learning tools, especially around the challenging topic of Narcissistic Personality Disorder (NPD).

First, why choose structured courses like the ones you might find on Udemy? Imagine deciding to build a house with no blueprint. You may know that walls, windows, and a roof are necessary, but if these pieces aren't planned and put together in a certain order, you might end up with a mess. The same idea applies when learning about something as intricate as NPD. The course on Udemy, designed by professionals, takes you step by step through the understanding of the disorder. It's like having a blueprint. With each lesson building on the last, you create a solid structure of knowledge.

This NPD course doesn't just touch on surface facts; it delves into the why and how. Why do narcissists behave the way they do? How can you identify such behaviors? Knowledge is layered, ensuring you get a detailed picture. Because of its organized layout, you won't find yourself lost or overwhelmed. This could make a huge difference in your ability to grasp and retain information. Plus, you can revisit the material as many times as you need.

Now, imagine you live or work with someone who has narcissistic tendencies. Reading about the disorder is helpful, but applying what you've learned is a different challenge. This is where webinars come in handy. The webinar "Living with a Narcissist" on Eventbrite is an excellent example. It's like attending a live class without leaving your home. You can hear real-life stories, ask questions, and even share experiences if you're comfortable.

The webinar offers practical tips and strategies to respond to the difficult behaviors of narcissists. This sharing of skills is crucial. Think about learning a dance. You can't just watch; you need to step onto the dance floor and try the moves. Webinars provide this hands-on approach, giving you a chance to practice coping strategies in a supportive environment.

Lastly, for daily bits of wisdom and encouragement, exploring resources like Kelly's YouTube channel, "The Little Shaman Healing," can complement structured learning. Here, you get insights in smaller pieces, perfect for when you're on the go or need a quick reminder of how to deal with challenging situations involving narcissists. Videos offer a personal touch, as if you're getting advice from a friend who understands.

BLOGS AND WEBSITES: QUICK READS AND INSTANT HELP

In our modern world, if you want to learn something fast, the internet is your go-to helper. No matter where you are, as long as you've got a phone or computer with internet, you can just tap or click, and boom, you have answers. It's like having a huge library in your pocket!

Now, let's talk about a topic a lot of folks are curious about these days: narcissism. Narcissism is when someone thinks very highly of themselves, maybe too highly, and it can cause problems for them and the people around them. Luckily, there are online places that dig deep into this subject so you can understand it better, and they're just a quick search away.

First, there's this cool blog on a website called Psychology Today. The blog is called "Narcissism Decoded," and, as the name suggests, they make the complex ideas of narcissism easier to get. Imagine having a smart friend who can break down heavy books into simple words you get in a snap—that's what this blog does. They've got a bunch of articles on different shades of narcissism, like what it's like, how to spot it, and what you can do if someone close to you might be a narcissist.

Then, there's the "Narcissist Family Files" blog. How does that ring a bell? Sometimes, a person can have a mom, dad, sister, brother, or even a close relative who always wants all eyes on them. It can be a lot to deal with, and that's where this blog comes in. It has stories, guidance, and resources to help people who are trying to tackle having a narcissist in the family. Think of it as a helpful buddy who understands what you're going through and has some wise advice.

Lastly, there's a website called "Out of the FOG." No, it's not about the weather—it stands for "Fear, Obligation, Guilt," things people often feel when dealing with someone who has a personality disorder, like narcissism. This website is like a warm, welcoming community center. It has discussions, tools, and all sorts of helpful stuff for folks trying to navigate the tricky storms that can come from relationships with complex personalities.

These online spaces open the door to heaps of knowledge that was once tucked away in thick, hard-to-read books. Now, in just a few clicks, anyone can get a clearer picture of narcissism. It's all about making life a little easier and giving people a helping hand. With information available around the clock, no one has to feel alone in figuring out how to deal with difficult personal issues. And that's the beauty of the internet—it connects us to the support and answers we need when we need them.

SUPPORT NETWORKS: FINDING YOUR TRIBE

Support networks and forums play a crucial role in the healing journey from any form of abuse, especially narcissistic abuse. Engaging with a community that truly understands what you are going through can be incredibly healing. Here, we will explore the benefits of joining such groups.

Firstly, a Facebook group called "Narcissistic Abuse Recovery" has become a beacon of support for many survivors. When you enter this community, you're not just finding a group; you're joining a family of individuals who empathize with your struggle because they've faced similar challenges. This support network brings people together from all walks of life, who connect over their shared experiences.

One of the greatest benefits of the "Narcissistic Abuse Recovery" group is the continuous flow of encouragement. Here, you can tell your story and receive responses of solidarity and understanding, rather than disbelief, which you might find elsewhere. Positive inter-actions in the group can help rebuild your sense of self-worth and empower you to reclaim your life. Additionally, the network offers practical advice, from dealing with the legal aspects of separation to setting boundaries and self-care routines.

Next, there's the platform called Reddit, a place where people gather to discuss just about any topic. On this website, there is a special space named "r/NarcissisticAbuse". One of the key advantages of this subreddit is the anonymity it provides. You can share your thoughts and feelings without the fear of being identified, which can be espe-cially important if you're concerned about privacy or backlash from the abuser.

The subreddit is a wellspring of collective wisdom. Members share stories and support each other through the complexities of narcissistic abuse. You can read about how others have coped with gaslighting, manipulation, or emotional neglect, and learn strategies for healing and moving forward. By learning from others' experiences, you can gain insights and tools to cope with your own situation.

Lastly, the "Narcissist Support Group" on DailyStrength is another valuable resource. This site is designed to be a safe haven, where individuals can talk about their experiences and emotions without judgment. The forum provides an opportunity for members to chat with others who truly get what it's like to face the challenges of recovering from narcissistic abuse.

The group often discusses topics that help in regaining confidence and strength, and in the process, many find friendships with others who can relate to their battle. Finding these connections can be life-altering; realizing you are not alone in your journey can be an incredibly healing realization.

By joining these supportive networks and forums, survivors of narcissistic abuse can find solace, solidarity, and strength. By connecting with others, learning from shared experiences, and receiving advice, healing becomes not just a personal journey, but a shared one. Each network serves a unique purpose, yet they all strive towards the same goal: to help survivors navigate the troubled waters of recovery and steer towards a more peaceful horizon.

CONCLUSION

As we draw near the end of our exploration, let's circle back to what we set out to achieve. This book aimed to be a friendly guide for anyone trying to wrap their head around some tough topics: narcissism, dark psychology, gaslighting, and manipulation. It gave hands-on advice for dealing with toxic individuals, guided you through recovery, and showed you how to take good care of your well-being.

Let's summarize what we've learned:

- We started by defining narcissism and dark psychology. We looked at what makes a person a narcissist, different types of narcissists, and how dark psychology influences their actions.
- We then broke down the sneaky ways narcissists twist reality – gaslighting and manipulation. Understanding these tactics is key to knowing when you're being targeted.
- The third leg of our journey was about defense strategies. We talked about setting limits, staying calm and distant

using the grey rock method, and how to deal with people who take the narcissist's side.

- Next, we tackled recovery. We learned about the bonds formed from shared trauma and how to break free. We also explored coping with legal issues and steps to heal after leaving the narcissistic environment.
- Self-care took center stage in the fifth part. We discussed how mindful actions and journaling can be a balm for your soul.
- And we didn't stop at theory. We shared real stories of others' battles with narcissism, showing how the tools from this book could work for you, too.
- Lastly, the book wrapped up with extra help and resources to keep you learning and growing.

Now, remember the major points: dealing with narcissism is a journey, healing doesn't happen overnight, and taking good care of yourself should always be a priority. Putting up boundaries, seeking expert advice when needed, and continuing to educate yourself are all vital steps on this path.

So, as we turn the final page, hold onto the message of hope and strength we've built. You're not alone. Armed with the right knowledge and tactics, you can move past these challenges.

Think of this not as a goodbye, but as a "see you later." Take this knowledge into your everyday life, reach out if you hit a rough patch, and pass on what you've learned to help others in need.

A heartfelt thanks for joining me on this adventure. Continue to grow, heal, and thrive. Remember to check out talks like "The Narcissistic Parent" by Dr. Ramani Durvasula for more insights, and keep your eyes on the road ahead; your future is waiting, bright and full of promise.

Keep healing, keep growing, and keep moving towards a future where you're in charge of your own story. And if you ever need a reminder of how far you've come, just flip through these pages again. Thank you, and take good care of yourself.